THE GARLAND
LIBRARY
OF
LATIN POETRY

ౠ

selected by
Steele Commager
Columbia University

AD TOPICA CARMINUM AMATORIORUM SYMBOLAE

Bruno Lier

ↄ

STUDIES IN THE DICTION OF THE SERMO AMATORIUS IN ROMAN COMEDY

Keith Preston

ↄ

MILITAT OMNIS AMANS

Alfons Spies

GARLAND PUBLISHING, INC.

NEW YORK & LONDON

1978

The volumes in this series have been printed on
acid-free, 250-year-life paper.

Library of Congress Cataloging in Publication Data

Lier, Bruno, 1878-
  Ad topica carminum amatoriorum symbolae.

  (The Garland library of Latin poetry)
  Reprint of B. Lier's thesis presented to Greifsund,
in 1914, and published by Herrcke & Lebeling, Stettin,
in 1914; K. Preston's thesis presented to the University
of Chicago, in 1914, and published by G. Banta Pub. Co.,
Menasha, Wis., in 1916; and A. Spies's thesis presented
to the Universität zu Tübingen, in 1928, and published
by H. Laupp jr., Tübingen, in 1930.

  1. Latin literature--History and criticism.
2. Latin language--Style. 3. Love in literature.
I. Preston, Keith, 1884-1927. Studies in the diction
of the sermo amatorius in Roman comedy. 1978.
II. Spies, Alfons, 1905-   Militat omnis amans.
1978. III. Title. IV. Series.
PA6141.Z5L5 1978   870'.9'354   77-70837
ISBN 0-8240-2973-9

Printed in the United States of America

Ad topica
carminum amatoriorum
symbolae.

Scripsit
Dr. Bruno Lier.

..... ∞ .....

Wissenschaftliche Beilage

zum

Programm des Königl. Marienstifts-Gymnasiums
zu Stettin.

Ostern 1914.

———— • ■ • ■ • ————

STETTIN.
Druck von Herrcke & Lebeling.
1914.

1914. Progr.-No. 220.

‚Vos exemplaria Graeca
nocturna versate manu, versate diurna.‘

Graecos in litteris omnibusque fere ingenii studiis Roma-
norum magistros fuisse cum alii Romanorum scriptores
confirmaverunt tum Horatius non nescivit hisque verbis expressit:
‚Graecia capta ferum victorem cepit et artes
intulit agresti Latio.‘
Hodie quoque iis utriusque populi litterarum monumentis, quae ad
nostram aetatem pervenerunt, Romanos omnibus fere locis Grae-
corum vestigia pressisse perspicere licet. Ac perspectum est
iam pridem a viris doctis. Neque tamen in hac universa re est
acquiescendum, sed hominum doctorum est in singulis litte-
rarum generibus singula persequi et quod quisque Graecorum
exemplar scriptor Romanus ad imitandum sibi proposuerit,
investigare. Nam nisi ea quae mutuati sunt Romani discernuntur,
quae ipsi effecerunt plane cognosci non possunt.
Ad hanc rem perficiendam quamquam iam multa sunt in
litteris elaborata, tamen tantum abest, ut omnia sint explorata,
ut multa etiamnunc conficienda esse videantur. Itaque Ed.
Norden, vir ille et Graecis litteris et Latinis eruditissimus, de
iis rebus, quae in praesens sunt pertractandae, ita dicit:*) ‚Es
ist ein beneidenswert schöner Glaube, lateinische Schriftstücke
irgendwelcher Art rein aus sich selbst heraus erklären zu
können, aber es ist doch ein Wahnglaube und in Wahrheit
das Produkt der ἀνιστορησία, ein Rudiment aus den Zeiten der
Renaissance, die das Lateinische isolierte. Was wir brauchen,
das ist vielmehr, um es kurz so zu formulieren, eine Topik der
Motive in Poesie und Prosa‘.

---

*) Gercke-Norden, Einleitung in die Altertumswissenschaft ² I, p. 446.

Quarum rerum ad eam partem, quae spectat ad carmina amatoria, accedere huiusque litterarum generis locos communes colligere mihi est in animo. Qua in re semper fere apparet eosdem τόπους et in Graecorum litteris et in Romanorum inveniri semperque considerantibus nobis utri ab alteris pendeant iudicandum est Romanos ex Graecis fontibus hausisse; atque etiam si duorum locorum, in quibus eadem sententia occurrit, Graeci loci auctor post Latinum vixit, cavendum est, ne specie inducti Graecum a Romano mutuatum esse putemus: immo utrumque ex tertio aliquo fonte communi hausisse putandum est. *)

Graecarum litterarum ea aetas, qua Venus amoris dea regnabat, est Alexandrinorum, quae dicitur. Illis enim praecipue temporibus amatoria carmina et elegiae et, quae cum his arte cohaerent, epigrammata vigebant. Alexandrinorum elegiae amatoriae ipsae temporum iniquitate perierunt; qua re relinquitur, ut illorum elegiae ex carminibus Romanorum amatoriis Catulli, Tibulli, Properti, Ovidi, quos Alexandrinorum vestigia pressisse ex ipsorum testimoniis apparet, cognoscantur. At epigrammata Graecorum vetustatem tulerunt. Quae carmina quia singula ut parva facile perire poterant, mox in florilegia congerebantur, qua re permulta illa ad nostram aetatem pervenerunt, quae in Anthologia Palatina, quae fertur, exstant. Haec duo sunt ea litterarum genera, a quibus loci communes amatorii praecipue sunt petendi. Ac proficisci quidem ab epigrammatis expedit, utpote quibus id poetae plerumque spectent, ut singulas sententias brevitate quadam atque acumine versibus exprimant. Ad nostram quaestionem pertinent Anthologiae Palatinae epigrammata libri V, quo amatoria continentur; praeterea huc spectant carmina imprimis libri XII, Stratonis Musae puerilis, ac ne in aliis quidem libris amatoria carmina passim dispersa desunt.

Sed praeter elegias et epigrammata etiam tertium poesis genus exstat, quo Amor plurimum valebat: comoediam novam quae fertur Atticorum dico, quae Plauti et Terenti fabulis imitatione est expressa.

*) Conf. E. Rohde, Der griechische Roman und seine Vorläufer. ² Leipz. 1900, p. 148 et Mallet, Quaestiones Propertianae, Gottingae 1882, p. 56.

Cum Plauto et Terentio in sententiis amatoriis adhibendis et tractandis Tibullum, Propertium, Ovidium non raro consentire, eos viros doctos, qui illis poetis interpretandis operam dederunt, non fugit. Quae res quomodo explicanda sit, Fridericus Leo docuit.*) Ita rem se habere vir ille doctissimus ratiocinatur: res amatoriae a comicis poetis ex hominum vita desumptae in Alexandrinorum poesin transierunt praecipueque in elegiam, qua amplificatae sunt uberiusque exornatae. Cohaesisse autem Alexandrinorum elegiam cum Atticorum comoedia nova vel ex eo cognosci potest, quod Romanorum elegia saepe consentit cum Romanorum comoedia. Cum enim dubitari non possit, quin Tibullus, Propertius, Ovidius veteres Romanorum poetas minimi aestimaverint, fieri non potest, quin et elegiaci Romanorum poetae et comici ex communi tertio fonte, scilicet ex comoedia nova Atticorum hauserint. Quo ex fonte Plautum et Terentium recta via hausisse inter omnes constat. Elegiacos autem Romanorum poetas non ipsos comicos, sed eorum aemulatores, elegiacos Alexandrinos imitatos esse, veri est simillimum.**)

Haec universa satis sunto. Iam ad ipsam dissertationem transeamus.

§ 1. Initium disserendi faciam ab ea sententia, quae saepissime in poesi amatoria occurrit, amatores magno amore inflammatos contendere solere sua amica neminem usquam pulchriorem inveniri, at illam omnes alias mulieres pulchritudine longe superare. De quo loco communi universo iam Hoelzer***) disputavit. Neque vero satis habet amator suam puellam omnium pulcherrimam esse, sed ad tantam saepe procedit admirationem, ut amatae puellae pulchritudinem comparet cum dis. Quo in

*) Plautinische Forschungen ¹, p. 129.
**) De elegiae Romanorum origine aliter ac Leo iudicat Jacoby (Mus. Rhen. vol. LX, p. 38–105). Contendit enim a poetis Alexandrinis elegias ad ipsorum amores pertinentes omnino non esse compositas studetque demonstrare elegiam Romanorum originem duxisse ex Alexandrinorum epigrammatis amatoriis, quae ipsa recta via penderent ab Atticorum comoedia nova. Cf. Heinemann, Epistulae amatoriae quomodo cohaereant cum elegiis Alexandrinis. (Dissert. Argentor. XIV 3) Argentorati 1909.
***) Hoelzer, De poesi amatoria a comicis Atticis exculta, ab elegiacis imitatione expressa. Pars I. Dissert. inaug. Marpurgi 1899, p. 18 sqq.

τόπῳ non mirum est praecipue Venerem eiusque puerum, Cupidinem, in certamen vocari. Quod his exemplis et Graecis et Latinis confirmetur:

A. P. V 72*) Rufini:

> Δαίμονες, οὐκ ᾔδειν ὅτι λούεται ἡ Κυθέρεια,
> χερσὶ καταυχενίους λυσαμένη πλοκάμους.
> ἱλήκοις, δέσποινα, καὶ ὄμμασιν ἡμετέροισι
> μήποτε μηνίσῃς, θεῖον ἰδοῦσι τύπον.
> νῦν ἔγνων. Ῥοδόκλεια καὶ αἱ Κύπρις. εἶτα τὸ κάλλος
> τοῦτο πόθεν; σύ, δοκῶ, τὴν θεὸν ἐκδέδυκας.

Quid quod Venus ipsa, cum mulierem pulcherrimam in Nilo flumine membra lavantem conspexerit, se alteram Venerem, tamquam sui imaginem aspicere putat? A. P. IX 386 incerti:

> Ἁ Κύπρις πρῴαν γυμνάν σ᾽ ἐβόασεν ἰδοῦσα·
> „Φεῦ, φεῦ, πῶς σταγόνων ἔκτοθεν Οὐρανίων,
> ζαλώσας ὠδῖνα Θαλάσσας, ὁ θρασὺς ἄλλαν
> Νεῖλος ἀπὸ γλυκερῶν Κύπριν ἀνῆκε βυθῶν;"

Conferas etiam Claudianum, sedulum illum poetarum Alexandrinorum imitatorem [epigr. 91]:

> ,hic formosa iacet Veneris sortita figuram.'

Ovid. amor. III 11, 47:

> ,perque tuam faciem, magni mihi numinis instar. . .'

Huc illud quoque epigramma dedicatorium pertinet, quo amator puellam propterea pulcherrimam esse dicit, quod a Venere cestum venustatem omnem gratiamque tribuentem acceperit:

(A. P. VI 88 Antiphanis Macedon.)

> Αὐτή σοι Κυθέρεια τὸν ἱμερόεντ᾽ ἀπὸ μαστῶν,
> Ἰνώ, λυσαμένη κεστὸν ἔδωκεν ἔχειν,
> ὡς ἂν θελξινόοισιν ἀεὶ φίλτροισι δαμάζῃς
> ἀνέρας· ἐχρῆσω δ᾽εἰς ἐμὲ πᾶσι μόνον.

Simili modo puer amatus comparatur cum Cupidine, Veneris filio; A. P. XII 54 Meleagri:

> Ἀρνεῖται τὸν Ἔρωτα τεκεῖν ἡ Κύπρις, ἰδοῦσα
> ἄλλον ἐν ἠϊθέοις Ἵμερον Ἀντίοχον.
> Ἀλλά, νέοι, στέργοιτε νέον Πόθον· ἦ γὰρ ὁ κοῦρος
> εὕρηται κρείσσων οὗτος Ἔρωτος Ἔρως.

*) Antholog. Graec. ed. Stadtmüller.

A. P. XII 75 Asclepiadis:

> Εἰ πτερά σοι προσέκειτο, καὶ ἐν χερὶ τόξα καὶ ἰοί,
> οὐκ ἂν Ἔρως ἐγράφη Κύπριδος, ἀλλὰ σύ, παῖς.

A. P. XII 76 – 78; XVI 68.

Conf. nunc Alliae Potestatis elogium (Atene e Roma XVI 259) v. 18:

> ‚et nitor in facie permansit eburneus illae,
> qualem mortalem nullam habuisse ferunt.‘

Haec sententia ita augeri solet, ut amator puellam etiam superare Venerem praedicet; velut Paulus Silentiarius amatorem, qui puellae piscem tamquam a Venere marina sibi oblatum mittit, Venerem se ab illa victam pulchritudine fassam esse dicentem facit A. P. V 300, 5:

> εἰ δέ τί σοι στέλλω βύθιον γέρας, ἵλαθι, κούρη·
> εἰς σὲ θαλασσαίη τοῦτο φέρει Παφίη,
> κάλλεϊ νικηθεῖσα τεοῦ χροὸς ἱμερόεντος,
> τὸ πρὶν ἐπ᾽ ἀγλαΐη θάρσος ἀπωσαμένη.

Praeterea conferas velim Ovid. amor. III 2, 59:

> ‚quod dea promisit, promittas ipsa, rogamus:
> pace loquar Veneris, tu dea maior eris.‘

Tibull. IV 13, 13:

> ‚nunc licet e caelo mittatur amica Tibullo,
> mittetur frustra, deficietque Venus.‘ *)

Meleagri Heliodora Gratias gratia superat, id quod poeta his versibus praedicat (A. P. V 147):

> Φαμὶ ποτ᾽ ἐν μύθοις τὰν εὔλαλον Ἡλιοδώραν
> νικάσειν αὐτὰς τὰς Χάριτας χάρισιν.

Neque vero solum amata puella ab amatore cum dea comparatur, sed contra etiam ab amante muliere amator cum Jove. Catull. 70:

> ‚Nulli se dicit mulier mea nubere malle
> quam mihi, non si se Juppiter ipse petat.‘

---

*) Non mirum, quod deae cum mortalibus exaequatae vel ab iis victae ira invidiaque amantibus excitatur; conferas Propert. III 28, 9:

> ‚num sibi collatam doluit Venus ipsa paremque?
> per se formosis invidiosa deast.‘

Alia exempla huius sententiae collegit Hoelzer l. l. p. 21.

vel eiusdem c. 72:

> ‚Dicebas quondam solum te nosse Catullum,
> Lesbia, nec prae me velle tenere Jovem.'

Denique amator magno amore captus se ipse exaequat cum dis. Quae sententia iam legitur in illo Sapphus praeclaro carmine (Anth. lyr. 2 [Bergk]):

> Φαίνεταί μοι κῆνος ἴσος θέοισιν
> ἔμμεν ὤνηρ ὅστις ἐναντίος τοι
> ἰζάνει. . . .

Quam Catullum imitatum esse carmine 51 nemo nescit:

> ‚Ille mi par esse deo videtur,
> ille, si fas est, superare divos,
> qui sedens adversus identidem te
> spectat et audit.'

Iterum ac saepius occurrit haec sententia. A. P. V 93 Rufini:

> εὐδαίμων ὁ βλέπων σε · τρισόλβιος ὅστις ἀκούει ·
> ἡμίθεος δ' ὁ φιλῶν · ἀθάνατος δ' ὁ γαμῶν.

Propert. III 15, 39:

> ‚si dabit haec multas (scil. noctes), fiam immortalis in illis.
> nocte una quivis vel deus esse potest.'

Propert. III 14, 9:

> ‚quanta ego praeterita collegi gaudia nocte:
> immortalis ero, si altera talis erit.'

Plaut. Curc. 167, Merc. 603, Poen. 276, Pseud. 1258.

§ 2. Amatori puellam amatam in caelum extollenti facile in mentem venit iudicii illius praeclari, quod fecit Paris litem componere a Jove iussus trium dearum de pulchritudine certantium. Quod iudicium poetae ita in suum usum conferre solent, ut puellam amatam in Veneris locum substituant. Velut Rufinus Junonem et Minervam Μαιονίδος puellae pulchritudini invidentes ita loquentes facit (A. P. V 68, 3):

> Οὐκέτι γυμνούμεσθα · κρίσις μία ποιμένος ἀρκεῖ ·
> οὐ καλὸν ἡττᾶσθαι δὶς περὶ καλλοσίνης.

Saepe etiam in hoc sententiarum nexu puella Veneri praestat. Paris enim, si amata puella cum tribus deis in pulchritudinis certamen quarta descendisset, sententiam secundum Venerem dictam mutavisset pomo illi tributo. A. P. V 221, 5 Agathiae:

εἰ δὲ καὶ ἀγλαΐης κρίσις ἵστατο, μᾶλλον ἂν αὐτῇ
Κύπρις ἐνίκη.9η, κἀνεδίκαζε Πάρις.

Simili modo in Rufini carmine obscoeno A. P. V 34, 9 – 10. Propertius, Cynthiae suae laudes praedicans, his verbis deas alloquitur (II 2, 13):

,cedite iam, divae, quas pastor viderat olim
Idaeis tunicas ponere verticibus.'

A. L.*) 897, 81:

,De pretio formae cum tres certamen inissent
electusque Paris arbiter esset eis,
praefecit Venerem Paridis censura duabus
deque tribus victae succubuere duae.
Cum tribus ad Paridem si quarta probanda venires,
prae tribus a Paride quarta probata fores.
Pomaque si formae potiori danda fuere,
haec potius formae danda fuere tuae.'

Aliter ac Paris iudicat Rufinus poeta, arbiter factus pulchritudinis trium mulierum (A. P. V 35, 11 – 12):

ἀλλὰ σαφῶς ἃ πέπονθε Πάρις διὰ τὴν κρίσιν ᾿εἰδώς.
τὰς τρεῖς ἀθανάτας εὐθὺ συνεστεφάνουν.**)

§ 3. In alia etiam sententiarum ratione puella cum dea comparata in poesi amatoria occurrit; digna enim existimatur, quam, cum sit pulcherrima, artifices exemplar sibi sumant, si quando iis Venus vel alia dea sit effingenda.

A. P. V 14 Rufini:

Ποῦ νῦν Πραξιτέλης; ποῦ δ᾿ αἱ χέρες αἱ Πολυκλείτου,
αὐταῖς πρόσθε τέχναις πνεῦμα χαριζόμεναι;

*) Anthologia Latina, rec. Alexander Riese.
**) Ovidius iudicium Paridis eo modo in rem suam convertit, ut Veneris victoriam a duabus deis latam laudibus efferens et iuvenes et puellas ad amandum incitet. Conferas rem. am. 711:

,Utraque formosae Paridi potuere videri:
sed sibi collatam vicit utramque Venus.'

vel art. am. I 247:

,Luce deas caeloque Paris spectavit aperto,
cum dixit Veneri „vincis utramque, Venus.“

τίς πλοκάμους Μελίτης εὐώδεας ἢ πυρόεντα
ὄμματα καὶ δειρῆς φέγγος ἀποπλάσεται;
ποῖ πλάσται; ποῖ δ' εἰσὶ λιθοξόοι; ἔπρεπε τῇδε
μορφῇ νηὸν ἔχειν, ὡς μακάρων ξοάνῳ.

Petron. 126 (Büch.): ‚nec diu morata dominam producit e latebris
laterique meo applicat, mulierem omnibus simulacris
emendatiorem.' Conf. Aristaenet. epist. I 1*).
De hoc loco communi iam Rohde in libro, qui inscribitur
Der griechische Roman² p. 165 adn. 2 disseruit, ubi alia etiam
praeter haec exempla invenies allata; porro conf. Hoelzer l. l.
p. 19 sq.

Huc pertinent etiam ii loci, quibus quamquam deorum ratio
non habetur, puella tamen artifici exemplar commendatur:
Plaut. Poen 1271: **)

,o Apella, o Zeuxis pictor,
cur numero estis mortui? hinc exemplum ut pingeretis.'
Prop. II 3, 41:

,si quis vult fama tabulas anteire vetustas,
hic dominam exemplo ponat in arte meam.'
Praeterea Ps.-Anacr. 16 et 17; A. P. XII 56 – 57; XVI 161,
162, 168.

§ 4. Saepe mentio fit furtorum Jovis, quippe qui cum
Danae, Leda, Europa aliisve mulieribus amoris consuetudine
fuerit iunctus. Amator autem, quanto illis mulieribus a Jove
dilectis pulchriorem suam puellam esse putat, tanto magis
veretur, ne Juppiter pulchritudine puellae captus rursus mutetur
puellamque suam sectetur; alii etsi periculum non esse putant,
ne sibi eripiantur a Jove amores et deliciae, at tamen suam
puellam esse veram Danaen, amore Jovis dignissimam contendunt.

A. P. V 256 Palladae:

Νῦν καταγιγνώσκω καὶ τοῦ Διὸς ὡς ἀνεράστου,
μὴ μεταβαλλομένου τῆς σοβαρᾶς ἕνεκα —
οὔτε γὰρ Εὐρώπης, οὐ τῆς Δανάης περὶ κάλλος
οὐδ' ἁπαλῆς Λήδης ἐστ' ἀπολειπομένη —

---

*) Heinemann l. l., p. 59.
**) Jacobs ad A. P. V 14.

Petron. 126:

> ‚quid factum est, quod tu proiectis, Juppiter, armis
> inter caelicolas fabula muta taces?
> nunc erat a torva submittere cornua fronte,
> nunc pluma canos dissimulare tuos.
> Haec vera est Danae. Tempta modo tangere corpus. . .‘

A. L. 897:

> 51 ‚Non Helenae mater nec par tibi filia Ledae,
> quamvis haec Paridem moverit, illa Jovem.
> . . . . .
> 59 Tuque puellarum dum ludis in agmine princeps,
> inter virgineos lucida stella choros,
> si magno conspecta Jovi de nube fuisses,
> deposuisse deum non puduisset eum.‘
> 67 – 68.

Ovid. amor. I 10, 1:

> ‚Qualis ab Eurota Phrygiis avecta carinis
> coniugibus belli causa duobus erat,
> qualis erat Lede, quam plumis abditus albis
> callidus in falsa lusit adulter ave,
> qualis Amymone siccis erravit in agris,
> cum premeret summi verticis urna comas,
> talis eras: aquilamque in te taurumque timebam,
> et quidquid magno de Jove fecit amor.‘

Prop. II 2, 3:

> ‚cur haec in terris facies humana moratur?
> Juppiter, ignoro pristina furta tua.‘

Eiusdem I 13, 29:

> ‚nec mirum, cum sit Jove dignae proxima Ledae,
> et Ledae partu gratior, una tribus,
> illa sit Inachiis et blandior heroinis,
> illa suis verbis cogat amare Jovem.‘

Frequentata est haec sententia in carminibus Musae puerilis, in quibus puer iterum ac saepius comparatur cum Ganymede, quem Juppiter in aquilam conversus in caelum rapuit. Dubium non est amatori, quin Juppiter, si puerum videret, amore inflammatus Ganymede repudiato hunc, qui ministraret sibi pocula, abriperet.

A. P. XII 194 Stratonis:

> Εἰ Ζεὺς ἐκ γαίης θνητοῖς ἔτι παῖδας ἐς αἴθρην
> ἥρπαζεν, γλυκεροῦ νέκταρος οἰνοχόους.
> αἰετὸς ἂν πτερύγεσσιν Ἀγρίππαν τὸν καλὸν ἡμῶν
> ἤδη πρὸς μακάρων ἦγε διηκονίας.
> Ναὶ μὰ σὲ γάρ, Κρονίδη, κόσμου πάτερ, ἢν ἐσαθρήσῃς,
> τὸν Φρύγιον ψέξεις αὐτίκα Δαρδανίδην.

A. P. XII 20 Juli Leonidae:

> Θαῦμα γὰρ εἰ Περίανδρον ἰδὼν οἰχ ἥρπασε γαίης
> τὸν καλόν ἢ φιλόπαις οὐκέτι νῦν ὁ θεός.

Similia leguntur A. P. XII 64, 3–4; 65; 69; 70; 37. – Conferas etiam Hoelzerum l. l. p 22.

§ 5. Puellarum gratia saepe fit, ut amata mulier in numerum dearum relata tribus Gratiis exaequetur. Usitata huius sententiae forma ea est, qua amator puellam unam esse ex tribus Gratiis contendat.

A. P. V 148 Meleagri:

> Τίς μοι Ζηνοφίλαν λαλιὰν παρέδειξεν ἑταίραν;
> τίς μίαν ἐκ τρισσῶν ἤγαγέ μοι Χάριτα;
> ἄρ᾽ ἐτύμως ἀνὴρ κεχαρισμένον ἄνυσεν ἔργον
> δῶρα διδοὺς καὐτὰν τὰν Χάριν ἐν χάριτι.

Idem Meleager in maius extollit Heliodoram suam, cum eam vel Gratias ipsas superare dicit (A. P. V 147):

> Φαμὶ ποτ᾽ ἐν μύθοις τὰν εὔλαλον Ἡλιοδώραν
> νικάσειν αὐτὰς τὰς Χάριτας χάρισιν.*)

Interdum sententia ita conformatur, ut puella quarta Gratia tribus illis adnumeretur.

A. P. V 145 Callimachi:

> Τέσσαρες αἱ Χάριτες ποτὶ γὰρ μία ταῖς τρισὶ κείναις
> ἄρτι ποτεπλάσθη, κἤτι μύροισι νοτεῖ
> εὐαίων ἐν πᾶσιν ἀρίζαλος Βερενίκα,
> ἇς ἄτερ οὐδ᾽ αὐταὶ ταὶ Χάριτες Χάριτες.

---

*) Conf. Aristaenet. epist. l 2: δύο κόραι προσῆλθον ἀναβλέπουσαι χάριν ἔρωτος μειδιῶσαι καὶ μόνῃ (emend. Kroll; cod. μόναι) γε τῷ ἀριθμῷ λειπόμεναι τῶν Χαρίτων.

A. P. V 69 Rufini:

σὺν σοὶ δ'αἱ Χάριτες τέσσαρές εἰσι, φίλη.

Quid quod virtutes et laudes puellae ita cumulantur, ut eadem triplex sit dea, cum et Gratiae sit instar et Veneris et Musae; quo fit, ut iam quattuor numerentur Gratiae, Veneres duae, decem Musae.

A. P. V 94 incerti:

Τέσσαρες αἱ Χάριτες, Παφίαι δύο καὶ δέκα Μοῦσαι *)
Δερκυλὶς ἐν πάσαις Μοῦσα, Χάρις, Παφίη.

Saepissime puellae non ipsae Gratiae fiunt, sed deae iis favisse et gratiam aliaque bona et corporis et animi tribuisse dicuntur.

A. P. V 194 Meleagri:

Αἱ τρισσαὶ Χάριτες τρισσὸν στεφάνωμα συνεῖραν
Ζηνοφίλᾳ, τρισσᾶς σύμβολα καλλοσύνας ·
ἁ μὲν ἐπὶ χρωτὸς θεμένα πόθον ἁ δ' ἐπὶ μορφᾶς
ἵμερον, ἁ δὲ λόγοις τὸ γλυκίμυθον ἔπος.

A. P. V 259, 7 Pauli Silentiari:

μορφὴν τριχθαδίην Χαρίτων τριὰς ἀμφιπολεύει ·
πᾶσα δέ μοι μορφὴ πῦρ ἴδιον προχέει.

Similia inveniuntur A. P. V 139; 12; 121; XII 121.

Praeter Gratias aliae etiam deae, praecipue Venus eiusque filius, puellas ornaverunt omni venustate et gratia:

(A. P. V 195 Meleagri)

Ζηνοφίλᾳ κάλλος μὲν Ἔρως, σύγκοιτα δὲ φίλτρα
Κύπρις ἔδωκεν ἔχειν, αἱ Χάριτες δὲ χάριν.

A. P. V 136.

Quin etiam quattuor deae a Rufino poeta laudantur, quae Melitam suam pulchritudine ornaverint:

(A. P. V 93)

Ὄμματ' ἔχεις Ἥρης, Μελίτη, τὰς χεῖρας Ἀθήνης,
τοὺς μαζοὺς Παφίης, τὰ σφυρὰ τῆς Θέτιδος.

---

*) Conf. Auson. ep. 32:

Lesbia Pieriis Sappho soror addita Musis
Εἰμ' ἐνάτη Λυρικῶν, Ἀσπίδων δεκάτη.

Quo in epigrammate mirum est, quod Minerva casta copulata est cum Venere, id quod aliis etiam locis legitur:
(Prop. IV 20, 7)

,est tibi forma potens, sunt castae Palladis artes.'
(A. L. 704 Petroni)

,Hesperie lateri redimicula nectit eburno
facta suis manibus, pectore digna suo.
Jam veteres iras Venus et Tritonia ponit:
pectora nam Veneris Palladis ambit opus.'

§ 6. Inimicitias inter Venerem et Minervam antiquitus intercedere iam ex hoc carmine, quod proximum exscripsimus, satis patet. Ac profecto rem ita se habere mirum non est cogitantibus Minervam esse castitatis et sapientiae et artis bellicae deam, quam sectari Cupido non audet. Velut Lucianus Cupidinem a Venere interrogatum, cur etsi omnes alios deos, Jovem, Neptunum, Apollinem atque etiam matrem ipsam superavisset, Minervam unam non temptaret, ita respondentem fingit (deor. dial. 19, 1):

.Ιέδια, ὦ μῆτερ, αὐτήν · φοβερὰ γάρ ἐστι καὶ χαροπὴ καὶ δεινῶς ἀνδρική · ὁπόταν γοῦν ἐντεινάμενος τὸ τόξον ἴω ἐπ' αὐτήν, ἐπισείουσα τὸν λόφον ἐκπλήττει με καὶ ὑπότρομος γίνομαι καὶ ἀπορρεῖ μου τὰ τοξεύματα ἐκ τῶν χειρῶν.*)

Itaque et Venus et Pallas ut amantes homines ad se perducant, operam dant; Venus enim hominibus persuadere studet, ut

---

*) In eodem deor. dialog. capite etiam Musas a Cupidine non impugnari legimus: σεμναὶ γάρ εἰσι, Cupido ratiocinatur (19, 2), καὶ ἀεί τι φροντίζουσι καὶ περὶ ᾠδήν ἔχουσι καὶ ἐγὼ παρίσταμαι πολλάκις αὐταῖς κηλούμενος ὑπὸ τοῦ μέλους. Cum quo loco consentit A. P. IX 39 Musici:

'Α Κύπρις Μούσαισι · „Κοράσια, τὰν Ἀφροδίταν
τιμᾶτ', ἢ τὸν Ἔρων ὕμμιν ἐφοπλίσομαι.“
Χαὶ Μοῖσαι ποτὶ Κύπριν · „Ἄρει τὰ στωμύλα ταῦτα ·
ἡμῖν δ'οὐ πέτεται τοῦτο τὸ παιδάριον.“

Ut Minerva, ita Diana quoque venatrix a Cupidine vinci non potest; utraque dea virgo est. Conferas Ovid. met. V 375, ubi Venus apud filium his verbis queritur:

,Pallada nonne vides iaculatricemque Dianam
abscessisse mihi?'

Rohde, Griech. Roman ², p. 157 adnot. 4.

amori totos se dedant, Pallas autem ut ex animo amorem
eiciant. Ut autem utrique inserviant homines, fieri nullo modo
potest. Quae sententia in hoc carmine inest:

(A. P. V 292 Pauli Silentiari)

> Θεσμὸν Ἔρως οὐκ οἶδε βιημάχος, οἰδέ τις ἄλλη
> ἀνέρα νοσφίζει πρῆξις ἐρωμανίης.
> εἰ δέ σε θεσμοπόλοιο μελιδόνος ἔργον ἐρύκει,
> οὐκ ἄρα σοῖς στέρνοις λάβρος ἔνεστιν Ἔρως.
> ....
> (11) θεσμοὺς Παλλὰς ἔχει, Παφίη πόθον. εἰπέ, τίς ἀνὴρ
> εἰν ἑνὶ θητεύσει Παλλάδι καὶ Παφίη;

Etsi plerisque propositum est Venere repudiata Minervam sequi,
tamen paucis ut propositum assequantur contingit, velut huic
mulieri pulchrae castitati enixe studenti, quam laudat hoc carmen:

(A. L. 364)

> ‚Pulcrior et nivei cum sit tibi forma coloris,
> cuncta pudicitiae iura tenere cupis.
> Mirandum est, quali naturam laude gubernes,
> moribus ut Pallas, corpore Cypris eas.
> Tu neque coniugii libet excepisse levamen,
> saepius exoptas nolle videre mares.
> Haec tamen est animo quamvis exosa voluptas:
> numquid non mulier, cum paris, esse potes?‘

Sunt etiam, quae si minus omnino amori resistant, at certe
lectum negent.

A. P. V 271 Pauli Silentiari:

> Μαζοὺς χερσὶν ἔχω, στόματι στόμα, καὶ περὶ δειρὴν
> ἄσχετα λυσσώων βόσκομαι ἀργυφέην.
> οὔπω δ' Ἀφρογένειαν ὅλην ἕλον· ἀλλ' ἔτι κάμνω
> παρθένον ἀμφιέπων λέκτρον ἀναινομένην.
> ἥμισυ γὰρ Παφίη, τὸ δ' ἄρ' ἥμισυ δῶκεν Ἀθήνη·
> αὐτὰρ ἐγὼ μέσσος τήκομαι ἀμφοτέρων.

Eadem sententia subest his eiusdem Pauli Silentiari versibus:
(A. P. V 245)

> Μαλθακὰ μὲν Σαπφοῦς τὰ φιλήματα, μαλθακὰ γυίων
> πλέγματα χιονέων, μαλθακὰ πάντα μέλη.

ψυχὴ δ' ἐξ ἀδάμαντος ἀπειϑέος · ἄχρι γὰρ οἴων
ἔστιν ἔρως στομάτων, τἄλλα δὲ παρϑενίης.
καὶ τίς ἱποιλαίη: τάχα τις, τάχα τοῦτο ταλάσσας
δίψαν Τανταλέην τλήσεται εὐμαρέως.

Plerumque autem fit, ut Minerva plane vincatur a Venere, id
quod iam docet iudicium illud Paridis, quo Venus praecurrit
et Minervam et Junonem.

A. P. V 233 Pauli Silentiari:

Ὁ πρὶν ἀμαλϑάκτοισιν ὑπὸ φρεσὶν ἠδὶν ἐν ἥβῃ
οἰστροφόροι Παφίης ϑεσμὸν ἀπειπάμενος,
γυιοβόροις βελέεσσιν ἀνέμβατος ὁ πρὶν Ἐρώτων
αὐχένα σοι κλίνω, Κύπρι, μεσαιπόλιος.
δέξο με καγχαλόωσα, σοφὴν ὅτι Παλλάδα νικᾷς,
νῦν πλέον ἢ τὸ πάρος μῆλον ἐφ' Ἑσπερίδων.

A. P. XVI 174; Auson. epigr. 42 et 43.

Sero amatorem paenitet non id fecisse quod ratio iussit. Ita
fit, ut Minerva postrema superior discedat.

A. P. VI 283 incerti:

Ἡ τὸ πρὶν αὐχήσασα πολυχρύσοις ἐπ' ἐρασταῖς,
ἡ Νέμεσιν δεινὴν οὐχὶ κύσασα ϑεόν,
μίσϑια νῦν σπαϑίοις πενιχροῖς πηνίσματα κρούει.
ὀψέ γ' Ἀϑηναίη Κύπριν ἐληίσατο.

Denique inimicitiae quae inter Venerem et Minervam intercedunt,
notantur vocibus ἐρωμανεῖν et λογίζεσϑαι *), velut in hoc carmine
Agathiae Scholastici, in quo poeta amatorem puellam suam
laudantem deque eius dote loquentem his verbis compellat:
(A. P. V 266, 9)

. . . οὐ φιλέεις, ἐψεύσαο · πᾶς δύναται γὰρ
ψυχὴ ἐρωμανέειν ὀρϑὰ λογιζομένη;

*) Nominatim stoicorum sapientia Cupidini est infesta; Cupido autem
et Zenonem et Cleanthem vincit.
A. P. V 133 Posidippi:

σιγάσϑω Ζήνων ὁ σοφὸς κύκνος ἅ τε Κλεάνϑους
μοῦσα · μέλοι δ' ἡμῖν ὁ γλυκύπικρος Ἔρως.

Eadem ratione Zenonis et Cleanthis sapientia repudiatur A. P. XI 28.

Similia leguntur A. P. IX 132 incerti:

> Σωφροσύνη καὶ "Ερως κατεναντίον ἀλλήλοισιν
> ἐλθόντις. . .

et A. P. V 92 Rufini:

> "Ωπλισμαι πρὸς "Ερωτα περὶ στέρνοισι λογισμίν, ...

Quam sententiam a Graecis mutuati sunt Romani:
Publil. Syr. 22:

> ‚Amare et sapere vix deo conceditur.‘

ibid. 116:

> ‚cum ames, non sapias aut cum sapias, non ames.‘

ibid. 15:

> ‚Amans quid cupiat scit, quid sapiat non videt.‘

§ 7. Varie homines admonentur, ut Cupidinem fugiant, quippe qui in animos semel immissus nihil nisi perturbationem sollicitudinemque hominibus afferat.

A. P. V 123 Philodemi:

> φεύγωμεν δυσέρωτες, ἕως βέλος οὐκ ἐπὶ νευρῇ·
> μάντις ἐγὼ μεγάλης αὐτίκα πυρκαΐῆς.

A. P. IX 443 Pauli Silentiari:

> Μήποτε κοιλήνης Παφίη νόον . . . .
> (δ) 'Ελπίδι μὴ θέλξῃς φρένα μαχλάδι· γυιοβόρον γὰρ
> πῦρ ὑποριπίζει, θυμὸν ἐφελκομένη.

In insequenti carmine Pauli Silentiari oculi, ut qui sint in amore duces,*) appellantur:
(A. P. V 225)

> 'Οφθαλμοί, τέο μέχρις ἀφύσσετε νέκταρ 'Ερώτων,
> κάλλεος ἀκρήτου ζωροπόται θρασέες;
> τῆλε διαθρέξωμεν ὅπη σθένος·

Prop. I 1, 33:

> ‚In me nostra Venus noctes exercet amaras,
> et nullo vacuus tempore defit amor.

---

*) De sententia, oculos esse in amore duces, disseruit Mallet l. l. p. 14; de formosis oculis Hoelzer l. l. p. 23 et 40.

hoc, moneo, vitate malum: . . .

(37)   quod si quis monitis tardas adverterit aures,
heu referet quanto verba dolore mea!'

§ 8.   Atqui plerique Amori resistentes operam perdunt;
potentissimus enim omnium deorum est Amor, cui neque dei
neque homines unquam resistere possunt.*)   Cuius rei eam
esse causam saepe audimus, quod Amor sit penniger homi-
nesque, quippe qui pedibus fugiant, facile consequatur.

A. P. V 58 Archiae:**)

  'Φεύγειν δεῖ τὸν Ἔρωτα· κενὸς πόνος, οὐ γὰρ ἀλύξω
  πεζὸς ὑπὸ πτηνοῦ πυκνὰ διωκόμενος.

A. P. V 300 Pauli Silentiari:**)

  Εἰ καὶ τηλοτέρω Μερόης τεὸν ἴχνος ἐρείσεις,
    πτηνὸς Ἔρως πτηνῷ κεῖσε μένει με φέρει·
  εἰ καὶ ἐς ἀντολίην πρὸς ὁμόχροον ἵξεαι Ἠῶ,
    πεζὸς ἀμετρήτοις ἕψομαι ἐν σταδίοις.

Prop. III 30, 1:

  ,Quo fugis ah demens? nulla est fuga. tu licet usque
  ad Tanain fugias: usque sequetur Amor.'

Ovid. met. I 540:

  ,qui tamen insequitur pennis adiutus Amoris
  ocior est . . .'

Praeterea A. P. XII 111; 113; XVI 251.

§ 9.   Saepe iuvenis amore incensus comparatur cum ave
ab aucupe visco vel cum pisce a piscatore hamo capto.***)
Talibus vinculis fieri non potest ut exsolvatur amator.   Qui
τόπος proficisci videtur a comicis, qui saepe quaestum meretri-
cium cum aucupio vel piscatura comparant.   Quod iam vidit
Hoelzer (l. l. p. 73), qui exempla ex comoedia sumpta collegit,

---

*) Huius sententiae exempla iam Mallet l. l. p. 16 attulit, ut nihil habeam,
quod addam.

**) Conf. Malletum l. l. p. 51.

***) Anthologiae Palatinae poetas et eroticos scriptores oculum amatae
puellae comparasse cum venatore vel cum sagittario iam exemplis confirmavit
Mallet l. l. p. 14.

velut Plaut. Asin. 219: ‚aedes nobis area est, auceps sum ego, esca est meretrix . . ., amatores aves.' Retia autem vel plagas iuvenibus non solum a meretricibus sed etiam ab Amore ipso tendi complura exempla ab eodem Hoelzero (l. l. p. 74) allata docent. De puella cum piscatrice comparata accurate disseruit Dieterich, Mus. Rhen. LV 217 sq. Kl. Schr. 187 (cf. Cichorius, Untersuch. zu Lucilius 180); his verbis quid sentiat complectitur p. 217: Das Bild vom Liebesangeln gehört zu dem festen Bestand der erotischen Poesie von der Komödie an, durch die Elegie bis zum späten Liebesbrief.' Exemplis, quae Hoelzer et Dieterich collegerunt, nonnulla addere liceat:

A. P. V 95 Meleagri:*)

 'Ιξὸν ἔχεις τὸ φίλημα, τὰ δ' ὄμματα, Τιμάριον, πῦρ·
 ἢν ἐσίδῃς, καίεις· ἢν δὲ θίγῃς, δέδεκας.

A. P. V 230 Macedoni Hypatici:

 πάντοθεν ἀγρεύεις τλήμονας ἠϊθέους.

A. P. V 99 incerti:

 Εἴ μοί τις μέμψαιτο, δαεὶς ὅτι λάτρις "Ερωτος
  φοιτῶ θηρευτὴν ὄμμασιν ἰξὸν ἔχων,
 εἰδείη . . . . .

A. P. XII 132 Meleagri:

 Οὔ σοι ταῦτ' ἐβόων, ψυχή; „Ναὶ Κύπριν, ἁλώσει,
  ὦ δύσερως, ἰξῷ πυκνὰ προσιπταμένη."
 οὐκ ἐβόων; εἰλέν σε πάγη. Τί μάτην ἐνὶ δεσμοῖς
  σπαίρεις; αὐτὸς "Ερως τὰ πτερά σου δέδεκεν.

Similia inveniuntur A. P. XII 93, 1—2 et 142, 1—2.

De amatore, quem puella quasi hamo captavit, sunt haec exempla:

A. P. XII 241 Stratonis:**)

 "Αγκιστρον πεπόηκας, ἔχεις ἰχθὺν ἐμέ, τέκνον·
 ἕλκε μ' ὅπου βούλει· μὴ τρέχε, μή σε φύγω.

A. P. V 246, 5 Macedoni Hypatici:**)

 Κεντρομανὲς δ' ἄγκιστρον ἔφυ στόμα, καί με δακόντα
 εὐθὺς ἔχει ῥοδέου χείλεος ἐκκρεμέα.

*) Iam apud Hoelzerum legitur.
**) Iam Dieterich attulit.

Lucret. IV 1122:

„. . vitare, plagas in amoris ne iaciamur,
non ita difficilest quam captum retibus ipsis
exire et validos Veneris perrumpere nodos.‘

Eadem imagine Tibullus si non puellam at Spem deam alloquens utitur II 6, 23:

„haec (scil. Spes) laqueo volucres, haec captat arundine pisces,
cum tenues hamos abdidit ante cibus.‘

§ 10. Saepe homines amantes amori, quem sibi perniciosum fore cognoverint, summa vi repugnant; plerumque autem frustra repugnant. *)

A. P. V 23 [Meleagri]:

ψυχή μοι προλέγει φείγειν πόθον Ἡλιοδώρας,
δάκρυα καὶ ζήλους τοῖς πρὶν ἐπισταμένη.
φησὶ μίν · ἀλλὰ φυγεῖν οὔ μοι σθένος · ἡ γὰρ ἀναιδὴς
αὐτὴ καὶ προλέγει καὶ προλέγουσα φιλεῖ.

A. P. V 229, 5 Pauli Silentiari:

ὡς δὲ διαρρῆξαι (scil. δεσμὰ Δωρίδος) σθένος οὐκ
ἔχον, ἔστενον ἤδη,
οἷά τε χαλκείη σφιγκτὸς ἀλυκτοπέδῃ.

Prop. IV 21, 3:

„crescit enim adsidue spectando cura puellae:
ipse alimenta sibi maxima praebet amor.
omnia sunt temptata mihi, quacunque fugari
possit: at ex omni me premit iste deus.‘

*) At eos ipsos, qui tam vehementer resistunt, Cupido plus vexat quam eos, qui libenter se ei dedunt; crescit enim luctando Cupido.

A. P. V 175 Meleagri:

Δεινὸς Ἔρως, δεινός. τί δὲ τὸ πλέον, ἢν πάλιν εἴπω
καὶ πάλιν οἰμώζων πολλάκι 'δεινὸς Ἔρως';
ἦ γὰρ ὁ παῖς τούτοισι γελᾷ καὶ πυκνὰ κακισθεὶς
ἥδεται · ἢν δ'εἴπω λοίδορα, καὶ τρέφεται.

Ovid. amor. I 2, 9:

„Cedimus an subitum luctando accendimus ignem?‘
(17) acrius invitos multoque ferocius urget
quam qui servitium ferre fatentur, Amor.‘

Tibull. I 8, 7:

„desine dissimulare: deus crudelius urit
quos videt invitos succubuisse sibi.‘

Ovid. amor. I 6, 35:

,hunc (scil. Amorem) ego, si cupiam, nusquam dimittere possum:
ante vel a membris dividar ipse meis.'

§ 11. Quae cum ita sint, amatorem sic animo affectum
queri legimus, quod Cupido animo insideat neque ut avolet
moveri possit; pennis enim nisi ut advolet eum non uti.*)

A. P. V 211 Meleagri:

ὦ πτανοί, μὴ καί ποτ' ἐφίπτασθαι μέν, Ἔρωτες,
οἴδατ', ἀποπτῆναι δ' οὐδ' ὅσον ἰσχύετε;

A. P. V 267 Pauli Silentiari:

Μηκέτι τις πτήξειε πόθου βέλος· ἰοδόκην γὰρ
εἰς ἐμὲ λάβρος Ἔρως ἐξεκένωσεν ὅλην.
μὴ πτερύγων τρομέοι τις ἐπήλυσιν· ἐξότε γάρ μοι
λὰξ ἐπιβὰς στέρνοις πικρὸν ἔπηξε πόδα,
ἀστεμφής, ἀδόνητος ἐνέζεται, οὐδὲ μετέστη,
εἰς ἐμὲ συζυγίην κειράμενος πτερύγων.

A. P. V 57 Archiae:**)

Νήπι' Ἔρως πορθεῖς με, τὸ κρήγυον· εἰς με κένωσον
πᾶν σὺ βέλος, λοιπὴν μηκέτ' ἀφεὶς γλυφίδα,
ὡς ἂν μοῦνον ἕλοις ἰοῖς ἐμέ, καί τινα χρήζων
ἄλλον ἀιστεῦσαι μηκέτ' ἔχοις ἀκίδα.

A. P. V 197, 5 Meleagri:

οὐκέτι σοι φαρέτρη [γλαφυρῇ] πτερόεντας ὀιστοὺς
κρύπτει, Ἔρως· ἐν ἐμοὶ πάντα γάρ ἐστι βέλη.

Prop. III 12, 13:

,in me tela manent, manet et puerilis imago:
sed certe pennas perdidit ille suas,
evolat heu nostro quoniam de pectore nusquam,
assiduusque meo sanguine bella gerit.'

Quo cum loco Birt (apud Hoelzerum, I. I. p. 15) confert
A. L. 896, 5:

,Cur ita complicitis alis?' nunquam evolat.'

Alia huius sententiae exempla invenies apud Hoelzerum, I.I. p.17.

*) Cf. Leo, Plautinische Forschungen p. 137. — Mallet, I. I. p. 17. —
Hoelzer, I. I. p. 15 sq.

**) quod epigramma tam simile est illi Pauliano, ut eius vestigia pressisse
poetam Byzantinum Mallet (p. 17) colligat.

§ 12. Ita fit, ut amantes homines ab Amore petant, ut se agitare desinat; alios potius vexet, id quod plus laudis ei adferat.*)

A. P. V 178, 9 Meleagri:

> ἀλλ' ἴθι, δυσνίκητε, λαβὼν δ' ἔπι κοῦφα πέδιλα
> ἐκπέτασον ταχινὰς εἰς ἑτέρους πτέρυγας.

A. P. V 214 Meleagri:

> Λίσσομ', Ἔρως, τὸν ἄγρυπνον ἐμοὶ πόθον Ἡλιοδώρας
> κοίμισον. αἰδεσθεὶς Μοῦσαν ἐμὰν ἱκέτιν.
> ναὶ γὰρ δὴ τὰ σὰ τόξα, τὰ μὴ δεδιδαγμένα βάλλειν
> ἄλλον, ἀεὶ δ' ἐπ' ἐμοὶ πτανὰ χέοντα βέλη,
> εἰ καὶ ἐμὲ κτείναις, λείψω φωνὴν προϊέντα
> γράμματ'· "Ἔρωτος ὅρα, ξεῖνε, μιαιφονίαν."

A. P. V 97 incerti:

> Ὁπλίζευ, Κύπρι, τόξα καὶ εἰς σκοπὸν ἥσυχος ἐλθὲ
> ἄλλον· ἐγὼ γὰρ ἔχω τραύματος οὐδὲ τόπον.**)

A. P. V 9 Alcaei:

> Ἐχθαίρω τὸν Ἔρωτα· τί γὰρ βαρὺς οὐκ ἐπὶ θῆρας
> ὄρνυται, ἀλλ' ἐπ' ἐμὴν ἰοβολεῖν κραδίην;

Prop. III 12, 17:

> ‚Quid tibi iucundum est siccis habitare medullis?
> si pudor est, alio traice tela tua.
> Intactos isto satius temptare veneno:
> non ego, sed tenuis vapulat umbra mea.'

Ovid. amor. III 11, 27:

> ‚his et quae taceo duravi saepe ferendis:
> quaere alium pro me, qui queat ista pati.'

Ovid. amor. III 11, 1:

> ‚multa diuque tuli . . . . . .
> cede fatigato pectore, turpis amor!'

---

*) In mentem venit tituli illius precatorii in aedificiis hic illic inscripti: „Ich bitt' dich, heiliger Florian, behüt mein Haus, zünd' andere an!“
**) Leviter est inflexa sententia in A. P. V 223 Macedoni epigrammate, ubi amator, ne diutius pectus fatigatum Cupido vexet, sed in aliam corporis partem tela iaciat, petit:

> Λῆξον, Ἔρως, κραδίης τε καὶ ἥπατος· εἰ δ' ἐπιθυμεῖς
> βάλλειν, ἄλλο τί μου τῶν μελέων μετάβα.

Praeterea Tibull. II 1, 81; II 4, 6; Ovid. amor. I 2, 50; II 5, 1;
II 9, 1; Catull. 63, 91 – 93;*) Callim. hymn. I 69; II 113; Eurip.
Med. 632. (Cf. etiam Mallet, I. I. p. 49.)

Interdum sententia ita est conformata, ut amator amore
vexatus animo demisso et humili Cupidinis telis se ipse obiciat
Cupidinemque hortetur, ut nisi fatigare desistat statim se
interficiat.

A. P. XII 166 Asclepiadis:

Τοῦϑ᾽ ὅ τι μοι λοιπὸν ψυχῆς, ὅ τι δὴ ποτ᾽, Ἔρωτες,
    τοῦτό γ᾽ ἔχειν πρὸς ϑεῶν ἡσυχίην, ἄφετε·
ἢ μὴ δὴ τόξοις ἔτι βάλλετέ μ᾽, ἀλλὰ κεραυνοῖς·
    ναὶ πάντως τέφρην ϑέσϑε με κάνϑρακιήν.
Ναί, ναί, βάλλετ᾽, Ἔρωτες· ἐνεσκληκὼς γὰρ ἀνίαις,
    ἐξ ὑμέων τοῦτ᾽ οὖν, εἴ γέ τι, βούλομ᾽ ἔχειν.

Cuius epigrammatis versus 5 – 6 congruunt cum

A. P. XII 45 Posidippi:

ναί, ναί, βάλλετ᾽, Ἔρωτες· ἐγὼ σκοπὸς εἷς ἅμα πολλοῖς
    κεῖμαι. Μὴ φείσησϑ᾽, ἄφρονες·

Quo cum epigrammate Mallet (p. 52) confert Prop. II 9, 37
sq. et Ovid. amor. II 9, 6.

A. P. V 196 Meleagri:

βαιὸν ἔχω τό γε λειφϑέν, Ἔρως, ἐπὶ χείλεσι πνεῦμα·
    εἰ δ᾽ ἐϑέλεις καὶ τοῦτ᾽, εἰπέ, καὶ ἐκπτύσομαι.

§ 13. Cum iis sententiis, de quibus modo disseruimus,
amatores exoptent, ut animos ab amore avellant, alii inveniuntur
loci, quibus amatores tanto amore puellae sint capti, ut quidvis,
quin etiam mortem se perpeti velle dicant, dummodo iungantur
cum amoribus suis.

A. P. V 220 Pauli Silentiari:

. . . . κἢν τις ἐρύξῃ
    μαλϑακὰ λυσιπόνου πλέγματα συζυγίης,
φάρμακον ἀμφοτέροις ξίφος ἔσσεται· ἥδιον ἡμῖν
    ξυνὸν ἀεὶ μεϑέπειν ἢ βίον ἢ ϑάνατον.

A. P. V 227 eiusdem:

ὄμμασιν οἷς Ῥοδόπην οὐ δέρκομαι, οὐδὲ φαεινῆς
    φέγγος ἰδεῖν ἐϑέλω χρύσεον Ἠριπόλης.

_____

*) Cf. Morawski, Catulliana (Krakau 1903) 14.

A. P. V 247 eiusdem: Poeta cum periculum sit, ne mulier amata amicitiam sibi renuntiet, ab ea petit:

μή, λίτομαι, δέσποινα, τόσην μὴ λάμβανε ποινήν·
μᾶλλον ἐγὼ τλαίην φάσγανον ἀσπασίως.

A. P. V 237 Macedoni Hypatici:

σὺ δ᾽ ἢν ἀπ᾽ ἐμεῖο λάθηαι,
τί ξίφος ἡμετέρην δύσεται ἐς λαγόνα.

A. P. V 63 Asclepiadis:

Νεῖφε, χαλαζοβόλει, ποίει σκότος, αἶθε, κεραυνοῖ,
πάντα τὰ πορφύροντ᾽ ἐν χθονὶ σεῖε νέφη.
ἢν γάρ με κτείνῃς, τότε παύσομαι· ἢν δέ μ᾽ ἀφῇς ζῆν,
καὶ διαθεὶς τούτων χείρονα, κωμάσομαι.*)

Cf. Horat. c. I 22, 21 sqq.

A. P. V 167 incerti:

Καὶ πυρὶ καὶ νιφετῷ με καί, εἰ βούλοιο, κεραυνῷ
βάλλε καὶ εἰς κρημνοὺς ἕλκε καὶ εἰς πελάγη.
τὸν γὰρ ἀπαυδήσαντα πόνοις καὶ Ἔρωτι δαμέντα
οὐδὲ Διὸς τρύχει πῦρ ἐπιβαλλόμενον.

Ne in sepulcralibus quidem carminibus haec sententia deest:

A. P. VII 378 Apollonidis:

ἄμφω δ᾽ ὡς ἅμ᾽ ἔναιον, ὑπὸ πλακὶ τυμβεύονται,
ξυνὸν ἀγαλλόμενοι καὶ τάφον ὡς θάλαμον.

A. P. VII incerti:

σύν τε γυναικὶ Καληποδίῃ τεῦξεν τόδε σῆμα
ὡς ἵνα τὴν στοργὴν κἢν φθιμένοισιν ἔχοι.

Quae sententia etiam apud Romanos frequentissima est. Nonnulla exempla transscribere liceat.

Prop. I 6, 27:

‚multi longinquo periere in amore libenter,
in quorum numero me quoque terra tegat.‘

Tibull. III 2, 3:

‚durus et ille fuit, qui tantum ferre dolorem,
vivere et erepta coniuge qui potuit.‘

---

*) Simillimum est illud Simonis Dach: „Kâm' alles Wetter gleich auf uns zu schlahn, wir sind gesinnt bei einander zu stahn. Krankheit, Verfolgung, Betrübnis und Pein soll unsrer Liebe Verknotigung sein." (Aennchen von Tharau V. 2.)

Versu 29 eadem sententia in formam tituli sepulcralis redacta legitur:

> ,Lygdamus hic situs est: dolor huic et cura Neaerae,
> coniugis ereptae, causa perire fuit.'

Tibull. III 3, 35:

> ,aut si fata negant reditum tristesque sorores,
> stamina quae ducunt quaeque futura neunt,
> me vocet in vastos amnes nigramque paludem
> dives in ignava luridus Orcus aqua.'

§ 14. Quod Cupido tam superbe in amatores dominatur, mirum non est cogitantibus deum pugnare contra hominem; consentaneum enim est hominem deo parem esse non posse. Quodsi Cupidini, id quod non raro fit, socium se adiungit Venus vel Bacchus, ita ut duo di pugnent contra unum hominem, repugnare stultissimi est. Sed ne dis quidem illis vicisse gloriam affert.

Haec sunt huius sententiae exempla:

(A. P. V 9 Alcaei)

> τί πλέον, εἰ θεὸς (scil. Ἔρως) ἄνδρα καταφλέγει; ἢ τί τὸ σεμνὸν
> δῃώσας ἀπ᾽ ἐμῆς ἆθλον ἔχει κεφαλῆς;

Simillime ratiocinatur Tibull. I 6, 3:

> ,quid tibi (scil. Amori) saevitiae mecum est? an gloria magnast
> insidias homini composuisse deum?
> (30) iussit Amor: contra quis ferat arma deos?'

Iuno ubi Didonem amore insano erga Aeneam captum esse sensit, hoc modo Venerem puerumque eius illudens alloquitur:

(Verg. Aen. IV 93)

> ,egregiam vero laudem et spolia ampla refertis
> tuque puerque tuus; magnum et memorabile nomen,
> una dolo divom si femina victa duorum est.'

Rufinus quidem poeta Cupidini soli obsistere se posse gloriatur, deum autem cum Baccho coniunctum se vincere posse desperat.

(A. P. V 92)

> Ὥπλισμαι πρὸς Ἔρωτα περὶ στέρνοισι λογισμόν,
> οὐδέ με νικήσει, μοῦνος ἐὼν πρὸς ἕνα.
> θνατὸς δ' ἀθανάτῳ συστήσομαι· ἢν δὲ βοηθὸν
> Βάκχον ἔχῃ, τί μόνος πρὸς δύ'*) ἐγὼ δύναμαι;

A. P. V 111 Philodemi:

> Ἠράσθην· τίς δ' οὐχί; κεκώμακα· τίς δ' ἀμύητος
> κώμων; ἀλλ' ἐμάνην· ἐκ τίνος; οὐχὶ θεοῦ;

subauditur: deo autem obsistere nefas est.

§ 15. Cupidini etiam deos, imprimis Jovem ipsum, deorum atque hominum rectorem, subiectos esse, omnium est opinio iterumque ac saepius legitur in litteris et Graecorum et Romanorum.**) Quam deorum cladem homines amori indulgentes ita in suam rem convertunt, ut ipsi quoque Cupidinem a se vinci posse desperent, nisi vero fortiores se dis esse putent; quin etiam multi ut amori se dedant, deorum exemplo incitantur.***)

Quem τόπον frequentatum iam apud Euripidem plus quam semel legimus; velut Helena adultera, ut Menelao coniugi se purget, his verbis in deos culpam transfert:

(Troad. 946)

> τί δὴ φρονοῦσ' ἐκ δόμων ἅμ' ἑσπόμην
> ξένῳ προδοῦσα πατρίδα καὶ δόμους ἐμούς;
> τὴν θεὸν κόλαζε καὶ Διὸς κρείσσων γενοῦ,
> ὃς τῶν μὲν ἄλλων δαιμόνων ἔχει κράτος,
> κείνης δὲ δοῦλός ἐστι· συγγνώμη δ' ἐμοί.

---

*) Duobus adversariis ne Herculem quidem obsistere posse proverbii loco dicitur, id quod monet Jacobs Libanio auctore usus (I 101, 18): δυοῖν γὰρ ἕνα οὐκ εἶναι κρατεῖν οὐδὲ τὸν Ἡρακλέα. De quo proverbio nuper disseruit von Prittwitz-Gaffron, Das Sprichwort im griech. Epigramm. Giessen 1912 p. 48.

**) De hac sententia egit Hoelzer l. l. p. 8 sq.

***) Nonnulla huius loci communis exempla iam collegerunt Mallet l. l. p. 27 et Hoelzer l. l. p. 52.

Nutrix Phaedrae ne amori Hippolyti diutius obsistat persuasura ita monet:

(Hippol. 473)

> ἀλλ', ὦ φίλη παῖ, λῆγε μὲν κακῶν φρενῶν,
> λῆξον δ' ὑβρίζουσ' · οὐ γὰρ ἄλλο πλὴν ὕβρις
> τάδ' ἐστί, κρείσσω δαιμόνων εἶναι θέλειν ·
> τόλμα δ' ἐρῶσα · θεὸς ἐβουλήθη τάδε.

Hippol. 451 sq. – Jon. 449 sq. – Bacch. 29.

Exempla a comoedia petita nonnulla attulit Hoelzer p. 52.

Ne Plato quidem huius sententiae est ignarus (de rep. II p. 378): . . . . ἀλλὰ δρώη ἂν ὅπερ θεῶν οἱ πρῶτοί τε καὶ μέγιστοι.

Iam transeo ad ipsa epigrammata amatoria.

A. P. V 99 incerti:

> Εἴ μοί τις μέμψαιτο, δαεὶς ὅτι λάτρις Ἔρωτος
>   φοιτῶ θηρευτὴν ὄμμασιν ἰξὸν ἔχων,
> εἰδείη καὶ Ζῆνα καὶ Ἄιδα τόν τε θαλάσσης
>   σκηπτοῦχον μαλερὰν δοῦλον ἐόντα Πόθων.
> εἰ δὲ θεοὶ τοιοίδε, θεοῖς δ' ἐνέπουσιν ἕπεσθαι
>   ἀνθρώπους, τί θεῶν ἔργα μαθὼν ἀδικῶ;

A. P. V 63 Asclepiadis: *)

> Νεῖφε, χαλαζοβόλει, ποίει σκότος, αἶθε, κεραύνου,
>   πάντα τὰ πορφύροντ' ἐν χθονὶ σεῖε νέφη.
> ἢν γάρ με κτείνῃς, τότε παύσομαι · ἢν δέ μ' ἀφῇς ζῆν,
>   καὶ διαθεὶς τούτων χείρονα, κωμάσομαι.
> ἕλκει γάρ μ' ὁ κρατῶν καὶ σοῦ θεός, ᾧ ποτε πεισθείς,
>   Ζεῦ, διὰ χαλκείων χρυσὸς ἔδυς θαλάμων.

A. P. V 166, 6 eiusdem:

> Ζεῦ φίλε. σίγησον, καὐτὸς ἐρᾶν ἔμαθες.

Qui locus animo obversatus esse videtur Theocriti hos versus scribentis:

> (VIII 59) . . . . . ὦ πάτερ ὦ Ζεῦ,
> οὐ μόνος ἠράσθην · καὶ τὺ γυναικοφίλας.

*) iam Hoelzer l. l. attulit.

Hos autem Theocriti versus Callimachi epigrammate (A. P. XII 230 [= Wilam. 52]) nutu vel potius digito significatos esse, Fritzsche (ad Theocr. VIII 56 ʰ) contendit. Sunt enim hi versus Callimachi:

> ναιχὶ πρὸς εὐχαίτεω Ἰανυμήδεος οὐράνιε Ζεῦ ·
> καὶ σύ ποτ᾽ ἠράσθης — οὐκέτι μακρὰ λέγω.

A. P. XII 117 Meleagri:

> ἐρρίφθω σοφίας ὁ πολὺς πόνος · ἓν μόνον οἶδα
> τοῦθ᾽ ὅτι καὶ Ζηνὸς λῆμα καθεῖλεν Ἔρως.

A. P. XII 101, 6 eiusdem: *)

> καὐτὸν ἀπ᾽ Οὐλύμπου Ζῆνα καθεῖλεν Ἔρως.

A Graecis Romanos mutuatos esse hi loci docent:

A. L. 144:

> ‚Mentitus taurum Europam Juppiter aufert,
>   virgineos ardens pandere fraude sinus.
> Humani tandem venia donentur amores,
>   si tibi, summe deum, dulcia furta placent.‘

Ovid. art. am. II 239:

> ‚Cynthius Admeti vaccas pavisse Pheraei
>   fertur et in parva delituisse casa:
> quod Phoebum decuit, quem non decet? exue fastus,
>   curam mansuri quisquis amoris habes!‘

Prop. III 30, 27:

> ‚illic adspicies (scil. Cynthia) scopulis haerere sorores
>   et canere antiqui dulcia furta Jovis,
> ut Semela est combustus, ut est deperditus Io,
>   denique ut ad Troiae tecta volarit avis.**)
> quod si nemo extat qui vicerit alitis arma,
>   communis culpae cur reus unus agor?‘

Ovid. art. am. III 83:

> ‚Latmius Endymion non est tibi, Luna, rubori,
>   nec Cephalus roseae praeda pudenda deae;

*) iam Hoelzer l. l. attulit.
**) ut Ganymedem raperet.

ut Veneri, quem luget adhuc, donetur Adonis,
unde habet Aenean Harmoniamque suos?
Ite per exemplum, genus o mortale, dearum
gaudia nec cupidis vestra negate viris!'

Tibull. II 3, 29:

,felices olim, Veneri cum fertur aperte
servire aeternos non puduisse deos.
Fabula nunc ille*) est: sed cui sua cura puellast,
fabula sit mavult quam sine amore deus.'

Etiam heroum amores commemorantur, ut hominum excusationem habeant.

Ovid. amor. II 8, 13:

,Nec sum ego Tantalide maior, nec maior Achille;
quod decuit reges, cur mihi turpe putem?'

Prop. II 8, 39 (agitur de eodem Achille deque eius erga Briseida amore):

,inferior multo cum sim vel matre vel armis,
mirum, si de me iure triumphat Amor?'

Ovid. art. am. II 221:

,paruit imperio dominae Tirynthius heros (scil. Hercules):
i nunc et dubita ferre, quod ille tulit!'

§ 16. Amorem hominibus graves dolores commovere atque etiam in summum discrimen eos deducere vel variis epithetis Cupidini inditis significatur; appellatur enim Ἔρως γλυκύπικρος (A. P. V 133, 4), δεινός (ibid. V 175), θρασύς (ibid. V 24, 5), σχέτλιος (ibid. V 56), βαρὺς θεός (Theocr. III 15). Similis est de Cupidine existimatio his locis:

(Theocr. XXIII 19)

Ἄγριε παῖ καὶ στυγνέ, κακᾶς ἀνάθρεμμα λεαίνας,
λάϊνε παῖ καὶ ἔρωτος ἀνάξιε, . . .

(A. P. V 176, 7 Meleagri)

πάντῃ γὰρ καὶ πᾶσιν ἀπέχθεται (Ἔρως).

---

*) Apollo Admeti tauros pascens.

(A. P. V 308 Diophanis)

Φηλήτης ὁ Ἔρως καλοῖτ᾽ ἂν ὄντως·
ἀγρυπνεῖ, ϑρασύς ἐστιν, ἐκδιδύσκει.

Apud Romanos saepissime ‚saevus‘ notatur Cupido.

§ 17. Sed etiam disertis verbis amatores varie queruntur, quod Cupido se vexet atque etiam absumat. Cuius querellae praecipuae conformationes afferantur exemplisque comprobentur!

a) Cupido perdit amatores.

A. P. V 65 Rufini: (amator alloquitur puellam)

„*Σῶσον*“ *ἔφην* „*ἄνϑρωπον ἀπολλύμενον παρὰ μικρόν,*
καὶ φεῦγον ζωῆς πνεῦμα σύ μοι χάρισαι“.

A. L. (Meyer) 989, 24:

‚Saeva non cernis, quod ego langueo?
Sic me destituis iam semimortuum?‘

Amori adiuncta sunt *οἶνος* et *λοετρά*

A. P. X 112 (incerti):

Οἶνος καὶ τὰ λοετρὰ καὶ ἡ περὶ Κύπριν ἐρωὴ
ὀξυτέρην πέμπει τὴν ὁδὸν εἰς Ἀίδην.*)

quod distichon iam Buecheler vidit imitatione expressum esse hoc titulo sepulcrali:

(Bch. 1499)

‚Balnea vina Venus corrumpunt corpora nostra,
sed vitam faciunt balnea vina Venus.‘ **)

b) Comparatur amor cum igni, quo amatores carpuntur; plus enim quam semel illi queruntur, quod amoris aestu et febri iactentur aut etiam absumantur.

A. P. V 110 Antiphili:

Εἶπον ἐγὼ καὶ πρόσϑεν, ὅτ᾽ ἦν ἔτι φίλτρα Τερείνης
νήπια· „συμφλέξει πάντας ἀεξομένη“.
οἱ δ᾽ ἐγέλων τὸν μάντιν· ἴδ᾽, ὁ χρόνος, ὃν ποτ᾽ ἐφώνουν,
οὗτος· ἐγὼ δὲ πάλαι τραύματος ᾐσϑανόμην.
καὶ τί πάϑω; λεύσσειν μὲν ὅλαι φλόγες· . .

---

*) Jacobs adnotat Plutarch. T. II p. 128 D: *ἀφροδίσια καὶ ὕφα καὶ βαλανεῖα καὶ οἶνος μιγνύμενα — φλέγμα καὶ χολὴν κινεῖ.*

**) Cf. Lier, Philolog. vol. LXIII (N. F. XVII) p. 59.

A. P. V 138 Meleagri:

> ποῖ σε φύγω; πάντῃ με περιστείχουσιν Ἔρωτες,
> οὐδ' ὅσον ἀμπνεῦσαι βαιὸν ἐῶσι χρόνον.
> . . . . πυρὶ φλέγομαι.

Cf. A. P. V 86, 6; V 123, 6; V 238, 1−2; XII 89.

A. P. V 209 Asclepiadis:

> Τῷ θαλλῷ Διδύμη με συνήρπασεν · ὤμοι, ἐγὼ δὲ
> τήκομαι, ὡς κηρὸς πὰρ πυρί, κάλλος ὁρῶν.

Vox τήκομαι eadem sententia usurpata est A. P. V 271, 6; V 258, 7−8; V 259, 1 aliisque locis.

Tibull. I 2, 97:

> ,at mihi parce, Venus: semper tibi dedita servit
> mens mea: quid messes uris acerba tuas?'

Tibull. I 8, 7:

> ,desine dissimulare: deus crudelius urit
> quos videt invitos succubuisse sibi.'

Ovid. amor. III 1, 20: ,. . . . quem ferus urit Amor.'

c) Cupidinem arcu sagittisque esse instructum, quibus armis hominibus amantibus vulnera infligat animosque inflammet, quis est quin sciat? Quae opinio tam usitata est et pertrita, ut ex multis exemplis haec pauca transscribere satis sit:

(A. P. V 86 Rufini)

> Ἀρνεῖται τὸν ἔρωτα Μελισσιάς, ἀλλὰ τὸ σῶμα
> κέκραγεν, ὡς βελέων δεξάμενον φαρέτρην,
> καὶ βάσις ἀστατέουσα καὶ ἄστατος ἄσθματος ὁρμή,
> καὶ κοῖλαι βλεφάρων ἰοτυπεῖς βάσιες.

(A. P. V 187 [Leonidae][*])

> . . . . βέβλημαι δ' ἐκ δολίου κέραος
> καὶ πᾶς τεφροῦμαι : θερμὸν δ' ἐπὶ θερμῷ ἰάλλει
> ἄτρακτον, λωφᾷ δ' οὐδ' ὅσον ἰοβολῶν.

(A. P. V 197, 5 Meleagri)

> οὐκέτι σοι φαρέτρη [γλαφυρῇ] πτερόεντας ὀϊστοὺς
> κρύπτει, Ἔρως · ἐν ἐμοὶ πάντα γάρ ἐστι βέλη.

---

[*] Cf. Reitzenstein, Pauly-Wissowa R.-E. s. v. Epigramm, p. 88.

(Tibull. II 6, 15)

> ,acer Amor, fractas utinam tua tela sagittas,
> si licet, extinctas adspiciamque faces!'

A. P. XII 89; Horat. c. II 8 15.

d) Non solum interdiu Cupido vexat homines, sed etiam noctu, ut somnum amatores capere non possint.*)

A. P. V 118 Crinagorae:

> Κῆν ῥίψῃς ἐπὶ λαιὰ καὶ ἢν ἐπὶ δεξιὰ ῥίψῃς,
> Κριναγόρη, κενεοῦ σαυτὸν ὕπερθε λέχευς,
> εἰ μή σοι χαρίεσσα παρακλίνοιτο Γέμελλα,
> γνώσῃ κοιμηθεὶς οὐχ ὕπνον, ἀλλὰ κόπον.

A. P. V 211, 3 Meleagri:

> οὐδ' ἡ νὺξ, οἱ φέγγος ἐκοίμισεν . . .

Prop. I 1, 33:

> ,in me nostra Venus noctes exercet amaras,
> et nullo vacuus tempore defit amor.'

Multa alia collegerunt Hoelzer l. l. p. 48 et Rohde, Der griech. Roman ², p. 168 adnot. 3.

e) Quin etiam tanti esse ducuntur dolores amantium, ut miseriae Tantali apud inferos graves poenas luentis illis minores esse videantur.

A. P. V 235 Pauli Silentiari:

> Λαὶ τάχα Τανταλέης Ἀχερόντια πήματα ποινῆς
> ἡμετέρων ἀχέων ἐστὶν ἐλαφρότερα.
> οὐ γὰρ ἰδὼν σέο κάλλος ἀπείργετο χείλεα μῖξαι
> χείλεΐ σῷ, ῥοδέων ἁβροτέρῳ καλύκων,
> Τάνταλος ἀκριτόδακρυς · ὑπερτέλλοντα δὲ πέτρον
> δείδιεν, ἀλλὰ θανεῖν δεύτερον οὐ δύναται.
> αὐτὰρ ἐγὼ ζωὸς μὲν ἐὼν κατατήκομαι οἴστρῳ,
> ἐκ δ' ὀλιγοδρανίης καὶ μόρον ἐγγὺς ἔχω.

---

*) Amorem amatori somnum adimere tam consentaneum est, ut mulier, si quando amatorem somnus complectitur, illi animum durum exprobret; nam εὕδειν τοῖς φιλέουσι οὐ θέμις.

A. P. V 119 Philodemi:

> τοὔνεκ' ἐν ἀπρήκτοισι καθήμεθα, κοὐχὶ τελεῦντες
> εὕδομεν, ὡς εὕδειν τοῖς φιλέουσι θέμις;

quo cum loco Jacobs confert Propert. II 15, 7:

> ,Illa meos somno lapsos patefecit ocellos
> ore suo, et dixit: siccine, lente, iaces?'

A. P. V 245, 5 eiusdem:

> καὶ τίς ὑποτλαίη; τάχα τις, τάχα τοῦτο ταλάσσας
> δίψαν Τανταλέην τλήσεται εἱμαρέως.

§ 18. Cupidinem etiam dis superiorem esse iam supra p. 26 vidimus. Itaque poeta quidam eum de Iove ceterisque dis triumphum agentem facit. Lactantius quidem, id quod ille nescio qui poeta finxit, servavit (instit. div. I, 11, 1): ‚Non insulse quidam poeta Triumphum Cupidinis scripsit: quo in libro non modo potentissimum deorum Cupidinem, sed etiam victorem facit. Enumeratis enim amoribus singulorum, quibus in potestatem Cupidinis dicionemque venissent, instruit pompam, in qua Juppiter cum ceteris dis ante currum triumphantis ducitur catenatus.‘ Rohde, cui hunc Lactanti locum debeo, quis ille poeta fuerit secum reputans, haec coniecit (Roman² 115, 1): ‚Es soll natürlich nicht mehr als eine ganz leichte Vermutung sein, dass in hellenistischer Zeit ein griechischer Dichter diesen übermütigen Gedanken ausgeführt haben könne. Die Vorstellung eines glänzenden Triumphzuges konnte den Griechen damaliger Zeit aus zahlreichen eben damals üblichen ähnlichen Schaustellungen siegreicher Könige vertraut genug sein.‘ Rohde disertis verbis quid sentiat cautissime coniecturam tenuissimam dicit. Sed quoquo modo se illud habet, alia sententia cum illa Lactantiana arte cohaerens non a Graecis originem duxisse, sed apud Romanos ipsos videtur orta esse: sententiam dico, qua amor comparatur cum militia Cupidinis.*) Quae sententia, etsi apud Graecorum poetas non occurrit, apud Romanos adeo est frequentata, ut in loci communis consuetudinem venerit. An miraris, quod Romani, gens illa bellicosissima rebusque militaribus deditissima, pugnas, victorias, castra aliasque eius modi res in amorem transtulerunt amantesque homines milites Cupidinis duxerunt? Haec sint exempla:

(Ovid. am. I 9, 1)

> ‚Militat omnis amans, et habet sua castra Cupido:
> Attice, crede mihi, militat omnis amans.‘

---

*) Christiani hanc sententiam in suum usum ita contulerunt, ut eos, qui fidem christianam confitebantur, milites Christi appellarent; de qua militia Christi conferas Perdrizet in Arch. f. Relig. XIV 101 et Cumont, Mithras I 317.

(Ovid. art. am. II 233)

,Militiae species amor est: discedite, segnes!
Non sunt haec timidis signa tuenda viris;
Nox et hiems longaeque viae saevique dolores
mollibus his castris et labor omnis inest;
Saepe feres imbrem caelesti nube solutum
frigidus et nuda saepe iacebis humo.'

(Prop. V 1, 135) Astrologus poetam carmini heroico operam daturum ad molles elegos reducit his verbis:

,at tu finge elegos, fallax opus, (haec tua castra)
scribat ut exemplo cetera turba tuo.
militiam Veneris blandis patiere sub armis
et Veneris pueris utilis hostis eris.
Nam tibi victrices, quascunque labore parasti,
eludet palmas una puella tuas.'

Similia leguntur Ovid. am. I 2, 29–37; II 9, 3–4; Tibull. I 3, 64; 82; Prop. I 1, 4; III 12, 16; I 6, 29; Ovid. art. am. II 674; Tibull. I 1, 75.

§ 19. Amantium sollicitudines et inter spem metumque fluctuatio cum maris aestu comparari solent, id quod Hoelzer l. l. p. 49 exemplis confirmavit.*) Quae imago ex eo videtur orta esse, quod 'Ἀφροδίτη non solum amoris dea putatur, sed etiam moderatrix fluctuum maris, ex cuius spuma emersisse fertur. Itaque ποντία vel εὔπλοια vel γαληναία 'Ἀφροδίτη appellatur eique non modo ab amantibus, sed etiam a nautis in periculis versantibus supplicatur et sacrificatur.

A. P. IX 143 Antipatris:

Λιτός τοι δόμος οὗτος (ἐπεὶ παρα κύματι πηγῷ
ἵδρυμαι νοτερῆς δεσπότις ῃιόνος),
ἀλλὰ φίλος· πόντῳ γὰρ ἐπὶ πλατὺ δειμαίνοντι
χαίρω, καὶ ναίταις εἰς ἐμὲ σωζομένοις.
'Ἰλάσκευ τὴν Κύπριν· ἐγὼ δέ σοι ἢ ἐν ἔρωτι
οὖριος, ἢ χαροπῷ πνεύσομαι ἐν πελάγει.

*) Haec addere liceat:
(A. P. V 234 Macedoni Hypatici)
καὶ τρομέω, κραδίη δὲ βυθῷ πελεμίζεται οἴστρῳ,
ψυχῆς πνιγομένης κύματι κυπριδίῳ.
Eadem imago subest voci ἐρωτοπλοεῖν in A. P. V 155.

A. P. V 16 Gaetulici:

οὔριος ἀλλ᾽ ἐπίλαμψον ἐμῷ καὶ ἔρωτι καὶ ἱστῷ,
δέσποτι καὶ θαλάμων, Κύπρι, καὶ ἠϊόνων.

Conf. etiam A. P. IX 144 et X 21.

Amor, quippe cuius symbolum sit ignis, maxime est contrarius mari. Itaque interdum admirationem poetis movet, quod Ἀφροδίτη et aquae et ignis est domina ac regina.

P. A. V 175 Meleagri:

θαῦμα δέ μοι, πῶς ἄρα διὰ γλαυκοῖο φανεῖσα
κύματος ἐξ ὑγροῦ, Κύπρι, σὺ πῦρ τέτοκας.

A. P. IX 420 Antipatris:

Μὴ κλαίων τὸν Ἔρωτα δόκει, Τηλέμβροτε, πείσειν,
μηδ᾽ ὀλίγῳ παύσειν ὕδατι πῦρ ἀπνεές.
. . . . ἐσβέσθη δὲ
οὐδὲ τότ᾽ ἐν πολλῷ τικτόμενος πελάγει.

Quae cum ita sint, facile intellegitur hominem mari amoris iactatum componi cum naufrago Veneremque implorari ut deam hominum terra marique naufragorum.

A. P. V 10 incerti:

Εἰ τοὺς ἐν πελάγει σώζεις, Κύπρι, κἀμὲ τὸν ἐν γᾷ
ναυαγόν, φιλίη, σῶσον ἀπολλύμενον.

A. P. V 208 Posidippi aut Asclepiadis:

Σήν, Παφίη Κυθέρεια, παρ᾽ ἠϊόν᾽ εἶδε Κλέανδρος
Νικοῦν ἐν χαροποῖς κύμασι νηχομένην.
καιόμενος δ᾽ ὑπ᾽ Ἔρωτος ἐνὶ φρεσὶν ἄνθρακας ἀνὴρ
ξηροὺς ἐκ νοτερῆς παιδὸς ἐπεσπάσατο.
χὠ μὲν ἐναυάγει γαίης ἔπι· τὴν δὲ θαλάσσης
ψαύουσαν πρηεῖς εἴχοσαν αἰγιαλοί.
νῦν δ᾽ ἴσος ἀμφοτέροις φιλίης πόθος· οὐκ ἀτελεῖς γὰρ
εὐχαί, τὰς κείνης εὔξατ᾽ ἐπ᾽ ἠϊόνος.

A. P. V 234 Macedoni Hypatici:

καὶ τρομέω, κραδίη δὲ βυθῷ πελεμίζεται οἴστρῳ,
ψυχῆς πνιγομένης κύματι κυπριδίῳ.
ἀλλ᾽ ἐμὲ τὸν ναυηγὸν ἐπ᾽ ἠπείροιο φανέντα
σῶε, τεᾶν λιμένων ἔνδοθι δεξαμένη.

A. P. X 21. − Catull. LXVIII 3.

3*

§ 20. Quod amore dolores amantibus commoventur, non est mirum eaque ipsa re verus amor cognosci solet. Quae opinio etiam hodie valet; hoc enim simili sententia est nostratibus in proverbio: „Was sich neckt, das liebt sich." Quid, quod rixis, quae sunt inter amantes, et iurgiis amor augeri putatur?

Menandri frg. 797 (Kock):

οργὴ φιλούντων ὀλίγον ἰσχύει χρόνον.

A. P. V 255 Pauli Silentiari:

„Ὕβρις ἔρωτας ἔλυσε." μάτην ὅδε μῦθος ἀλᾶται ·
ὕβρις ἐμὴν ἐρέθει μᾶλλον ἐρωμανίην.

Terent. Andr. 555:

,Amantium irae amoris integratiost.'

Catull. LXXIII 7:

. . . . ,Quod amantem iniuria talis
cogit amare magis.'

A. L. 76:

,Iurgia conflat amor, ut blandius urat amantes:
ad tumulum fidei iurgia conflat amor.'

Itaque poetae elegiaci iuvenibus puellisque aperte praecipiunt, ut ipsi iurgia nectant: puella amatorem deludat, amator autem quamvis sit inflammatus amorem puellae dissimulet.

Ovid. am. II 19, 33:

,Si qua volet regnare diu, deludat amantem!'

Ovid. am. I 8, 95:

,ne securus amet nullo rivale, caveto:
non bene, si tollas proelia, durat amor.'

Prop. II 25, 29:

,tu tamen interea, quamvis te diligat illa,
in tacito cohibe gaudia clausa sinu:
namque in amore suo semper sua maxima cuique
nescio quo pacto verba nocere solent.'

Tibull. IV 12, 5:

,hesterna quam te solum quod nocte reliqui,
ardorem cupiens dissimulare meum.'

Prop. II 14, 19:

> ‚hoc sensi prodesse magis: contemnite amantes:
> sic hodie veniet, si qua negavit heri.'

Prop. IV 5, 29:

> . . . . ‚utere causis:
> maior dilata nocte recurret amor.'

Similiter Terent. Eunuch. 812:

> . . . . ‚novi ingenium mulierum:
> Nolunt ubi velis; ubi nolis cupiunt ultro.' . .

Ne in puerilis quidcm Musae carminibus haec sententia deest.

A. P. XII 203 Stratonis:

> Οὐκ ἐθέλοντα φιλεῖς με, φιλῶ δ᾽ ἐγὼ οὐκ ἐθέλοντα·
> εὔκολος ἦν φεύγω, δύσκολος ἦν ἐπάγω.

Conferas supra p. 20 adnot.

Sed plerumque amantibus et puellis et iuvenibus his praeceptis omnino opus non est; sua enim sponte inter se vexant, quoniam amor et odium, quamvis contraria esse videantur, simul hominum animos tenere solent.

Catull. LXXXV:

> ‚Odi et amo . quare id faciam, fortasse requiris.
> Nescio, sed fieri sentio et excrucior.'

Cuius epigrammatis praeclari sententias pluribus rhetorice exposuit et in elegiae formam redegit Ovidius in amor. III 11.*) Hos versus transscribere liceat:

> (33) ‚Luctantur pectusque leve in contraria tendunt
> hac amor hac odium, sed, puto, vincit amor.
> Odero, si potero; si non, invitus amabo:
> nec iuga taurus amat; quae tamen odit, habet.'

Catull. XCII:

> ‚Lesbia mi dicit semper male nec tacet unquam
> de me: Lesbia me dispeream nisi amat.
> Quo signo? quia sunt todidem mea: deprecor illam
> assidue, verum dispeream nisi amo.'

---

*) Conf. Jacoby, Mus. Rh. LX 86, ubi plura de hac sententia eiusque origine invenies.

38

Catull. LXXXIII 3:

,Mule, nihil sentis. si nostri oblita taceret,
sana esset: nunc quod gannit et obloquitur,
non solum meminit, sed, quae multo acrior est res,
irata est, hoc est, uritur et coquitur.'

A. P. XI 252 Nicarchi:

Εἴ με φιλεῖς, μισεῖς με · καὶ εἰ μισεῖς, σὺ φιλεῖς με ·
εἰ δέ με μὴ μισεῖς, φίλτατε, μή με φίλει.

A. P. XII 172 Eveni:

Εἰ μισεῖν πόνος ἐστί, φιλεῖν πόνος, ἐκ δύο λυγρῶν
αἱροῦμαι χρηστῆς ἕλκος ἔχειν ὀδίνης.

A. P. V 23; 106; XII 103; 126, 6.

§ 21.   Aegritudinum, quibus amantes conficiuntur, ea est
saepissime causa, quod alterius amor ab altero non redditur.
Qua re non semel amantes a Cupidine petere legimus, ut aut
utrumque amoris flammis urat aut ex alterius quoque animo
amorem restinguat.   De hoc τόπῳ Fridericus Leo in libro suo
„Plautinische Forschungen" p. 130 his verbis disputavit:
„Der Wunsch Tib. IV 5, 13 *vel serviat aeque vinctus uterque
tibi vel mea vincla leva* kehrt mit derselben Alternative wieder
Ter. Eun. 91 *utinam esset mihi pars aequa amoris tecum ac
pariter fieret, ut aut hoc tibi doleret 'itidem ut mihi dolet aut
ego istuc abs te factum nihili penderem*, d. h. bei Menander;
die Stelle war berühmt und klingt in der Elegie vielfach nach
(Catull. 76, 23, Tib. I 2, 63, Ovid. met. XIV 24, Rufinus
A. P. V 88, auch bei Aristaenetus (I 16 ὡς ταύτην, Ἔρως,
βέβληκας τὴν ψυχήν, οὕτως ἴσῃ βολῇ τὴν ἐμὴν κατατόξευσον
ἐρωμένην)." Haec Leo. Ex numero exemplorum, quae vir ille
doctissimus collegit, illud Rufini epigramma transscribo:

(A. P. V 87 [ed. Stadtm.])

Εἰ δυσὶν οὐκ ἴσχυσας ἴσην φλόγα, πυρφόρε, καῦσαι,
τὴν ἑνὶ καιομένην ἢ σβέσον ἢ μετάθες.

Jacobs adscripsit: Imitatus est Auson. ep. 80:

,Aut restingue ignem, quo torreor, alma Dione,
aut transire iube: vel face utrumque parem.'

Haec alia huius loci communis exempla mihi enotuerunt:

(A. P. V 67 Lucilli alii Polemonis)

>Ἢ τὸ φιλεῖν περίγραψον, Ἔρως, ὅλον ἢ τὸ φιλεῖσθαι
πρόσθες, ἵν᾽ ἢ λύσῃς τὸν πόθον ἢ κεράσῃς.

(A. P. V 96 Rufini)

Εἰ μὲν ἐπ᾽ ἀμφοτέροισιν, Ἔρως, ἴσα τόξα τιταίνεις,
εἰ θεός· εἰ δὲ ῥέπεις πρὸς μέρος, οὐ θεὸς εἶ.

(A. P. V 168, 3 Asclepiadis)

ἥδιον δ᾽, ὁπόταν κρύψῃ μία τοὺς φιλέοντας
χλαῖνα, καὶ αἰνῆται Κύπρις ὑπ᾽ ἀμφοτέρων.

(Auson. epigr. 76)

,Hoc quod amare vocant, misce, aut dissolve, Cupido.
Aut neutrum flammis ure, vel ure duos.'

(A. L. 24)

,Dic quid agis, formosa Venus, si nescis amanti
ferre vicem? perit omne decus, dum deperit aetas.
(5) Haec metuas exempla precor et semper amanti
redde vicem, quia semper amat, qui semper amatur.'

(A. L. 78)

,Mens, ubi amaris, ama. rarum est agnoscere amicos,
rarum invenire [est]. mens, ubi amaris, ama.'

(Ovid. amor. II 10, 29)

,Felix, quem Veneris certamina mutua perdunt!'

(Quintil. declam. 14, 9) ,Amatoris unum remedium est: amari.'

§ 22. Amatores id fere ultimum spectant, ut puellae
amatae pulchritudine fruantur corporisque voluptates expleant;
sed quo plus puella voluptatis amatori praebet, eo magis
augetur illius ἐρωμανία, ut in dies plus optet. Talem hominem
insatiabili voluptatum cupiditate accensum ostendit Paulus
Silentiarius in A. P. 271:

Μαζοὺς χερσὶν ἔχω, στόματι στόμα, καὶ περὶ δειρὴν
ἄσχετα λυσσώων βόσκομαι ἀργυφέην.
οὔπω δ᾽ Ἀφρογένειαν ὅλην ἕλον· ἀλλ᾽ ἔτι κάμνω
παρθένον ἀμφιέπων λέκτρον ἀναινομένην.

et in A. P. V 290:

> *Εἰ μὲν ἐμοί, χαρίεσσα, τεῶν τάδε σύμβολα μαζῶν*
> *ὤπασας, ὀλβίζω τὴν χάριν ὡς μεγάλην·*
> *εἰ δ' ἐπὶ τοῖς μίμνεις, ἀδικεῖς, ὅτι λάβρον ἀνῆψας*
> *πυρσόν, ἀποσβέσσαι τοῦτον ἀναινομένη.*

Ubi autem primum omnia optata amatori ita contigerunt, ut
ei ne concubitum quidem puella negaret, cupiditates celeriter
satiatae defervescunt amorque languescit. Rufinus quidem ut
expertus hoc docet in

A. P. V 46:

> *Πολλάκις ἠρασάμην σε λαβὼν ἐν νυκτί, Θάλεια,*
> *πληρῶσαι θαλερῷ θυμὸν ἐρωμανίῃ.*
> *νῦν δ', ὅτε [μοι] γυμνὴ γλυκεροῖς μελέεσσι πέπλησαι,*
> *ἔκλυτος ὑπναλέῳ γυῖα κέκμηκα κόπῳ.*

et in A. P. V 76:

> *Εἰ τοίην χάριν εἶχε γυνή μετὰ Κύπριδος εὐνήν,*
> *οὐκ ἄν τοι χρονέεσκεν ἀνήρ ἀλόχοισιν ὁμιλῶν.*
> *πᾶσαι γὰρ μετὰ Κύπριν ἀτερπέες εἰσὶ γυναῖκες.*

Itaque ii, qui voluptatibus venereis sunt delectati, appetitum
multo iucundiorem esse voluptatum magisque titillare sensus
quam ipsas voluptates iudicant. Cuius sententiae haec sunt
exempla:

A. P. IX 620 Pauli Silentiari:

> *Ἄγχι μὲν ἐλπὶς ἔρωτος· ἑλεῖν δ' οὐκ ἔστι γυναῖκας·*
> *εἶρξε πυλὶς Παφίην τὴν μεγάλην ὀλίγη.*
> *Ἀλλ' ἔμπης γλυκὺ τοῦτο· ποθοβλήτοις γὰρ ἐπ' ἔργοις*
> *ἐλπὶς ἀληθείης ἐστὶ μελιχροτέρη.*

Ovid. amor. II 9, 43:

> ‚Me modo decipiant voces fallacis amicae,
> sperando certe gaudia magna feram;
> et modo blanditias dicat, modo iurgia nectat;
> saepe fruar domina, saepe repulsus eam.‘

A. L. 700 [Petroni]:

> ‚Foeda est in coitu et brevis voluptas
> et taedet Veneris statim peractae.

5. Nam languescit amor peritque flamma.
   Sed sic sic sine fine feriati
   et tecum iaceamus osculantes.
   Hic nullus labor est ruborque nullus:
   hoc iuvit, iuvat et diu iuvabit.
   Hoc non deficit incipitque semper.'

§ 23. Venerem vel Cupidinem furta sua occultare consentaneum est. Itaque homines, si qui amori se dedunt, nisi arbitris remotis voluptatibus venereis non fruuntur, velut Philodemus puellam amatam amplexurus ancillae mandat (A. P. V 3):

> Τὸν σιγῶντα, Φιλαινί, συνίστορα τῶν ἀλαλήτων
> λύχνον ἐλαιηρῆς ἐκμεθύσασα δρόσου
> ἔξιθι· μαρτυρίην γὰρ Ἔρως μόνος οὐκ ἐφίλησεν
> ἔμπνουν·*) καὶ πηκτὴν κλεῖε. Φιλαινί, θύρην.
> καὶ σὺ φίλει, Ξανθώ με· . . . . .

Tibullus vero ita monet (I 2, 33):

> ,Parcite luminibus, seu vir seu femina fiat
> obvia: celari vult sua furta Venus.'

Quae cum ita sint, amantes homines cavent, ut ne temere effutiant amores suos; timent enim, ne garrulitatis poenas Cupidini aliisque dis expendant hominumque invidiam sibi conflent. Qua sententia iam Plato usus est in A. P. VII 100**), quod epigramma ut amatorium falso inter sepulcralia legitur:

> Νῦν ὅτε μηδέν, Ἄλεξις. ὅσον μόνον εἶφ', ὅτι καλός,
> ὦπται καὶ πάντῃ πᾶσι περιβλέπεται.
> θυμέ, τί μηνύεις κυσὶν ὀστέον;***) εἶτ' ἀνιήσεις
> ὕστερον; οὐχ οὕτω Φαῖδρον ἀπωλέσαμεν:

quod epigramma videtur imitatus esse Dioscorides in A. P. V 55, 7:

> ἀλλὰ τί μηνύω κυσὶν ὀστέα; μάρτυρές εἰσι
> τῆς ἀθυροστομίης οἱ Μίδεοι κάλαμοι.

*) At quod mortalibus nefas, deae licet: (A. P. V 122, 3 Philodemi)
ἐς τὰ φιλεύντων
ἔργα κατοπτεύειν οὐ φθόνος ἀθανάτη.
**) De hoc epigrammate disseruit Wilamowitz, Philolog. Untersuch. I 222.
***) Proverbii locum obtinet. Cf. von Prittwitz-Gaffron, Das Sprichw. im griech. Epigr. p. 6.

42

A. P. V 251, 5 Pauli Silentiari:

σπήθεα δ' ἐξεύχθω τά τε χείλεα · τἄλλα δὲ σιγῇ
κρυπτέον · ἐχθαίρω τὴν ἀθυροστομίην.

Ovid. art. am. II 704:

,ad thalami clausas, Musa, resiste fores.'

Alios locos ex Romanorum poetis sumptos collegit multos
F. Wilhelm, Mus. Rh. LIX p. 288.

Etiamsi quis alterius amores casu comperit, illos ut celandos
vulgare non licet.

Tibull. I 2, 37:

,si quis et imprudens adspexerit, occulat ille
perque deos omnes se meminisse neget:
nam fuerit quicunque loquax, is sanguine natam,
is Venerem e rapido sentiet esse mari.'

Accedit, quod vel pudore amantes impediuntur, quominus si
non amorem at tamen thalami voluptates disertis verbis efferant;
immo tecte illa secreta significare satis habent.

A. P. V 127 Marci Argentari:

Στέρνα περὶ στέρνοις, μαστῷ δ' ἐπὶ μαστὸν ἐρείσας
χείλεά τε γλυκεροῖς χείλεσι συμπιέσας
Ἀντιγόνης καὶ χρῶτα λαβὼν πρόσχρωτα — τὰ λοιπὰ
σιγῶ, · · · · ·

Ovid. am. I 5 19:

,Quos umeros, quales vidi tetigique lacertos!
Forma papillarum quam fuit apta premi!
Quam castigato planus sub pectore venter!
Quantum et quale latus, quam iuvenale femur!
Singula quid referam? nil non laudabile vidi
et nudam pressi corpus ad usque meum.
Cetera quis nescit? lassi requievimus ambo.'

Ovid. epist. [XV] 133:

,Ulteriora pudet narrare, sed omnia fiunt.'*)

---

*) Conf. Goethii nostri poema, quod inscribitur ,Brautnacht', extr.:
,Dann hält er (scil. Amor) schalkhaft und bescheiden
sich fest die beiden Augen zu.'

Ovid. amor. III 2, 83:

>,Risit et argutis quiddam promisit ocellis:
>hic satis est; alio cetera redde loco!'

Huc pertinet etiam Lucian. deor. dial. XI: Luna Veneri interroganti amorem erga Endymionem aperit hisque verbis narrandi finem facit: τότε τοίνυν ἐγὼ ἀψοφητὶ κατιοῦσα ἐπ' ἄκρων ἰᾶν δακτύλων βεβηκυῖα, ὡς ἂν μὴ ἀνεγρόμενος ἐκταραχϑείη — οἶσϑα. τί οὖν ἄν σοι λέγοιμι τὰ μετὰ ταῦτα;

Quae aposiopesis simili modo adhibita est a Plauto; cf. Pseud. 216 (Lorenz ad 760); 1178; Asin. 703.

§ 24. Cum Cupido omnes arbitros, ne furta sua vulgentur, ex cubiculo removeat, tamen adest lucerna testis quasi inanima; quam quippe amoribus faventem saepe poetae alloquuntur vel ipsam loquentem inducunt. Conscia omnium thalami voluptatum, tamen semper est taciturna.*)

A. P. V 3 Philodemi:

>Τὸν σιγῶντα, Φιλαινί, συνίστορα τῶν ἀλαλήτων
>λύχνον . . .

A. P. V 127 Marci Argentari: . . . . τὰ λοιπὰ
>σιγῶ, μάρτυς ἐφ' οἷς λύχνος ἐπεγράφετο.

A. P. V 196 Meleagri: . . . . ναὶ φιλάγρυπνον
>λύχνον ἐμῶν κώμων πόλλ' ἐπιδόντα τέλη.

A. L. 711:

>,Ludite: sed vigiles nolite exstinguere lychnos.
>Omnia nocte vident, nil cras meminere lucernae.'

Martial. XIV 39: ,Lucerna cubicularis.

>Dulcis conscia lectuli lucerna,
>quidquid vis facias licet, tacebo.'

Lucerna autem non solum fidam, sed etiam infidam videt puellam, si qua in Venerem prona fidem violavit rivalemque in cubiculum intromisit. Tum amator suspecti amoris stimulis agitatus lucernam implorat, ne periurae puellae rivalique luceat sed exstinguens voluptates illorum imminuat.

---

*) De hoc loco communi multa iam collegit E. Pertsch, De Valerio Martiale Graecorum poetarum imitatore. Dissert. inaug. Berolini 1911, p. 33.

A. P. V 6 Asclepiadis:

> Λύχνε, σὲ γὰρ παρεόντα τρὶς ὤμοσεν Ἡράκλεια
> ἥξειν κοὐχ ἥκει· λύχνε, σὺ δ᾽, εἰ θεὸς εἶ,
> τὴν δολίην ἀπάμυνον· ὅταν φίλον ἔνδον ἔχουσα
> παίζῃ, ἀποσβεσθεὶς μηκέτι φῶς πάρεχε.

A. P. V 164, 3 Meleagri:

> εἴ τις ὑπὸ χλαίνῃ βεβλημένος Ἡλιοδώρας
> θάλπεται, ὑπναπάτῃ χρωτὶ χλιαινόμενος,
> κοιμάσθω μὲν λύχνος· ὁ δ᾽ ἐν κόλποισιν ἐκείνης
> ῥιπτασθεὶς κείσθω δεύτερος Ἐνδυμίων.

A. P. V 165, 7 eiusdem:

> ἢ νέος ἄλλος ἔρως, νέα παίγνια: μήποτε, λύχνε,
> ταῦτ᾽ ἐσίδῃς, εἴης δ᾽ ἧς παρέδωκα φύλαξ.

A. P. V 4 Statylli Flacci:

> Ἀργύρεον νυχίων με συνίστορα πιστὸν ἐρώτων
> οὐ πιστῇ λύχνον Φλάκκος ἔδωκε Νάπῃ,
> ἧς παρὰ νῦν λεχέεσσι μαραίνομαι, εἰς ἐπίορκον
> παντοπαθῆ κούρης αἴσχεα δερκόμενος.
> Φλάκκε, σὲ δ᾽ ἄγρυπνον χαλεπαὶ τείρουσι μέριμναι·
> ἄμφω δ᾽ ἀλλήλων ἄνδιχα καιόμεθα.

Lucernae est proprium sternuere; id quod in eam partem accipiunt homines amantes, ut lucernam ter sternuentem quasi oraculum amoris esse putent, quo quid futurum sit cognosci possit. Itaque cum Apolline, deo fatiloquo, eam comparari invenimus.

A. P. VI 333 Marci Argentari:

> Ἴδῃ, φίλτατε λύχνε, τρὶς ἔπταρες· ἢ τάχα τερπνὴν
> εἰς θαλάμοις ἥξειν Ἀντιγόνην προλέγεις;
> εἰ γὰρ, ἄναξ, εἴη τόδ᾽ ἐτήτυμον, οἷος Ἀπόλλων
> θνητοῖς μάντις ἔσῃ καὶ σὺ παρὰ τρίποδι.

Neque vero semper amori hominum favet lucerna, sed etiam fit, ut amantium hominum voluptatibus invideat iisque insidietur.*) Lucernae enim invidae culpa factum est, ut Leander ad Hero suam Hellespontum transnaturus undis periret.

---

*) Conf. Grillparzer, Des Meeres und der Liebe Wellen III extrem.: ‚Die Lampe soll's nicht sehn.‘

A. P. V 262 Agathiae Scholastici:

Μήποτε λύχνε, μύκητα φέροις, μηδ' ὄμβρον ἐγείροις,
μὴ τὸν ἐμὸν παύσῃς νυμφίον ἐρχόμενον.
αἰεὶ σὺ φθονέεις τῇ Κύπριδι· καὶ γὰρ ὅθ' Ἡρὼ
ἥρμοσε Λειάνδρῳ . . . θυμέ, τὸ λοιπὸν ἔα.

Non solum lucernae veterum superstitio tribuebat numen quoddam,
sed etiam nocti appositis vocibus vel ἱερή vel πότνια vel φίλη;
quae modo cum lucerna copulata modo sola in veterum car-
minibus amatoriis ab amantibus imploratur.

A. P. V 7 Meleagri:

Νὺξ ἱερὴ καὶ λύχνε, συνίστορας οὔτινας ἄλλους
ὅρκοις, ἀλλ' ὑμέας εἱλόμεθ' ἀμφότεροι ·

A. P. V 164 eiusdem:

Ἐν τόδε, παμμήτειρα θεῶν, λίτομαί σε, φίλη Νύξ,
ναὶ λίτομαι, κῶμον σύμπλανε, πότνια Νύξ,

A. P. V 165 eiusdem:

Ὦ Νύξ, ὦ φιλάγρυπνος ἐμοὶ πόθος Ἡλιοδώρας

A. P. V 190 eiusdem:

Ἄστρα*) καὶ ἡ φιλέρωσι καλὸν φαίνουσα Σελήνη**)
καὶ Νὺξ καὶ κῶμον σύμπλανον ὀργάνιον,
ἆρά γε τὴν φιλάσωτον ἔτ' ἐν κοίταισιν ἀθρήσω
ἄγρυπνον, λύχνῳ πόλλ' ἀποδυρομένην;***)
ἤ τιν' ἔχει σύγκοιτον;

A. P. V 163 Asclepiadis:

Νύξ, σὲ γάρ, οὐκ ἄλλην μαρτύρομαι, οἷά μ' ὑβρίζει
Πυθιὰς ἡ Νικοῦς, οὖσα φιλεξαπάτης.

§ 25. Imprimis autem lectus, gravissimus complexuum
testis, in carminibus amatoriis et Graecorum et Latinorum
appellatur.****)

---

*) Cf. Prop. II 9, 41: ‚Sidera sunt testes' . . .

**) Jacobs cum hoc loco confert Theocr. II 10: ἀλλὰ Σελάνα | φαῖνε καλόν. —
Aliis etiam locis Luna ut amantibus faveat imploratur; ipsa enim Endymionis
amore est capta; cf. A. P. V 122 Philodemi et Ovid. epist. XVII 61–64.

***) Jacobs adnotat Apulei met. p. 213: ‚multumque cum lucerna secreta
collocuta.' Mulierem cum lucerna loquentem suasque cum ea res com-
municantem habemus in Aristoph. Ecclesiaz. initio.

****) Nonnulla iam collegerunt Mallet I. I. p. 37 et Pertsch I. I. p. 33.

A. P. V 3, 5 Philodemi:

καὶ σὺ φίλει, Ξανθώ, με· σὺ δ᾽, ὦ φιλεράστρια κοίτη,
    ἤδη τῆς Παφίης ἴσθι τὰ λειπόμενα.

A. P. V 180, 12 Asclepiadis:

. . ὧν κλίνη μάρτυς ἐπεγράφετο.

Catull. LXI 111:

,O cubile, quod omnibus
. . . .
candido pede lecti,
quae tuo veniunt hero,
quanta gaudia.‘

eiusdem VI 6:

,Nam te non viduas iacere noctes
nequicquam tacitum cubile clamat.‘

Ovid. am. III 14, 26:

,spondaque lasciva mobilitate tremat!‘

eiusdem art. am. II 703:

,Conscius, ecce, duos accepit lectus amantes.‘

Prop. II 18, 35:

,ipse tuus semper tibi sit custodia lectus.‘

eiusdem II 15, 1:

,O me felicem! o nox mihi candida! et o tu
    lectule deliciis facte beate meis!
Quam multa adposita narramus verba lucerna,
    quantaque sublato lumine rixa fuit!‘

Martial. X 38, 6:

,O quae proelia, quas utrimque pugnas
    felix lectulus et lucerna vidit.‘

A. L. 699 Petroni:

,Sit nox illa diu nobis dilecta, Nealce,
    quae te prima meo pectore composuit;
sit torus et lecti genius secretaque sponda,
    queis tenera in nostrum veneris arbitrium.‘

A. L. 760, 5:

, „Nate“ dies audit, nox et torus audit „amice“,
    et pro temporibus nomina mutat ei.‘

§ 26. Amantes homines promptissimi sunt ad amores suos non solum fatendos, sed etiam iure iurando firmandos; talia autem iura iuranda quo promptius dantur, eo minus conservantur.*) Quae cum ita sint, iterum ac saepius in carminibus amatoriis amantium periurium perfidiaque notatur, hominesque monentur, ne amatorum iuri iurando fidem tribuant.

Periurii autem amantium ea est causa, quod id ius iurandum, quod ad res amatorias pertinet, ὅρκος ἀφροδίσιος qui dicitur, iustum vulgo non putatur; quod qui violaverit, poenas eum non daturum esse ferunt. Quam sententiam iam antiquitus vulgatam esse disertis verbis confirmat Plato in Conviv. p. 183, quo loco Pausaniam de Cupidine sic verba facientem fingit: ὃ δὲ δεινότατον, ὥς γε λέγουσιν οἱ πολλοί, ὅτι καὶ ὀμνύντι μόνῳ συγγνώμη παρὰ θεῶν ἐκβάντι τὸν ὅρκον οἳ φασιν εἶναι. οὕτω καὶ οἱ θεοὶ καὶ οἱ ἄνθρωποι πᾶσαν ἐξουσίαν πεποιήκασι τῷ ἐρῶντι, ὡς ὁ νόμος φησὶν ὁ ἐνθάδε. Idem in Phileb. p. 65: καὶ ἐν ταῖς ἡδοναῖς ταῖς περὶ τἀφροδίσια, αἳ δὴ μέγισται δοκοῦσιν εἶναι, καὶ τὸ ἐπιορκεῖν συγγνώμην εἴληφε παρὰ θεῶν

Sed ne Plato quidem hunc locum communem primus aperuit; scholion enim priori Platonis loco ascriptum exstat, ex quo iam Hesiodum illam sententiam non ignorasse apparet; dicit enim scholiasta: Ἀφροδίσιος ὅρκος οὐκ ἐμποίνιμος, ἐπὶ τῶν δι' ἔρωτα ὀμνυόντων πολλάκις καὶ ἐπιορκούντων. μέμνηται δὲ ταίτης καὶ Ἡσίοδος, λέγων·

> ἐκ τοῦδ' ὅρκον ἔθηκεν ἀμείνονα ἀνθρώποισι
> νοσφιδίων ἔργων περὶ Κύπριδος,

καὶ Πλάτων ἐν Συμποσίῳ.

Scholiastae autem illud Ἀφροδίσιος ὅρκος οὐκ ἐμποίνιμος Graecis in proverbio vetustate trito fuisse Diogenianus

---

*) Conf. Goethium nostrum in poemate, quod inscribitur ‚Wer kauft Liebesgötter?‘, extr.:

,Sie (scil. Cupidines) lieben sich das Neue;
doch über ihre Treue
verlangt nicht Brief und Siegel;
sie haben alle Flügel.'

affirmat.*) Itaque non mirum, quod hic τόπος in poesi amatoria est frequentatus.**)

a) Exempla primum quidem ea afferam, quibus amantes homines temere peierare vel fidem fallere demonstretur.

A. P. V 6 Asclepiadis:

. . . ὤμοσεν Ἡράκλεια ἥξειν κοὐχ ἥκει ·

A. P. V 278 Pauli Silentiari:

ἃ πόσα τὴν Κυθέρειαν ἐπώμοσεν ἕσπερος ἥξειν ·
ἀλλ᾽ οὔτ᾽ ἀνθρώπων φείδεται οὔτε θεῶν.

ad quem locum Jacobs ascripsit Verg. Aen. X 880:

, ... nec divom parcimus ulli.'

A. P. V 249, 8 eiusdem Pauli Silentiari:

Λείδια μή με λίπῃς · ἐστὲ γὰρ ὁρκαπάται.

Ovid amor. III 11, 21:

,Turpia quid referam vanae mendacia linguae
et periuratos in mea damna deos?'

Ovid. epist. [XV] 55:

,Nec vos decipiant blandae mendacia linguae!
Quae dicit vobis, dixerat ante mihi.'

Ovid. art. am. I 645:

,Fallite fallentes: ex magna parte profanum
sunt genus; in laqueos, quos posuere, cadant!

(657) Ergo ut periuras merito periuria fallant,
exemplo doleat femina laesa suo!'

b) Interdum amator, ut amoris vinculis se liberet, iusiurandum sibi ipse dat aliquamdiu puellam amatam se vitaturum esse; neque vero ullo modo peierare non potest; nam vel iram deorum subire quam puellam dimittere mavult.

A. P. V 132 Maeci:

Ὤμοσ᾽ ἐγώ, δύο νύκτας ἀφ᾽ Ἡδυλίου, Κυθέρεια,
σὸν κράτος, ἡσυχάσειν · . . . .
(5) αἱροῦμαι δ᾽ ἀσεβεῖν κείνης χάριν, ἢ τὰ σὰ τηρῶν
ὅρκι᾽ ἀποθνήσκειν, πότνι᾽, ὑπ᾽ εὐσεβίης.

---

*) Cf. Paroemiogr. Graec. edd. Leutsch et Schneidewin. Gottingae 1839, p. 221.

**) De hoc loco communi nonnulla iam collegerunt Jacobs, Animadvers. in epigr. Anthol. Graec. I 2, p. 260 et Mallet l. l. p. 19 sq. et von Prittwitz-Gaffron l. l. p. 13.

A. P. V 255, 5 Pauli Silentiari:

> ὤμοσα γὰρ λυκάβαντα μένειν ἀπάνευθεν ἐκείνης ·
> ὦ πόποι · ἀλλ' ἱκέτης πρωΐος εὐθὺς ἔβην.

A. P. V 253 eiusdem:

> Ὤμοσα μιμνάζειν σέο τηλόθεν, ἀργέτι κούρη,
> ἄχρι δυωδεκάτης, ὦ πόποι, ἠριπόλης ·
> οὐδ' ἔτλην ὁ τάλας · τὸ γὰρ αὔριον ἄμμι φαάνθη
> τηλοτέρω μήνης, ναὶ μὰ σέ, δωδεκάτης.
> ἀλλὰ θεοῖς ἱκέτευε, φίλη, μὴ ταῦτα χαράξαι
> ὅρκια ποιναίης νῶτον ὑπὲρ σελίδος ·
> θέλγε δὲ σαῖς χαρίτεσσιν ἐμὴν φρένα · μηδέ με μάστιξ,
> πότνα, καταισμύξῃ καὶ σέο καὶ μακάρων.

Tibull. II 6, 13:

> ,iuravi quotiens rediturum ad limina nunquam!
> cum bene iuravi, pes tamen ipse redit.'

Similiter Tibull. I 5, 1 sq.

c) Talia periuria ideo tam saepe fiunt, quod di amantes homines periuros impunitos dimittere putantur. Nam ipse Juppiter semel atque iterum huiusmodi culpam in se admisit.

A. P. V 5 Callimachi:

> ὤμοσεν · ἀλλὰ λέγουσιν ἀληθέα, τοὺς ἐν ἔρωτι
> ὅρκους μὴ δύνειν οὔατ' ἐς ἀθανάτων.

A. P. V 51 Dioscoridis:

> Ὅρκον κοινὸν Ἔρωτ' ἀνεθήκαμεν · ὅρκος ἱ πιστὴν
> Ἀρσινόης θέμενος Σωσιπάτρῳ φιλίην.
> ἀλλ' ἡ μὲν ψευδής, κενὰ δ' ὅρκια · τῇ δ' ἐφυλάχθη
> ἵμερος · ἡ δὲ θεῶν οὐ φανερὴ δύναμις.

Haec duo Anthologiae Palatinae exempla iam Mallet p. 22 vulgavit.

Publil. Syr. 38:

> ,Amantis iusiurandum poenam non habet.'

Ovid. am. III 3, 1:

> ,Esse deos hic crede: fidem iurata fefellit,
> et facies illi, quae fuit ante, manet!
> (11) Scilicet aeterno falsum iurare puellis
> di quoque concedunt, formaque numen habet.'

4

Ovid. am. III 11, 45: . . . . . . ,per omnes,
    qui dant fallendos se tibi saepe, deos.' . .

Tibull. III 6, 49:
    . . . . ,periuria ridet amantum
    Juppiter et ventos inrita ferre iubet.'

Tibull. I 9, 5:
    ,parcite, caelestes: aequum est impune licere
    numina formosis laedere vestra semel.'

Quid, quod amatores monentur, ne iurare timeant, quod
amantium periuria Juppiter non curet?

Tibull. I 4, 21:
    ,nec iurare time: Veneris periuria venti
    inrita per terras et freta summa ferunt.
    gratia magna Jovi: vetuit pater ipse valere,
    iurasset cupide quidquid ineptus amor.'

Ovid. art. am. I 631:
    ,nec timide promitte: trahunt promissa puellas;
    pollicito testes quoslibet adde deos!
    Juppiter ex alto periuria ridet amantum
    et iubet Aeolios inrita ferre Notos.
    Per Stryga Junoni falsum iurare solebat
    Juppiter: exemplo nunc favet ipse suo.'

Ovid. am. I 8, 85:
    ,nec, si quem falles, tu periurare timeto:
    commodat in lusus numina surda Venus.'

At etiam contraria monentur: caveant amantes, ne peierent,
quod non semper eorum periuria impune relinquantur.

Prop. II 16, 47:
    ,non semper placidus periuros ridet amantes
    Juppiter et surda neglegit aure preces.
 (53) periuras tunc ille solet punire puellas,
    deceptus quoniam flevit et ipse deus.'

  d) Amantium iura iuranda quia nihil valere homines haud
ignorant, fidem non habent.

A. P. V 174 Meleagri:
    Οἶδα · τί μοι κενὸς ὅρκος, . . .

A. P. V 183 eiusdem:

> Ἔγνων, οὐ μ' ἔλαθες· τί θεούς; οἳ γάρ με λέληθας
> ἔγνων· μηκέτι νῦν ὄμνυε· πάντ' ἔμαθον·
> ταῦτ' ἦν, ταῦτ', ἐπίορκε; . . .

Tibull. III 6, 47:

> ‚etsi perque suos fallax iuravit ocellos
> Junonemque suam perque suam Venerem
> nulla fides inerit . . .‘

Horat. c. II 8, 1:

> ‚Ulla si iuris tibi peierati
> poena, Barine, nocuisset umquam,
> dente si nigro fieres vel uno
> turpior ungui,
> crederem: sed . . .‘

Quin etiam disertis verbis monentur amantes, ne credant his iuribus iurandis.

Ovid. rem. am. 687:

> ‚At tu nec voces (quid enim fallacius illis?)
> crede nec aeternos pondus habere deos.‘

e) Iura iuranda amatoria laedere vel promissis non stare scriptores et Graeci et Latini ita verbis efferre solent, ut vota ventis et undis rapta esse dicant; id quod nos simili imagine usi dicimus: ‚etwas ist in den Wind geredet.‘ *) De qua formula pertrita cum alii tum Mallet l. l. uberius disputaverunt exemplaque multa collegerunt, ut nihil habeam quod addam.

§ 27. Amor desideriumque saepe ita apparet, ut invideat amator iis omnibus rebus, quibus a puella amata attingi vel una cum ea saepe esse licet, sive vesti qua puella tegitur, sive aurae quam spiritu ducit, sive rosae quam manibus decerpit, sive poculo quod labris attingit, sive aliis rebus; quin etiam eo desiderii procedit, ut in illas omnes res

---

*) Conf. Körner, Zriny V 6: ‚Wenn deine Schwüre nicht der Wind verwehte.‘

mutari cupiat. Quae sententia imprimis a Graecorum poetis est usurpata. *)

Ps.-Anacr. 22, 5:

> ἐγὼ δ' ἔσοπτρον εἴην,
> ὅπως ἀεὶ βλέπῃς με·
> ἐγὼ χιτὼν γενοίμην,
> ὅπως ἀεὶ φορῇς με.
> ὕδωρ θέλω γενέσθαι,
> ὅπως σε χρᾶτα λούσω·
> μύρον, γύναι, γενοίμην,
> ὅπως ἐγώ σ' ἀλείψω
> καὶ ταινίη δὲ μαστῶν
> καὶ μάργαρον τραχήλῳ
> καὶ σάνδαλον γενοίμην·
> μόνον ποσὶν πάτει με.

Theocr. III 12:

> αἴθε γενοίμαν
> ἁ βομβεῦσα μέλισσα καὶ ἐς τεὸν ἄντρον ἱκοίμαν
> τὸν κισσὸν διαδὺς καὶ τὰν πτέριν ἅ τυ πυκάσδει.

A. P. V 82 incerti:

> Εἴθ' ἄνεμος γενόμην, σὺ δ' ἐπιστείχουσα παρ' αὐγὰς
> στήθεα γυμνώσαις καί με πνέοντα λάβοις.

A. P. V 83 incerti:

> Εἴθε ῥόδον γενόμην ὑποπόρφυρον, ὄφρα με χερσὶν
> ἀρσαμένη χαρίσῃ στήθεσι χιονέοις.

A. P. XV 35 Theophanis:

> Εἴθε κρίνον γενόμην ἀργένναον, ὄφρα με χερσὶν
> ἀρσαμένη μᾶλλον σῆς χροτῆς κορέσῃς.

---

*) Sententia etiam apud nostros poetas est frequentata; conferas, ut exemplum afferam, Goethii nostri poema, quod inscribitur „Liebhaber in allen Gestalten":

> ‚Ich wollt', ich wär' ein Fisch,
> so hurtig und frisch;
> und kämst du zu angeln,
> ich würde nicht mangeln.
> Ich wollt', ich wär' ein Fisch,
> so hurtig und frisch.' et sqq.

A. P. V 173 Meleagri:

> Εἴδεις, Ζηνοφίλα, τρυφερὸν θάλος · εἴθ᾽ ἐπὶ σοὶ νῦν
> ἄπτερος εἰσῄειν ὕπνος ἐπὶ βλεφάροις,
> ὡς ἐπὶ σοὶ μηδ᾽ οὗτος, ὁ καὶ Διὸς ὄμματα θέλγων,
> φοιτήσαι, κάτεχον δ᾽ αὐτὸς ἐγώ σε μόνος.

A. P. XII 52 Meleagri:

> Οὔριος ἐμπνεύσας ναύταις Νότος, ὦ δυσέρωτες,
> ἥμισύ μευ ψυχᾶς ἄρπασεν Ἀνδράγαθον.
> Τρὶς μάκαρες νᾶες, τρὶς δ᾽ ὄλβια κύματα πόντου,
> τετράκι δ᾽ εὐδαίμων παιδοφορῶν ἄνεμος·
> Εἴθ᾽ εἴην δελφίς, ἵν᾽ ἐμοῖς βασταχτὸς ἐπ᾽ ὤμοις
> πορθμευθεὶς ἐσίδῃ τὰν γλυκόπαιδα Ῥόδον.

A. P. V 294 Leonti:

> Ψαῦε μελισταγέων στομάτων, δέπας· εὗρες, ἄμελγε·
> οἳ φθονέω· τὴν σὴν δ᾽ ἤθελον αἶσαν ἔχειν.

A. P. XII 142 Rhiani:

> Ἰξῷ Δεξιόνικος ὑπὸ χλωρῇ πλατανίστῳ
> κόσσυφον ἀγρεύσας, εἷλε κατὰ πτερύγων·
> χὠ μὲν ἀναστενάχων ἀπεκώκυεν ἱερὸς ὄρνις.
> Ἀλλ᾽ ἐγώ, ὦ φίλ᾽ Ἔρως καὶ θαλεραὶ Χάριτες,
> εἴην καὶ κίχλη καὶ κόσσυφος, ὡς ἂν ἐκείνου
> ἐν χερὶ καὶ φθογγὴν καὶ γλυκὺ δάκρυ βάλω.

A. P. XII 190 Stratonis:

> Ὄλβιος ὁ γράψας σε, καὶ ὄλβιος οὗτος ὁ κάλλει
> τῷ σῷ νικᾶσθαι κηρὸς ἐπιστάμενος.
> Θριπὸς ἐγὼ καὶ σύρμα τερηδόνος εἴθε γενοίμην,
> ὡς ἀναπηδήσας τὰ ξύλα ταῦτα φάγω.

A. P. VII 669 (carm. sepulcr.) Platonis:

> Ἀστέρας εἰσαθρεῖς ἀστὴρ ἐμός · εἴθε γενοίμην
> οὐρανός, ὡς πολλοῖς ὄμμασιν εἰς σὲ βλέπω.

Romanorum poetarum exemplum hoc mihi enotuit: (Ovid. am. II 15, 7) Amator anulum, quem puellae donaturus est, sic appellat:

> ,Felix, a domina tractaberis, anule, nostra:
> invideo donis iam miser ipse meis.

O utinam fieri subito mea munera possem
artibus Aeaeae Carpathiive senis!
Tunc ego te cupiam, domina, et tetigisse papillas
et laevam tunicis inseruisse manum:
elabar digito quamvis angustus et haerens
inque sinum mira laxus ab arte cadam.' et sqq.

§ 28. Amatores eo plerumque spectant, ut osculentur
puellas. Quae cum ita sint, non est mirum, quod saepe in
carminibus amatoriis mentio fit osculandi. Quod ita intellegi
solet, ut anima utriusque osculantis labris ab altero in alterum
transfundatur. Quam sententiam iam apud Platonem legimus:
(A. P. V 77)

Τὴν ψυχήν, Ἀγάθωνα φιλῶν, ἐπὶ χείλεσιν ἔσχον ·
ἦλθε γὰρ ἡ τλήμων ὡς διαβησομένη.

Hoc aliaque exempla multa, quae apud eroticos et Graecos et
Romanos exstant, iam ab aliis viris doctis sunt collecta.*)
Hunc unum Theocriti locum addere mihi liceat (XXVII 61):

αἴθ' αὐτὰν δυνάμαν καὶ τὰν ψυχὰν ἐπιβάλλειν.

Huic loco communi subest imago bibendi; bibit enim, ut ita
dicam, alter alterius animam. Sed aperte quoque osculum
amantium praecipue apud Graecos comparatur cum nectari,
id quod haec exempla doceant: (Lucian. deor. dial. 5, 4)
φιλεῖ (scil. ὁ Γανυμήδης) ἥδιον τοῦ νέκταρος.

(A. P. V 304 incerti)

Κούρη, τίς με φίλησεν ὑφ' ἕσπερα χείλεσιν ὑγροῖς.
νέκταρ ἔην τὸ φίλημα · τὸ γὰρ στόμα νέκταρος ἔπνει ·
καὶ μεθύω τὸ φίλημα, πολὺν τὸν ἔρωτα πεπωκώς.

Horat. c. I 13, 15:

. . . . . ,oscula quae Venus
quinta parte sui nectaris imbuit.'

Alia etiam ratione poculum in usum suum conferunt amantes
homines. Abutuntur enim poculo, quo oscula clam inter se
ferant, ita ut puella quasi oscula simul cum vino offerens

---

*) Conf. Jacobs, Animadvers. in Anthol. Graec. I 1, p. 337, Hertzberg
ad Propert. I 13, 17, Mallet l. l. p. 37.

poculum, postquam ipsa labris attigit, amatori praebeat, qui eidem ipsi poculi loco cui puella labra admovet. Quo lusu, ut ipso amantes delectantur, ita praecipue id agunt, ut coram aliis etsi osculis fruantur, tamen se osculari dissimulent.

A. P. V. 260 Agathiae Scholastici:

Εἰμὶ μὲν οὐ φιλόοινος · ὅταν δ᾽ ἐθέλῃς με μεθύσσαι,
πρῶτα σὺ γευομένη πρόσφερε, καὶ δέχομαι.
εἰ γὰρ ἐπιψαύσεις τοῖς χείλεσιν, οὐκέτι νήφειν
εὐμαρὲς οὐδὲ φυγεῖν τὸν γλυκὺν οἰνοχόον ·
πορθμεύει γὰρ ἔμοιγε κύλιξ παρὰ σοῦ τὸ φίλημα
καί μοι ἀπαγγέλλει τὴν χάριν ἣν ἔλαβεν.

Quo cum carmine Jacobs confert Aristaen. I 25: τοῦτον δὴ τὸν τρόπον, ὥσπερ ἐκ στομάτων ὑπεφίλουν ἀλλήλους, καταπίνοντες τὰ φιλήματα, καὶ τὸν οἶνον τοῖς χείλεσι κεκραμένον καὶ μέχρι καὶ αὐτῆς παρέπεμπον τῆς καρδίας.

Ovid. amor. I 4, 31:

,quae tu reddideris, ego primus pocula sumam
et, qua tu biberis, hac ego parte bibam.‘

Ovid. art. am. I 575:

,fac primus rapias illius tacta labellis
pocula, quaque bibit parte puella, bibas.‘

Lucianus Junonem de Ganymede Jovem maritum his verbis obiurgantem fingit (deor. dial. 5, 2): καὶ τὸ φίλημά σοι ἥδιον τοῦ νέκταρος, καὶ διὰ τοῦτο οὐδὲ διψῶν πολλάκις αἰτεῖς πιεῖν · ὁτὲ δὲ καὶ ἀπογευσάμενος μόνον ἔδωκας ἐκείνῳ, καὶ πιόντος ἀπολαβὼν τὴν κύλικα ὅσον ὑπόλοιπον ἐν αὐτῇ πίνεις, ὅθεν καὶ ὁ παῖς ἔπιε καὶ ἔνθα προσήρμοσε τὰ χείλη, ἵνα καὶ πίνῃς ἅμα καὶ φιλῇς ·

Ibid. 6, 2 Juno apud Jovem Ixionem, qui se sectetur, accusat: ὁ δὲ (scil. Ἰξίων) καὶ ἔστενε καὶ ὑπεδάκρυε, καὶ εἴ ποτε πιοῦσα παραδοίην τῷ Γανυμήδει τὸ ἔκπωμα, ὁ δὲ ᾔτει ἐν αὐτῷ ἐκείνῳ πιεῖν καὶ λαβὼν ἐφίλει μεταξὺ καὶ πρὸς τοὺς ὀφθαλμοὺς προσῆγε καὶ αὖθις ἀφεώρα ἐς ἐμέ · ταῦτα δὲ ἤδη συνιεῖν ἐρωτικὰ ὄντα.

Etiam per alias res puella oscula mittit amatori, sive zona abutitur sive pomis sive placenta.

A. P. V 284 Agathiae Scholastici:

Εἰργομένη φιλέειν με κατὰ στόμα δῖα Ῥοδάνϑη
ζώνην παρϑενικὴν ἐξετάνυσσε μέσην
καὶ κείνην φιλέεσκεν· ἐγὼ δέ τις ὡς ὀχετηγὸς
ἀρχὴν εἰς ἑτέρην εἷλκον ἔρωτος ὕδωρ,
αἳ ἐρύων τὸ φίλημα· περὶ ζωστῆρα δὲ κούρης
μάστακι ποππύζων τηλόϑεν ἀντεφίλουν.
ἦν δὲ πόνου καὶ τοῦτο παραίφασις· ἡ γλυκερὴ γὰρ
ζώνη πορϑμὸς ἔην χείλεος ἀμφοτέρου.

A. L. (Riese) 218, 7:

,at si dissimulas, multum mihi cara, venire,
oscula cum pomis mitte: vorabo libens.‘

A. L. (Meyer) 257, 9:

,Misit dente levi paullum libata placentae
munera, de labris dulcia mella suis.
Nescio qui plus melle sapit, quod contigit, ipsa
spirans Cecropium, dulcis odore, thymum.‘

Index.

•-•-•

The University of Chicago

Studies in the Diction of the Sermo Amatorius in Roman Comedy

A DISSERTATION
SUBMITTED TO THE FACULTY OF THE GRADUATE SCHOOL OF ARTS AND
LITERATURE IN CANDIDACY FOR THE DEGREE OF
DOCTOR OF PHILOSOPHY
(DEPARTMENT OF LATIN)

BY

KEITH PRESTON

A Private Edition
Distributed by
The University of Chicago Libraries
1916

The Collegiate Press
GEORGE BANTA PUBLISHING COMPANY
MENASHA, WISCONSIN
1916

PREFACE

These studies in the Sermo Amatorius of Roman Comedy were undertaken at the suggestion of Professor Henry W. Prescott, of the University of Chicago. I am indebted to him for constant aid and criticism at all stages of my work.

INTRODUCTION

The sermo amatorius of Roman Comedy has been by no means neglected by modern scholars, though it has been studied chiefly for what it might contribute to the history of Elegy. Scholars have endeavored to settle the important question as to whether Roman Elegy was an original type by comparing parallels, largely erotic, drawn from the comic fragments, Menander, the Palatine Anthology, Lucian, Alciphron, Philostratus, Aristaenetus, and the Scriptores Erotici on the one side, and Roman Comedy and Elegy on the other. It is perhaps open to question whether the main point at issue has been settled decisively, but these studies have at least resulted in clearly demonstrating the Greek sources for most of the erotic material in Plautus, Terence, and the elegiac poets. Most of the more important parallels have been noted, and literary relationships at least partially established.

In my detailed study of erotic diction in Roman Comedy I have, of course, been greatly indebted to previous studies of the sort mentioned above. Among these, Leo, in his many contributions to this subject, has been most suggestive. In addition to the sections in his Plautinische Forschungen to which I have so frequently referred, I have found his review of Rothstein's Propertius (Gött. G. A., 1898, p. 746) full of hints. The dissertations of Volkmar Hoelzer[1] and Maximilian Heinemann[2] have been particularly helpful.

In the introductory chapters of his erotic lexicon to Ovid, Tibullus, and Propertius, René Pichon has drawn some interesting comparisons between the Greek erotic vocabulary, and the erotic diction of Roman Elegy and Comedy. There seemed to be room for a closer study of the erotic portions of Roman Comedy, such study to be devoted primarily to diction. The existence of a Greek background for Comedy may be taken as proved. My main idea has been to see how far this background might contribute to the closer interpretation of words and phrases in the erotic vocabulary of Plautus and Terence. My first task was to collect the Greek erotic vocabulary from sources already indicated, and determine, so far as possible, what words were technical; I have not confined my Greek parallels entirely to those authors that could be placed in an immediate relation to Comedy, though it has been my aim to do so

---

[1] De Poesi Amatoria a Comicis Atticis exculta ab elegiacis imitatione expressa, Marburg, 1899.

[2] Epistulae Amatoriae quomodo cohaereant cum Elegiis Alexandrinis, Strassburg, 1910, Vol. XIV, Fasc. 3 of Dissertationes Philologicae Argentoratenses.

to a large extent. The word for word comparison that I have made
of the Greek and Latin sermo should require no defense in principle,
and I have endeavored to use all due caution in its application. In
general, I have contented myself with placing side by side what seemed
to be similar or equivalent expressions in the Greek or Latin sermo,
and have allowed the results to speak for themselves. In some cases
it may be stated with a fair degree of certainty that a given word or
phrase came directly from a Greek original; for a case of this sort cf.
pernoctare (παννυχίζειν) p. 46. More often the Greek may only be
said to contribute something in atmosphere or direct interpretation;
for example, cf. Leo (Gött. G. A., 1898, p. 740) on Propertius I.1.33 in
me nostra Venus *noctes* exercet *amaras*; Leo compares Aristoph. Lysis.
764 and context: ἀργαλέας γ'εὖ οἶδ' ὅτι ἄγουσι νύκτας. The fact that a
word is technical in Latin may often be missed without the evidence
of the Greek.

In determining Latin usage, I have not stopped with Comedy or
Elegy, but have included prose writers, notably Petronius, and other
poets as late as Martial. Many words have been discussed solely from
the Latin side, where the Greek did not seem to offer significant com-
parisons.

In the effort to group my material I have adopted certain classifica-
tions, which have proved convenient, if not convincingly valid. Part I
is devoted to the abstract nouns which figure in the sermo, and is largely
an interpretation of Mercator 18 sqq. The sections that follow are
devoted to different aspects of what I have termed the sermo meretricius.

I should perhaps say a word as to omissions and inclusions. In my
treatment of particular rubrics I have not hesitated to refer to the
Latin Thesaurus, Pichon, or other compilations, for supplementary
material, where the word under consideration was there adequately
treated. I have omitted altogether many words that had no special
interest, or were sufficiently treated in existing lexica or special com-
mentaries. Unfortunately I have not been able to consult all that has
been written on the sermo amatorius. Among the things that I have
been unable to consult are several erotic dictionaries, known to me
only by title.[3] From the comment of others who had these works at
their disposal I have not been led to believe that my loss was serious.

[3] I have consulted the Glossarium Eroticum Linguae Latinae of P. Pierrugues,
Berlin, 1908 (2nd edition).

I

In the body of words composing what we may call the sermo amatorius of Roman Comedy, no other group is more interesting than those abstract nouns that have to do with the emotions. The querulous and introspective lover of Comedy has a particular fondness for analyzing his condition, and employs, to this end, a curious diversity of terms. The same situation and the same passion may involve error, aegritudo, cupiditas, terror, etc. The extreme example of such combinations is the catalogue of vitia that occurs in the Mercator 18 sqq. In this passage the reader is at once impressed by the variety of terms, the apparent remoteness of their application to the passion of love, and the resulting difficulty of exact interpretation. A failure to solve this difficulty, perhaps, in some measure accounts for Leo's contention that the list is, in the main, a mere farrago (cf. Leo crit. note ad 1). The passage has been discussed, with particular attention to the grouping of terms, by Prescott (Classical Philology IV.11 sq). In this discussion a very suggestive comparison is drawn between the Mercator passage and Cicero Tusc. 4.80, where many of the same terms are used in a philosophical context. A certain similarity, in point of diction, is evident, and this resemblance need not be thought of as entirely accidental. The close and somewhat artificial analysis of love that we find in Plautus, and, to some extent, in Terence also, is singular in a Roman comic poet; moreover, not a few of the words employed suggest the vocabulary of philosophy. The same words represent, in Cicero, definite equivalents from the Greek philosophical vocabulary, but so direct a comparison is not possible for Comedy. It does seem likely, on the internal evidence afforded by such resemblances in diction, that Plautus, in the Mercator catalogue, was rendering, with more or less fidelity, his Greek original. We may not assume that the list of vitia, as found in this original, was lifted bodily from philosophical sources. Such lists are, it is true, of frequent occurrence in the philosophers, but the listing of virtues and vices of typical persons is also characteristic of Comedy (cf. Leo Plaut. Forsch.[2], p. 131). It ought to be added that several of the abstracts in this particular list have no exact equivalents in the philosophical categories. To admit these facts is not to destroy the value of the philosophical material. After all necessary exceptions have been made, there remain a number of words that compare very neatly with stock terms in the Stoic categories; in most cases, also, such a comparison gives to the Latin word a distinctness of meaning that was often lacking before.

The Greek poets of the New Comedy were thoroughly familiar with Hellenistic philosophy[4] and lampooned it with the more success because of this familiarity. Philemon, the author of the Ἔμπορος, which served as a model for Plautus' Mercator, was a conspicuous example of this tendency. His Φιλόσοφοι was directed against the philosophers, and a fragment, 85 K., contains a slighting allusion to the φιλοσοφία καινή—φιλοσοφίαν καινὴν γὰρ οὗτος φιλοσοφεῖ· πεινῆν διδάσκει καὶ μαθητὰς λαμβάνει etc. Other fragments of Philemon, however, show a philosophizing tendency on the part of the poet himself, cf. Philemon 92K. 1-4, 88K. Whatever the real attitude of these poets toward Stoic tenets, it would be strange if their diction were not at times affected by the familiar jargon, even consciously, perhaps, in passages of a mock serious character, like the Mercator catalogue.[5] Hence the philosophical material may be supposed to have a distinct value, in such places, to interpret shades of meaning and explain juxtapositions. The pages that follow will be chiefly concerned with the interpretation of Mercator 18-31.

> Nam amorem haec cuncta vitia sectari solent:
> Cura aegritudo nimiaque elegantia—
> Haec non modo illum qui amat, sed quemque attigit   20
> Magno atque solido multat infortunio:
> Nec pol profecto quisquam sine grandi malo,
> Prae quam res patitur studuit elegantiae—
> Sed amori accedunt etiam haec quae dixi minus:
> Insomnia, aerumna, error, (et) terror et fuga,   25
> Ineptia stultitiaque adeo et temeritas(t),
> Incogitantia, excors immodestia,
> Petulantia et cupiditas, malivolentia:
> [6]Inhaeret etiam aviditas, desidia, iniuria,

[4]For fragments alluding to the Stoics cf. Susemihl Gesch. d. gr. Lit. d. a. Z. p. 249 n. 10; note particularly Theognetus ap. Athen. III.104 b (Leo Plaut. Forsch.[2] p. 130).

[5]Leo has noted certain Stoic echoes in Comedy: cf. Plaut. Forsch.[2] p. 130 and note 4 with the citations Capt. 271 (cf. Stich. 120) Trin. 485 sq. Note also Lambinus on Cist. 60-1 doleo ab animo, doleo ab oculis, doleo ab aegritudine. Quid dicam, nisi stultitia mea me in maerorem rapit. Lamb. "Stoicum est hoc. Nam Stoici aiunt omnem aegritudinem, atque adeo omnem animi morbum ex stultitia, stultaque opinione nasci."

[6]29—inertia L: ineret et iam . . . . residia.

Inopia, contumelia et dispendium,
Multiloquium, parumloquium:
That the Mercator catalogue is at least not out of keeping with
the manner of Philemon can best be attested by one of the fragments
already referred to, 92K.

ἀεὶ τὸ πλουτεῖν συμφορὰς πολλὰς ἔχει
φθόνον τ' ἐπήρειάν τε καὶ μῖσος πολύ
πράγματά τε πολλὰ κἀνοχλήσεις μυρίας
πράξεις τε πολλὰς συλλογάς τε τοῦ βίου. κτλ.

Aside from the listing tendency, and the introduction of certain abstract
nouns that appear in the Stoic categories (φθόνος, μῖσος, etc.) this
fragment is interesting because of the introductory line ἀεὶ τὸ πλουτεῖν
συμφορὰς πολλὰς ἔχει, which is certainly not far removed from the intro-
ductory formula Mercator 18: nam amorem haec cuncta vitia sectari
solent. I am not inclined to believe that the word vitia, Mercator 18,
represents any technical equivalent in Greek, despite the fact that it is
technical in Cicero.[7] Vitia is a natural Latin equivalent for any term
representing unfavorable consequences. Propertius calls love a vitium II.1.
65 hoc si quis vitium poterit mihi demere, etc., where the word is equiva-
lent to morbus (νόσημα), cf. Rothstein ad l.; vitium is a failing or defect
Prop. II.22.17, and a blemish or stain, apparently, Prop. III.17.5 per te
iunguntur, per te solvuntur amantes, tu vitium ex animo dilue, cf. amoris
macula Plaut. Poen. 198. The only other list of vitia or concomitants
of love is found Eunuchus 59 sq. in amore haec omnia insunt vitia:
iniuriae, suspiciones, inimicitiae, indutiae, bellum, pax rursum. If we
were to look for a philosophical parallel ἁμαρτία would perhaps be
nearest to the sense, cf. V. Arnim o. c. 468, Plutarch de virtute morali
cp. 10 p. 449 d πᾶν μὲν γὰρ πάθος ἁμαρτία κατ' αὐτούς ἐστι καὶ πᾶς ὁ λυ-
πούμενος ἢ φοβούμενος ἢ ἐπιθυμῶν ἁμαρτάνει but a neutral expression such as
συμφοραί, for example, is more likely in Mercator 18 and Eunuch. 59.
Comparisons are much more suggestive in connection with the particular
vitia that follow; for convenience, I shall examine these in approximately
the order of occurrence.

Aegritudo (Mercator 19) is used in Cicero to render the Stoic λύπη
Cic. fin. III.35 (= V. Arnim III.381) omnes eae (perturbationes) sunt

[7]Cf. Cicero Tusc. IV.30 (V. Arnim Frag. Stoic. III.425) vitia enim adfectiones sunt
manentes, perturbationes autem moventes. Also Tusc. IV.10. (V. Arnim 424) ex per-
turbationibus autem primum morbi conficiuntur quae vocant illi νοσήματα eaque
quae sunt eis morbis contraria, quae habent ad res certas vitiosam offensionem atque
fastidium, deinde aegrotationes, quae appellantur a Stoicis ἀρρωστήματα.

genere quattuor . . . . . aegritudo, formido, libido, quamque
Stoici . . . . . ἡδονήν appellant; cf. also Melcher Chrysippus'
Lehre von den Affekten p. 23 sq. This fourfold division of the emo-
tions is Stoic, cf. Zeno ap. Diog. Laër. VII.110 (=V. Arnim I.211)
φησιν . . . . .Ζήνων ἐν τῷ περὶ παθῶν εἶναι γένη τέτταρα, λύπην,
φόβον, ἐπιθυμίαν, ἡδονήν, Aristo=V. Arnim I.370 (Clemens Alex. Stromat.
II.20 p. 195 Sylb., Vol. I.p. 486 Pott.) ὅθεν, ὡς ἔλεγεν 'Αρίστων, πρὸς ὅλον
τὸ τετράχορδον, ἡδονὴν λύπην φόβον ἐπιθυμίαν κτλ. For Chrysippus mater-
ial cf. V. Arnim III.377-420. The general terms aegritudo (λύπη)
formido (φόβος) are used to include a variety of emotions which are
further listed and defined[8] in a somewhat arbitrary manner.[9] This
Stoic tendency to subdivide and classify and collect more or less related
terms in lists and catalogues may partly account for a like tendency in
Comedy.

Aegritudo in Cicero is not ordinarily coupled with words which it
properly includes. It may be used in the generalizing plural to indicate
the several varieties of aegritudo: Tusc. I.80 aegritudines irae libidines.
The antithesis between aegritudo (λύπη) and gaudium, laetitia (ἡδονή)
is sharply drawn fin. I.57 tum fit ut aegritudo sequatur si illa mala sint,
laetitia si bona, fin. I.56 non placet detracta voluptate . . . . .
aegritudinem statim consequi.

The word aegritudo was particularly well adapted to rendering the
Stoic λύπη, as involving the idea of disease, and as applicable both to
mind and body. The comparison between diseases of the mind and
body was emphasized by Chrysippus[10]: Cicero Tusc. IV.10.23 (V. Arnim
III.424). The glosses also emphasize this same idea, cf. Corpus Gloss.
II.245. 58, II.247.29, II.377.3, III.600.42. The word was used in medicine
as a term for insanity: Plin. N. H. 7.171 iam signa letalia: in furoris
morbo risum, sapientiae vero aegritudine fimbriarum curam, etc. Aegri-
tudo in the mind corresponds to aegrotatio in the body: Cicero Tusc.
III.23 doloris origo . . . . . explicanda est, id est causa efficiens

---

[8]V. Arnim III.415 (= Cicero Tusc. IV.17.18) angor aegritudo premens . . . . .
aerumna aegritudo laboriosa, etc., V. Arnim III.413 (Stobaeus ecl. II.92), V. Arnim
III.412 (Diog. Laer. VII.110.111). These lists compared, and common elements
noted, Zeller, Die Philosophie der Griechen in ihres geschichtlichen Entwicklung
1865 (2nd ed.) III.p. 213, n. 3. Cf. also Melcher o. c. pp. 23-27, V. Arnim III.394-420.

[9]Zeller o. c. III p. 213. Die vier Hauptklassen der Affekte wurden dann weiter in
zahlreiche Unterarten getheilt bei deren Aufzählung sich aber unser Philosophen mehr
von dem Sprachgebrauch als von psychologischen Erwägungen leiten lassen.

[10]Cf. also Pohlenz "Das Dritte und Vierte Buch der Tusculanen" Hermes 41, p.
336. Melcher o. c. p. 18. In general also Von Arnim III.421.430.

aegritudinem in animo tamquam aegrotationem in corpore. The same reason apparently dictates the preference for aegritudo in Comedy, where the conception of love as a disease[11] is exceedingly common and seems to go beyond mere metaphor. The lover's mind is ailing: Ter. And. 559 animus aegrotus, ibid. 309. The loved one is the only physician: Cist. 74 si medicus veniat qui huic morbo facere medicinam[12] potest.

As used in Comedy, aegritudo, the general term, includes a variety of painful emotions which range from grief or vexation to anxiety or painful anticipation. For the former meaning cf. Adelphoe 312 ut ego hanc iram . . evomam omnem, dum aegritudo haec est recens; Curc. 223-5 si recte facias, Phaedrome, auscultes mihi atque istam exturbes ex animo aegritudinem. paves, parasitus quia non rediit; here for aegritudo one might substitute cura (φροντίς), properly a subhead of aegritudo (for the various subheads of aegritudo [λύπη] cf. particularly Von Arnim III.414, 415). But nice philosophical distinctions[13] are naturally not observed in Comedy. Thus aegritudo is occasionally coupled with what are properly subheads under the main term: cf. Thesaurus Linguae Latinae, I.952.60 sq., Lodge, s. v. So with maeror Stich. 215, cura Merc. 19 cura aegritudo. Such synonyms as dolor miseria, etc., frequently replace the main term. Similarly, in Greek poetry, there is no perceptible difference in value between λύπη Diphilus 88K., Eur. Orest. 398, and ἄλγος A. P. V.289, 297 and ὀδύνη A. P. V.106, XII.49. But the generalizing plural serves as an occasional reminder that aegritudo is the general and all inclusive word: cf. Ter. Haut. 539, Plaut. Stich. 526.

The contrast between voluptas, gaudium (ἡδονή) and aegritudo (λύπη) so much emphasized by the Stoics, and in Cicero, is reproduced in Comedy. Each state is thought of as excluding the other; they may not, therefore, be combined in a person at any single time: Merc. 359 ubi voluptatem aegritudo vincat, quid ibi inest amoeni, Ter. Eunuchus 552 ne hoc gaudium contaminet vita aegritudine aliqua, Haut. 679-80

[11]Aegritudo is used of other emotional weaknesses than love. Trin. 1091 adimit animam mihi aegritudo, Men. prol. 35 eaque is aegritudine paucis diebus post Tarenti emortuost, Merc. 140, Phorm. 750, Cist. 60.

[12]Cf. A. P. V.116 οἶδα διδάξαι φάρμακον ᾧ παύσεις τὴν δυσέρωτα νόσον, A. P. V.130 λύπης φάρμακ' ἐπιστάμεθα, Longus I.22 τῆς ἐρωτικῆς λύπης φάρμακον.

[13]Cf. Cicero Tusc. III.83 sed ratio una omnium est aegritudinum plura nomina. Nam et invidere aegritudinis est et aemulare et obtrectare et misereri et angi, lugere, maerere, aerumna adfici, lamentari, sollicitari, dolere, in molestia esse, adflictari, desperare, 84 haec omnia definiunt Stoici eaque verba quae dixi, singularum rerum sunt, non, ut videntur, easdem res significant, sed aliquid differunt.

res nulla mihi posthac . . . . . tanta quae mi aegritudinem adferat: tanta haec laetitia obortast, And. 961, Haut. 506.

Aegritudo and its various subheads have a particular affinity for cura: Merc. 162 cruciatum curam, ibid. 19 cura aegritudo, ibid. 870 cura, miseria, aegritudo, Pseud. 21 miseria et cura. The distinction between the two words is fairly well brought out: Truc. 455 quantast cura in animo quantum corde capio dolorem. Ciceronian usage corresponds (cf. T. L. L. s. v.). In Tusc. IV.18 sollicitudo (=cura) is defined as aegritudo cum cogitatione. Cicero combines cura with dolor (5 times), angor (2), molestia (1), and with sollicitudo (3), as in Ter. Phorm. 441. The Greek equivalent, φροντίς, of cura, sollicitudo belonged to the Stoic categories, and was there regarded as a variety of λύπη: cf. Andronicus περὶ παθῶν 2 (p. 12 Kreuttner) (V. Arnim III.414) φροντὶς δὲ λογισμὸς λυπουμένου. Φροντίς and μέριμνα are frequently combined with λῦπαι;cf. Diph. fr. 88K. λύπας μερίμνας ἁρπαγάς, Antipho Tetr. I. 2.2 λύπας καὶ φροντίδας προσβέβληκεν; cf. Isocr. 408 E, and again Apollod. 3 K. τοῖς μεριμνῶσίν τε καὶ λυπουμένοις. The painful character of φροντίς is emphasized also in Aesch. Pers. 161 καί με καρδίαν ἀμύσσει φροντίς, A. P. V.5 χαλεπαὶ τείρουσι μέριμναι. Compare such phrases as curae exanimales (Rudens 221), though this is not the erotic cura.

Somewhat similar to the conception of love as a disease (aegritudo) of the mind is the idea that love is an aberration (insania). According to Stoic ideas, the emotions were of necessity irrational; the sapiens was necessarily free from all harmful emotions, and all men but the sapiens were mad: Diog. Laer. VIII.124 (V. Arnim 664) πάντας τε τοὺς ἄφρονας μαίνεσθαι· οὐ γὰρ εἶναι φρονίμους, ἀλλὰ κατὰ τὴν ἴσην τῇ ἀφροσύνῃ μανίαν πάντα πράττειν; cf. also V. Arnim 657-676. The Stoic categories include under ἐπιθυμία (V. Arnim III.394=Stobae. ecl. II.90. 7 W.) ἔρωτες σφοδροί, πόθοι, ἵμεροι. In ἔρωτες σφοδροί is implied the distinction between a virtuous, rational love, such as became the sapiens, and the technical ἐρωτομανία, an excessive or vicious passion. This distinction is amplified elsewhere: cf. V. Arnim III.717 (Stobae. ecl. II.65. 15 W.) τὸν δὲ ἐρωτικὸν καὶ διχῇ λέγεσθαι, τὸν μὲν κατὰ τὴν ἀρετὴν ποιὸν σπουδαῖον ὄντα, τὸν δὲ κατὰ τὴν κακίαν ἐν ψόγῳ. ὡς ἂν ἐρωτομανῆ τινα. Ἔρως as a φιλία κατὰ πάθος (Aristotle Nicom. Eth. 8.3) is defined by Andronicus (V. Arnim III.397) as ἐπιθυμία σωματικῆς συνουσίας but this may not be a Stoic definition (Pohlenz, Hermes 41 p. 350, n. 5) The whole conception of a rational and an irrational love is somewhat confused: in general cf. V. Arnim III.716.722, Pohlenz p. 349-50, Melcher p. 40. The general idea may, however, be reflected in Mercator

262-3 quam ego postquam aspexi, non ita amo ut sanei solent homines, sed eodem pacto ut insanei solent. In numerous other passages we have love as an aberration, cf. Merc. 325.443.446, Curc. 187, Ter. And. 692, Haut. 257. Certain other words should perhaps be mentioned in this context. Folly and madness were synonyms according to the Stoics: Cicero Tusc. IV.54 (V. Arnim 665) Stoici qui omnes insipientes insanos esse dicunt. So, in the Mercator catalogue such expressions as ineptia, stultitia, etc., may well be grouped as varieties of ἐρωτομανία.[14]

Somewhat similar to ἐρωμανία (insania) is terror (Merc. 25) as a vitium amoris. The natural equivalent of φόβος in the Stoic categories is metus, formido: Cicero Tusc. IV.7.14 (V. Arnim III.393). Among the varieties of metus Cicero lists terror, defining it, Tusc. IV.19 (V. Arnim III.410) as metum concutientem, ex quo fit ut pudorem rubor, terrorem pallor et tremor et dentium crepitus consequatur. This is not a translation of any existing Stoic definition, but the phenomena listed suggest an identification with ἔκπληξις defined Diog. Laer. VII. 112 (V. Arnim III.407) as φόβος ἐκ φαντασίας ἀσυνήθους πράγματος; cf. also V. Arnim III.408, 409.[15] Ἔκπληξις occurs elsewhere in erotic contexts: cf. Ach. Tat. I.4 πάντα δέ μ' εἶχον ὁμοῦ ἔπαινος, ἔκπληξις, τρόμος, αἰδώς. The general term φόβος is not unknown in such connections: Aristaen. II.5 θεωροῦσα τὸν καλὸν αἰδοῦμαι, φοβοῦμαι, ὑφ' ἡδονῆς πνευστιῶ.[16] An erotic idea in φόβος is justified also by certain combinations in Plato: cf. Philebus 50 B ὀργὴν μὴν καὶ πόθον καὶ θρῆνον καὶ φόβον καὶ ἔρωτα, Rep. 579 B πολλῶν καὶ παντοδαπῶν φόβων καὶ ἐρώτων μεστός, Phil. 50 C τήν γ' ἐν τοῖς φόβοις καὶ ἔρωσι.... κρᾶσιν. Outside of the Mercator catalogue, where terror is grouped with other terms that have technical force, the words for fear do not seem to be technical in Roman Comedy, although they are frequently found in erotic passages: cf. Miles 1233,

[14]This idea was a commonplace in later Greek poetry: A. P. V.267 οὐ φιλέεις . . . . . πῶς δύναται γὰρ ψυχὴ ἐρωμανέειν ὀρθὰ λογιζομένη. A. P. XII.117 τί δ' ἔρωτι λογισμός. Cf. Ter. Eunuchus 61 sq. incerta haec (amoris) si tu postules ratione certa facere, nihilo plus agas, quam si des operam ut cum ratione insanias, Men. 59K. φύσει γάρ ἐστ' ἔρως τοῦ νουθετοῦντος κωφόν to which Ribbeck compares Afranius 348 amentes, quibus animi non sunt integri, surde audiunt. Cf. also A. P. V.89, V.132, V.272 (λυσσώων), V.47, 220, 225, 267. The ἐρωτομανία of Greek epigram is of course the furor of Latin elegy. Pichon p. 157.

[15]Cf. Tischer-Sorof on Cicero Tusc. IV.19, where this identification is made, with a reference to the Diogenes passage, and also to Stob. ecl. II.7. Cf. also Melcher o. c. p. 25.

[16]Cf. Nemesius de nat. hom. 19-21 (V. Arnim III.416) Διαιρεῖται δὲ καὶ φόβος εἰς ἕξ, εἰς ὄκνον, εἰς αἰδώ, εἰς αἰσχύνην, εἰς κατάπληξιν, εἰς ἀγωνίαν, εἰς ἔκπληξιν . . . . . αἰδὼς δὲ φόβος ἐπὶ προσδοκίᾳ ψόγου.

1272, 996a; in such cases various specific causes for fear are mentioned, and metus, timor, etc., have no consistent technical meaning in themselves.

In Mercator 25 we find the grouping error terror fuga. As Prescott suggests, error and terror fall naturally together as similar perturbationes. The same combination occurs (though not in an erotic context), Rudens 215 algor error pavor me omnia tenent, and in Ovid Amor. I.10.9. We may point also to the use of πλάνη: Plato Phaed. 81 A πλάνης καὶ ἀνοίας καὶ φόβων καὶ ἀγρίων ἐρώτων καὶ τῶν ἄλλων κακῶν τῶν ἀνθρωπείων ἀπηλλαγμένη. The grouping here might seem to suggest an erotic connection for πλάνη if it did not appear from other passages (cf. p. 9) that the combination φόβων καὶ ἐρώτων was the significant one; πλάνη = error (Corp. Gloss. II.408. 38) is not technical, as appears, in the Greek sermo amatorius. As used in Comedy, cf. Merc. 347, Amph. 470, and in Cicero, who reflects the Greek distinctly (cf. Cicero ph. fr. 9.8 error et ignorantia veri, Plato Phaedo 81 A πλάνη καὶ ἄνοια) error retains its original idea of uncertainty or confusion. Starting with this idea error becomes technical in the later sermo amatorius, where it seems to be practically a synonym for insania, or furor: cf. Vergil Ecl. VIII.41 Ut vidi, ut perii! ut me malus abstulit error (Theocr. Id. II.82 χὼς ἴδον, ὡς ἐμάνην, ὡς μευ πέρι θυμὸς ἰάφθη). The comment of Servius "amor enim errare plerumque compellit" shows a desire to connect this usage with the ordinary idea. Cf. also the Ovidian use of error: Amores I.2.35 Blanditiae comites tibi erunt Errorque Furorque. Error, as a delusion, may also have been written by Ovid Met. X.342 retinet malus error[17] amantem ut praesens spectem Cinyram. Cf. also Met. III.431, where the idea of an optical illusion is more prominent.[18]

The third member, fuga, of the triad in Mercator 25, is of course natural after terror. It may be explained, as has been done, by reference to the plot of the play: cf. 644 certumst exsulatum hinc ire me, also 652 where the word fuga is used. Flight on the part of the lover, for one reason or another, is a common motif in Comedy: cf. Asin. 591 sq., Haut. 118, Eunuch. 216. Fuga is more probably purely formal in this context

[17]"Ardor" Ehwald, without comment, and so also most of the older editors. There is some MSS authority for error, however, cf. Jahn 1832 crit. note, Bach 1836, who reads ardor, remarking: "beides (error, ardor) oft verwechselt s. Heins. zu Amor. I.10.9. Wohl bezeichnet auch error heftige Liebe insofern als Leidenschaft ein Zustande des Wahns, der insania, ist Ovid Amor. I.10.9, Prop. I.13.28, Verg. Ecl. VIII. 41." Magnus (1914) rejects error.

[18]In Ovid error is used occasionally of a moral fault, a sense not found in Plautus, cf. Trabea 6 Rib. ego voluptatem animi nimium summum esse errorem arbitror.

and practically equivalent to terror, cf. Andronicus περὶ παθῶν 1 (p. 11 Kreuttner) = V. Arnim 391, φόβος δὲ ἄλογος ἔκκλισις ἢ φυγὴ ἀπὸ προσδοκουμένου δεινοῦ.

An exceedingly common word in erotic contexts in Plautus is aerumna, which is used objectively, where aegritudo is subjective. The idea of labor is inherent in the word: Paul. Fest 24 itaque (i. e. "ab aerumnulis quibus sarcinae portabantur") aerumnae labores onerosos significant; sive a Graeco sermone deducuntur; nam αἴρειν graece latine tollere dicitur (cf. also other etymologies: Char. gramm. I.98.12, Albin. gramm. VII. 297.8, T. L. L. s. v.). Plautus uses aerumna of the trials or hardships of the lover, who is compared to Hercules: Persa 1-2 qui amans egens ingressus est princeps in amoris vias superavit aerumnis suis aerumnas Herculi, Epid. 179 neque sexta aerumna acerbior Herculi, quam illa mihi obiectast. In Cicero aerumna is defined Tusc. IV.18 (V. Arnim 415) as aegritudo laboriosa. This may perhaps be intended as an equivalent for ἄχθος[19] in the Stoic categories, which is defined, Diog. Laer. VII.111, Stob. ecl. II.92.7 W. (V. Arnim 412, 413) as λύπη βαρύνουσα (cf. also V. Arnim 414, 416, etc.). In this connection note Lucr. IV.1069 furor atque aerumna gravescit (cf. βαρύνουσα). The distinction between cura and aerumna appears neatly in a fragment of Pacuvius trag. 276 lapit cor cura, aerumna corpus conficit. This idea of physical distress is regularly preserved in Comedy: cf. Capt. 195 sq. si di immortales id voluerunt vos hanc aerumnam exsequi, decet id pati aequo animo: si id facietis, levior labos erit, Capt. 1009, Miles 33, Rudens 257, Ter. Hec. 288, Trin. 839. Occasionally aerumna or the synonym, labor, mean simply distress of mind, aegritudo (cura), so Casina 415 cor de labore pectus tundit, Capt. 929, Curc. 142.[20]

The combination insomnia aerumna occurs in Mercator 25. The association is one of sense as well as sound. Sleeplessness is one of the commonest privations of the lover, and the phrase labores et vigiliae is too familiar to require examples. Insomnia is mentioned, apparently as a vitium amoris, Caec. Stat. 168 Rib. consequitur comes insomnia, ea porro insaniam affert, cf. also Pacuvius 9, Servius on Aeneid IV.9. So also, in Greek erotic writers, ἀγρυπνία is a familiar symptom or effect of love. Specific and technical force is indicated by such a phrase as Ach. Tat. I.7 ἐρωτικὴν ἀγρυπνίαν; cf. also A. P. V.5 σὲ δ' ἄγρυπνον χαλε-

---

[19] Cf., however, Tischer—Sorof on Cicero Tusc. IV.18: aerumna = ὀδύνη λύπη ἐπίπονος, angor = ἄχθος λύπη βαρύνουσα.

[20] πόνος (ἄχθος, μόχθος, ὀδύνη) are frequent in erotic contexts: Aristoph. Eccl. 972 διά τοί σε πόνους ἔχω, A. P. V. 162 ὁ πόνος δύεται εἰς ὄνυχα, A. P. V. 75, V.297.

παι τείρουσι μέριμναι, A. P. V.197 φιλάγρυπνον λύχνον, ibid. V.166 ἄγρυπνον πόθον, A. P. V.201 ἀγρυπνῶ in erotic sense. Compare also Hoelzer o. c., p. 48. This commonplace is reflected in the Latin elegiac poets much more than in Comedy: cf. Pichon s. v. vigilare.

Here I wish to turn directly to Mercator 28 sq. and discuss in some detail the grouping in lines 28-30. Before doing so I will quote a passage from Epictetus which shows possible combinations in such lists, and bears a striking resemblance (accidental, of course) to the list in question. Epict. II.16.45 ἐκ τῆς διανοίας ἔκβαλε ἀντὶ Προκρούστου καὶ Σκίρωνος λύπην, φόβον, ἐπιθυμίαν, φθόνον, ἐπιχαιρεκακίαν, φιλαργυρίαν, μαλακίαν, ἀκρασίαν. Both λύπη and a form of φόβος (ἔκπληξις) have already been paralleled in our Mercator passage. Petulantia and cupiditas in line 28 may loosely cover Greek ἐπιθυμία. The bearing of petulantia has been sufficiently indicated by Prescott. Cupiditas seems to be similar to cupido and lubido in Comedy. Lubido, like ἐπιθυμία, is distinctly erotic. Cf. Ter. And. 308 quo magis lubido frustra incendatur tua, and Haut. 367 ut illius animum cupidum inopia incenderet, Alciphron I.35 ἀπερρίπισε τὴν ἐπιθυμίαν, Ach. Tat. I.5 ὑπέκκαυμα ἐπιθυμίας, etc. For lubido=ἐπιθυμία in Stoic lists, cf. Cicero Tusc. IV.7.14 (V. Arnim III.393) lubido opinio venturi boni, Andronicus περὶ παθῶν 1 (V. Arnim III.391) ἐπιθυμία δὲ ἄλογος ὄρεξις· ἢ δίωξις προσδοκωμένου ἀγαθοῦ. Cupiditas is followed in the Mercator list by malevolentia=invidia, according to Prescott; cf. the combination ἐπιθυμίαν, φθόνον, ἐπιχαιρεκακίαν[21] in Epictetus. I hardly see the necessity for giving aviditas the same erotic meaning as cupiditas (cf. Prescott). It would seem rather to be an equivalent of the φιλαργυρία which is so common in Stoic discussions,[22] as, for example, here in Epictetus. This is a common meaning for aviditas[23] cf. T. L. L. II.1422.67, 1423.3, Corpus Gloss. II.471. 24. The idea fits the context, since in lines 52 sq. we have the father complaining of his son's rapacity, and the combination aviditas desidia (if the text be correct) is an extremely natural one, cf. Epict. φιλαργυρίαν μαλακίαν ἀκρασίαν. Rapacity and extravagance are often combined; so we may properly compare Plato Rep. 564 B τῶν ἀργῶν τε καὶ δαπανηρῶν ἀνδρῶν γένος. Desidia is frequent in Plautus, always in the sense of a vicious or wasteful idleness.

[21]Cf. V. Arnim 394 (end), 412, 414, 415, 418. Also Tischer-Sorof on Cicero Tusc. IV.17 "malevolentia griech. ἐπιχαιρεκακία."

[22]Cf. Andronicus περὶ παθῶν 4 (p. 16 Kreuttner)=V. Arnim 397 φιλοχρηματία δὲ ἐπιθυμία [ἄχρηστος ἤ] ἄμετρος χρημάτων.

[23]Festus defines aviditas as cupiditas (p. 14.9), but aviditas=cupiditas is rare. Cf. however, Pliny N. H. 20.277, 23.144 (T. L. L. II.1423. 24-27).

'Αργία, μαλακία, τρυφή, ῥαστώνη, ῥᾳθυμία, ἀπονία, are similarly used in Greek; of these, the first three are more frequent in erotic connections. In addition to the passages cited by Prescott for ἀργία versus ἔρως (Eur. frag. 324 N. Ἔρως γὰρ ἀργὸν κἀπὶ τοῖς ἀργοῖς ἔφυ. Stob. Flor. 64, 29 Θεόφραστος ἐρωτηθεὶς τί ἐστιν ἔρως πάθος ἔφη ψυχῆς σχολαζούσης) note the familiar passage from Xen. Anab. III.2.25 ἂν ἅπαξ μάθωμεν ἀργοὶ ζῆν καὶ ἐν ἀφθόνοις βιοτεύειν καὶ Μήδων δὲ καὶ Περσῶν καλαῖς καὶ μεγάλαις γυναιξὶ καὶ παρθένοις ὁμιλεῖν. Cf. also Plato Rep. 572 E ἐρωτά τινα . . . . προστάτην τῶν ἀργῶν καὶ τὰ ἕτοιμα διανεμομένων ἐπιθυμιῶν, Eur. Hipp. 380 sq., Xen. Oec. I.19.[24]

In the case of the words that follow desidia, i. e., iniuria inopia contumelia, the difficulties of interpretation increase, and we are obliged to rely entirely, or nearly so, on Latin usage. Iniuria and contumelia are, as Leo says, (cf. also Prescott p. 20) generally coupled in Latin.[25] In ordinary usage contumelia seems to be stronger than iniuria (cf. Nonius 430.15), only in the sense of adding insult to injury. Iniuria is the more general term, and may range from unfaithfulness, in the sermo amatorius, to undutiful conduct on the part of a son towards his father. The words are often practically synonymous (always remembering the special idea of insult in contumelia); so, in the passages cited above, Ter. Hec. 165, Haut. 566. In the sermo amatorius, contumelia is used particularly of the indignities inflicted by the meretrix upon the amator (Eun. 48). The meaning that I am inclined to press for contumelia in this passage is that of convicium, as in the phrase contumeliam dicere and elsewhere: cf. Curc. 478, Pseud. 1173, Truc. 299, Ter. Phorm. 376, Menaech. 520, Afr. com. 374 Rib. It seems to me that lines 43-55 of the Mercator prologue are intended as a loose running commentary on the latter portion of the catalogue, and serve to show at least what these words meant to the author of lines 43-55. In this way iniuria (29) would refer to the outrageous conduct of the son: cf. 54 intemperantem, non modestum, iniurium[26] trahere exhaurire me quod quirem ab se domo. Contumelia, then would refer to the criticism which such conduct provokes particularly, perhaps, from the father (cf. lines 46-60). Dis-

[24] Greek σχολή, like Latin otium, is generally favorable or neutral in meaning. It is occasionally an equivalent of ἀργία, τρυφή, etc., Soph. frag. 288 τίκτει γὰρ οὐδὲν ἐσθλὸν εἰκαία σχολή, Eur. Hipp. 384 σχολὴ τερπνὸν κακόν.

[25] In addition to the passage from Pacuvius (279, 80) patior facile iniuriam, si est vacua a contumelia, and the comment of Nonius (430, 15) iniuria enim levior res est, we have the combination Ter. Hec. 165, Haut. 566, Cicero inv. 1. 105 and elsewhere.

[26] Servius in Aen. IX.107 hinc est apud comicos iniurius qui audet aliquid extra ordinem iuris.

pendium is repeated from the prologue 53 amorem multos inlexe in dispendium, with a generalizing tone which is in itself significant. Inopia[27] as used in Mercator 30 can bear no other meaning, if the foregoing ideas be accepted, than that of lack of funds, inopia argenti. Cf. Caec. Stat. 199 Rib. in amore suave est summo summaque inopia, etc., Plaut. Pseud. 300 ita miser et amore pereo et inopia argentaria, Men. mon. 156 ἔρωτα παύει λιμὸς ἢ χαλκοῦ σπάνις. Accepting these meanings, I should assert that the grouping aviditas, desidia, iniuria, was quite logical; in line 54 the adjective iniurium sums up, as a more general term, the specific charges contained in intemperantem and non modestum; so with iniuria in its triad. The combination inopia contumelia dispendium is not quite so convincing; the suggestion made for contumelia does, however, make it distinct in meaning and separable from iniuria, thus accounting, to some extent, for the arrangement.

In the foregoing discussion, I have endeavored to present what seems to me strong evidence for a Greek original for this passage, and to explain and interpret those words and groupings that seem to reflect this original. It is quite clear that the Latin author handled this passage with some degree of freedom, and indeed, if that author was Plautus, we should not expect slavish imitation. The fact that these lines are not a "mere farrago" appears evident; if it be granted also that they show distinct traces of the Greek of Philemon, the probabilities will be all in favor of Plautine authorship for this portion of the Mercator prologue.

[27]For the other interpretation, i. e., inopia = the condition of being without the object of one's affections, cf. Prescott p. 20. In this sense a comparison with σπάνις, ἐπιθυμία ἀτελής Andronicus περὶ παθῶν p. 4 (p. 16 Kreuttner, V. Arnim 397) might be in order. Cf. also Cicero Tusc. disp. IV.21 indigentia libido inexplebilis (V. Arnim III.398) and Tischer-Sorof ad locum, Melcher o. c. p. 24. This meaning for σπάνις, though certainly not common in the Greek sermo, is attractive: A. P. XII.30.3 φύλαξαι μή σε καὶ ἡ πυγὴ ταὐτὰ παθοῦσα λάθῃ καὶ γνώσῃ φιλέοντος ὅση σπάνις.

II

The so-called sermo amatorius of Roman Comedy divides naturally into several different classes of words. The Plautine abstracts just considered are not closely related to the general sermo, and were best explained by comparison with other than strictly erotic sources. In contrast to these is what we may call the sermo meretricius, i.e., the somewhat specialized and quasi-technical vocabulary of the meretrix, the leno, and the young men "qui amant a lenone." This class of words is of peculiar interest because so many of the words included are technical in the narrowest sense, and may be fully interpreted only by comparison with the Greek words for which they stand.[28] As in the case of the abstract nouns, and perhaps to an even greater degree, the study of the sermo amatorius in the special phase which I have termed the sermo meretricius, may be expected to contribute toward the reconstruction of the Greek background for Comedy. The object of this study is to consider diction, rather than larger topics, as the material of Comedy, in this, as in most other respects, has been very thoroughly dealt with by other scholars.

The fact that the meretrix in Comedy is a somewhat conventionalized literary figure does not preclude a certain realism in treatment. In line with this realism is the constant use of a number of expressions that have to do with the business activities of the meretrix, and were undoubtedly in everyday use among the people. These terms are in the truest sense technical. The business itself is ordinarily referred to as a gainful occupation, (ἐργασία)[29] quaestus; from the moral standpoint this business is stigmatized as indignus or turpis (αἰσχρός): Poen. 1139-40 namque hodie earum mutarentur nomina facerentque indignum genere quaestum corpore, Sex. Turp. Rib. 42 mulier meretrix quae me quaesti causa cognovit sui (cf. also Turp. Rib. 84), Terence Hec. 756 si esset alia ex hoc quaestu. Cf. also Plaut. Asin. 511, Cist. 121, Miles 785, Rudens 541, Ter. Andr. 79. Cf. Aristaen. I.19 αὐτίκα τῆς αἰσχρᾶς αὐτὴν

[28]The Attic provenance of the meretrix in Roman Comedy is asserted by Leo (Gesch. d. röm. Literatur I. p. 144). "Die attische Hetäre ist etwas dem Rom des hannibalischen Krieges und auch der folgenden Jahrzehnte begrifflich Fremdes; in Tarent konnte man wohl dergleichen finden, aber die römischen Analogien waren nicht geeignet, Farben für das attische Spiel abzugeben" (cf. also Leo Plaut. Forsch.[2] p. 140 n. 2). Polybius XXXII. 11. 3 dates the influx of the hetaerae into Rome in the first half of the second century B. C.

[29]For comparisons from other trades cf. Asin. 198 sqq., Lucian meretr. dial. 7. 2, Leo Plaut. Forsch.[2] p. 150 n. 2.

ἀνέστησεν ἐργασίας, Hdt. II.135, Dem. 270.15.   The Latin quaestum corporis (corpore) facere represents the Greek ἐργάζεσθαι σώματι: Polyb. 12.13.2, Alex. Sam. ap. Ath. 572 F.   So in Greek we have ἐργάτις (operatrix) as a synonym for ἑταίρα (πόρνη), A. P. V.245 εἰσὶ γὰρ ἄλλαι κρέσσονες εὐλέκτρου κύπριδος ἐργάτιδες, and the Latin opera "service" is part of the same idea.   Cf. opera, operaria: Bacch. 74 opera, Asin. 721 opto annum hunc perpetuom huius operas (servitus amatoria, Ussing), ibid. 598, Bacch. 45[30], Cist. 740, Miles 1057, (1075), Rudens 440.   The commercial nature of such "service" is emphasized by various combinations: cf. Bacch. 74 Ah, nimium pretiosa es operaria, Cist. 740 at pol illi quoidam mulieri nulla opera gratuita est.   Cf. also Gr. ἐργαστήριον "workshop" = brothel Dem. 1367.26.   In elegy we have officium = opera in the erotic sense: cf. Propert. II.25.39, II.22.24, Ovid Am. III.7.24.

The public of the meretrix (ἑταίρα), those who resorted to her regularly, is commonly referred to as her adventores, "customers", and the verb in ordinary use is advenio (προσ or ἐπι-φοιτῶ) Truc. 96: ne quis adventor gravior abaetat quam adveniat, ibid. 616 si aequom facias adventores meos non incuses, quorum mihi dona accepta, Apul. met. 10.21 basiola. . . . . meretricum poscinummia . . . . . adventorum negantinummia, Varro Men. 263 (doubtful, cf. T. L. L. I.836.73, where adventores is cited as customers of a caupona, "caupona dub.") In general cf. T. L. L. I.836. 69-74, Lodge s. v.   Venio is also technical in this sense: Nov. 24 Rib. multum ames, paulum des, crebro venias, rarenter, Verg. Cat. I.1-3 Delia, Tucca, tibi venit . . . . . Delia. saepe tibi non venit adhuc mihi; cf. also Propertius I.5.32 quare quid possit mea Cynthia, desine, Galle, quaerere: non impune illa rogata venit, where the technical force is overlooked by Rothstein ("dazu tritt venire in der zu I.4.10 besprochenen Weise als Vertretung des einfachen Verbums esse"), ib. I.10.25.   Note also adire = advenire (technical): Bacch. 617 (indignior) . . . . . quem quisquam homo aut amet aut adeat, Asin. 141, Catullus 8.16 (Friedrich ad loc.).   On adeo in general cf. T. L. L. I.620, 54-57, Lodge s. v.   For the Greek cf. Alciphr. I.35 ἐπὶ τὰς θύρας φοιτᾶν (amatores), ibid. I.37 πρὸς ἡμᾶς καὶ κοιμησόμενος, ἐφοίτα, Lucian dial. meretr. X.1.[31]

[30]Leo, critical note ad 1., reads deddiderit operas, comparing Bacch. 93; he suggests as a possible reading reddiderit, comparing Cicero ad fam. 16.10.2 (tu Musis nostris para ut operas reddas), ad Att. 6.2.6.

[31]Technical force should be noted also for quaero: Pseud. 1125 scortum quaerit, Poen. 688 hospitium te aiunt quaeritare (a possible euphemism, as a leno is speaking, cf. infra 690-691), Men. 675 quis hic me quaerit? ME. Sibi inimicus magis quam aetati tuae. Cf. Greek δίζημι Odyss. 21. 160 ἄλλην δή τιν᾽ ἔπειτα ᾽Αχαιιάδων εὐπέπλων

The lover is said also to keep company, maintain relations, with the meretrix, consuescere, solere (ὁμιλεῖν): Ter. Hec. 555 nam si is posset ab ea sese derepente avellere quacum tot consuesset annos, Cist. 36³² viris cum suis praedicant nos solere, Lucian dial. meretr. X.2 ἀφ' οὗ γυναικὶ ὁμιλεῖν ἤρξατο-πρῶτον δὲ ὡμίλησέ μοι. An intimacy of this kind is called consuetudo (συνήθεια, ὁμιλία): Ter. And. 279 (cf. Donatus ad loc.) ut neque me consuetudo neque amor neque pudor commoveat (-moneat?), Phorm. 161 dum expecto quam mox veniat qui adimat hanc mihi consuetudinem,³³ Cist. 94, Pseud. 64, Turp. 94 Rib., cf. T. L. L. IV.561, 46-75 Lodge s. v.   For the Greek equivalents compare Men. frag. 726K. ἔργον ἐστί Φανία μακρὰν συνήθειαν βραχεῖ λῦσαι χρόνῳ, Samia 280 χρόνος συνήθει' οἷς ἐδουλούμην ἐγώ, Alciphr. I.33.³⁴

μνάσθω . . . . . διζήμενος, Aristoph. 451K. γυναῖκα δὴ ζητοῦντες ἐνθάδ' ἥκομεν (ζητῶ). In the Menaechmi passage, sibi inimicus, etc., seems to imply a hostile force in the verb quaerere; for this cf. Prop. III.5.12 et hostem quaerimus, Sen. quaest. nat. V.18.5 hostem in mare aut post mare quaeremus. For quaero in the sermo amatorius cf. Catullus VIII.13 nec te requiret nec rogabit invitam (Friedrich ad loc.), Horace Epod. 12.16, 15.13, Prop. II.24a.9, I.4.20 (possibly). Rogare is technical as a decided euphemism in elegy, cf. Fried. on Cat. VIII.13, but not, apparently, in Comedy.

³²Cist. 36 solere, "sc. rem habere" Ussing; so also most of the older commentators. More likely solere is itself a translation of Gr. ὁμιλεῖν, in which case there is no ellipsis. Cf. Catullus 113. 1 duo . . . . . solebant Moecillam (mecilia is the reading of O). Friedrich defends the MSS -ā citing Ter. Adelph. 666 where there is good authority (cod. Bemb.) for consuevit illā, though the metrically more difficult cum illa is offered by other MSS.   In both examples Friedrich postulates the ellipsis of uti or some other verb that governs the abl. Baehrens reads cum Moecilla, in the Catullus passage, emending the rest of the line.   It seems easier to read the accusative in Catullus 113. 1 but in the Adelph. passage cum should stand; consuescere is even more suggestive of Gr. ὁμιλεῖν than solere.

³³G. Ramain Quomodo Bembinus Liber, etc., Paris, 1894 and Rev. de Phil. XXX.34. defends aegritudo for this place, affirming that consuetudo, which he defines as an affectus animi amori proximus, is meaningless in this connection. Hauler (Phormio, Dziatzko-Hauler⁴ Anhang p. 231, defends consuetudo, as does Kauer Jahresbericht 143 p. 241. Hauler and Kauer rightly observe that consuetudo frequently refers to an intimate relationship, "living with" the mistress (And. 279, 439) or the legal wife (Phorm. 161, Hec. 404, And. 560). Note, however, that Ramain's definition is accurate for such an example as And. 110 (cited by Hauler, note on Phorm. 161) for the stronger meaning.

³⁴Consuetio in Plautus has a more specific meaning than consuetudo, cf. Plaut. Amph. 490 (but cf. also Donatus on Adelphoe IV.5.32, Paulus 61, Leo crit. note ad loc.).   So frequently ὁμιλία but not always; for the weaker meaning cf. Ach. Tat. I.9 Μέγιστον γάρ ἐστιν ἐφόδιον εἰς πειθὼ συνεχὴς πρὸς ἐρώμενον ὁμιλία, for the stronger Xen. Symp. VIII.22, Mem. III.11.14.   The glosses give συνήθεια or ἔθος, not ὁμιλία, as equivalent to consuetudo, cf. Corp. Gloss. II.113. 31, 446.12, III.158.49,

The commoner relations between the meretrix or the leno and the
amator are expressed in terms borrowed from the marriage ceremony.
The lover might remove his mistress from the house of the leno to quar-
ters provided by himself; he was then said to take or escort, ducere
(ἄγειν) and the leno to release, or dismiss, mittere (ἀποπέμπειν): Poen.
100 neque duxit umquam neque ille voluit mittere, ibid. 269 duxit
domum, cf. adduco Merc. 813 amicam adduxit intro in aedes, cf. εἰσάγω
Aristoph. Eccl. 983 ἀλλ' οὐχὶ νυνὶ τὰς ὑπερεξηκοντέτεις εἰσάγομεν. Adduco
is used also of the meretrix, who leads a man to her home: Truc. 114
eumpse ad nos si domi erit, mecum adducam, ibid. 514. Duco[35] in Comedy
is used indifferently of marriage or illicit love; ducto, with reference,
perhaps, to its proper frequentative force, refers only to the latter,
Phorm. 500 ut phaleratis ducas dictis me et meam ductes gratiis, Men-
aech. 694, Poen. 272 (ductito), ibid. 868, Merc. 786 obducto (in conspec-
tum ducere, Taub.). In general cf. Lodge s. v. duco, adduco, ducto etc.,
and T. L. L. I.593, 45-50, 57. Nubo, as used of illicit relations, is cons-
cious, and designedly facetious, so may better be mentioned elsewhere
in this discussion (cf. p. 42).

The commercial side of such transactions is expressed by the verb
conducere (μισθοῦσθαι) cf. Corp. Gloss. II.372.6, 108.7, Bacch. 1097
memoravit eam sibi hunc annum conductam, Amph. 288, T. L. L. IV.159.
48-60, Lodge s. v. Latin conduco may translate λαμβάνω, which is often
used instead of the more exact μισθοῦσθαι, sometimes with the price
subjoined. For the latter verb cf. Lucian Dial. meretr. VI.4 οἱ μισθούμενοι,
for the former Luc. Dial. meretr. XI.1 ἑταίραν δέ τις παραλαβὼν πέντε
δραχμὰς τὸ μίσθωμα δούς, Alexander frag. 3K. εἰς αὐριόν με δεῖ λαβεῖν

276.43, ἔθος II.285.1, III.142.4, etc. Consuescere is used regularly in malam partem:
Plaut. Asin. 222 (in word play), ibid. 703, Cap. 867, Cist. 87 (cf. Lodge s. v.), Caec. Stat.
149 Rib., Ter. Hec. 555, Phorm. 873, Adelph. 666 (T. L. L. IV.551. 69-75). Consues-
cere in these passages is similar to ὁμιλεῖν (=μιγῆναι) Aristaen. II.7 αὐτῶν ἐρωτικῶς
ὁμιλούντων or to συνεῖναι (συγγίγνεσθαι) for which the regular expression in Latin
Comedy is cum aliquo esse Truc. 362, 688, 706, 936, Most. 392, Merc. 102, Menaech.
188, Amph. 817, Ter. Hec. 156. For συνεῖναι cf. Aristoph. Pax 863, Eccl. 340, 619,
συνουσία Men. frag. 541K., Aristaen. II.7.

[35]The idiom scortum ducere becomes as general in meaning as uxorem ducere, i. e.,
all thought of the actual "taking" or escorting, is lost, and the phrase is often equiva-
lent to scortari, Bacch. 1080 duxi habui scortum, Pseud. 258. By an apparent confusion
of idioms ducere is used with noctem in the sense of conducere, Poen. 108 ducit noctem;
the phrase is so interpreted by the older commentators, and by Lodge (tentatively).
This is perhaps supported by Naev. 105 Rib. eius noctem nauco ducere, where the
idea of hiring seems predominant in duco; cf. the fact that we have the ablative of
price instead of the genitive as in the phrases nauci, flocci ducere (facere).

αὐλητρίδα. That λαμβάνω is not the habere of habui scortum may perhaps be inferred from such a passage as Alexis 213K. δύο λαβεῖν μαγείρους βούλομαι.³⁶ Πρίαμαι occurs Philemon 4K. 8, Eubul 67K. πρίασθαι κέρματος τὴν ἡδονήν³⁷ cf. emere Most. 286 nam amator meretricis mores sibi emit auro et purpura, Poen. 274 nebulai cyatho septem noctes non emam. Vendere is frequent, of both sexes, cf. Miles 312, Curc. 482. The consideration received is the merces; so merces annua Truc. 31, Bacch. 29, Ter. Phorm. 414; according to the charge, a meretrix is pretiosa (Bacch. 74), or vilis, cf. scorta diobolaria Poen. 270, amicae . . . . . diobolares Cist. 407 (cf. Varro L. L. VII.64. Fest. 329) Pseud. 659 (all modern editors read doliarem; diobolarem, Camerarius), Diobolaria (title of comedy) Fulg. 566-7, cf. Antiph. 300K. τριωβόλῳ δὲ πόρνην (ἐξελαύνειν), Plato com. 174K. (l. 17) Κυβδάσῳ τριώβολον, Epicrates 3K. l. 22. Corresponding to merces are μίσθωμα Luc. Dial. meretr. XI.1, μισθωμάτιον (mercedula) Alciphron I.36, ἐμπολή Artemid. I.78, Dio C. 79.13. Where a meretrix was retained for an extended period of time, a formal contract was concluded;³⁸ such a contract (συγγραφή) is burlesqued, Plaut. Asin. 746 sq., where Latin syngraphus is used.

Avarice is the most marked characteristic of the meretrix (cf. Hoelzer p. 68 sq.). In addition to the regular merx she is constantly soliciting gifts, dona (δῶρα); Asin. 512 lingua poscit, corpus quaerit, etc., Truc. 16, 51, Lucil. 684, Men. Thais 217K. αἰτοῦσαν πυκνά, Alciph. I.30 αἰτοῦσαι παρὰ τῶν ἐραστῶν ἀργύριον, A. P. V.121, etc. These gifts are a constant theme in Comedy: cf. Truc. 544, Cist. 133, Ter. Eun. 163, Pseud. 177, Truc. 425, etc. Hence the verbs do, dono (δίδωμι) are in frequent use of the lover, Bacch. 1080, Truc. 230, 239, 634, 911, etc. Defero is found in the same sense: Men. 133, 173, 561, Miles 960, etc., and degero Truc. 113b, Men. 741, 804. Lovers are called munigeruli (Pseud. 181). Accipio

³⁶Habeo, Bacch. 1080, Ter. And. 85, Adelph. 389 is Greek ἔχω Men. 295K. Χρυσίδα, Κορώνην . . . . . καὶ Ναννάριον ἔσχηκας, Antiph. 102K. εἶτ' οὐ δικαίως εἰμὶ φιλογύνης ἐγὼ καὶ τὰς ἑταίρας ἡδέως πάσας ἔχω, Baton 3K., Eup. 9K. For the precise meaning of the words cf. Donatus on Adelphoe 389 an domi est habiturus "proprie quia haberi uxor dicitur et haberi mulier cum coit." Petr. 130 paralysin . . . . quae abstulit mihi, per quod etiam te habere potui (Taub.). In many cases, particularly with the phrase γυναῖκα ἔχειν (of marriage) the erotic idea is in abeyance.

³⁷Cf. Hec. 69 quam minimo pretio suam voluptatem expleat. For mores (Most. 286) cf. Amphis 1K. ἡ δ' (meretrix) οἶδεν ὅτι ἡ τοῖς τρόποις ὠνητέος ἄνθρωπός ἐστιν ἢ πρὸς ἄλλον ἀπιτέον. Note Afranius 380 Rib. (morigeratio) but cf. also Leo Plaut. Forsch.² p. 145 " εὐγνώμων τρόπος ist nicht morigeratio."

³⁸Cf. Legrand Daos p. 275, Schömann-Lipsius Der att. Process p. 732-733, Beauchet Droit privé de la républ. ath. IV.p. 42.

is technical of the meretrix: Truc. 616 adventores meos . . . . .
quorum mihi dona accepta et grata habeo: tuaque ingrata quae abs te
accepi cf. λαμβάνω Philostr. Epist. 12.2, and Boissonade n. ad loc. λαβεῖν
"accipere et dare nota Latinis in amatoria vocabula aeque ac Graecis
χαρίζεσθαι et λαβεῖν: Olearius." With χαρίζεσθαι in this sense com-
pare the use of χάριτες = dona, munera, Alciphr. I.36, though this may be
rather parallel to Latin dona accepta, grata (Truc. 616 et al.).   Aufero
is also used of the meretrix: Truc. 16 sed relicuom dat operam ne sit
relicuom poscendo atque auferendo ut mos est mulierum.   For δῶρα
ἀποφέρω, δίδωμι, etc., cf. Alciph. I.6.2 κωμάζουσι εἰς αὐτὴν ἡ πρὸς θάλατταν
νεολαία καὶ ἄλλος ἄλλο δῶρον ἀποφέρει, Aristoph.Thesm. 345 ἢ δῶρά τις
δίδωσι μοιχῷ γραῦς γυνή.   For dare, auferre munera, in elegy cf. Pichon
s. vv.

Avarice, in the mistress, provokes extravagance in the lover, whose
prodigal gifts are usually referred to in Plautus as damna.   Damnum
(-a), as used in Latin Comedy, is of peculiar interest because of the
apparent lack of any adequate Greek background.   In its legal uses
(cf. T. L. L. V.23.30 sq. 24. 70 sq. 25. 58 sq.), damnum may often be
glossed by ζημία (cf. also Corp. Gloss. II.322. 20; 503. 22; 529. 43;
534. 61; III.4. 33).   The same thing is true of damnum in general usage,
outside of legal contexts, i. e., damnum = deminutio rei familiaris opposed
to lucrum (T. L. L. V.22. 55 sq.); note particularly Don. on Ter. Eunuch.
994 damnum rei est, malum ipsius hominis; this distinction seems to be
fairly apt for ζημία also.   ζημία and κέρδος are contrasted Chilon. ap.
Apost. 8. 34 b ζημίαν αἱροῦ μᾶλλον ἢ κέρδος αἰσχρόν (Otto Sprich. 197),
cf. Men. mon. 496 τὰ μικρὰ κέρδη ζημίας μεγάλας φέρει.   Note also Publil.
Syrus 113 Rib. damnum appellandum est cum mala fama lucrum,
Men. mon. 6 ἅπαν τὸ κέρδος ἄδικον ὂν φέρει βλάβην.[39]   This general use
of damnum outside the sermo amatorius is exceedingly common in
Comedy, in the idioms damnum facere, and damnum dare, in com-
bination with malum, and in opposition to lucrum (cf. Lodge I.349.C,
Otto loc. cit.).   The word is very evidently an old Latin word, with
certain technical (legal) associations.   It may occasionally translate
ζημία in Comedy, but in certain cases, even outside the sermo, this is
impossible; cf. the pun Men. 267 ne mihi damnum in Epidamno duis.

The damna of lovers (cf. T. L. L. V.23. 20 sq.) appear to be peculiar

[39]Damnum as an epithet for the meretrix (Men. 133) is apparently the Greek ζημία;
cf. Ter. Eunuch. 79 calamitas nostri fundi, and for the thought, Alciph. III.33 ὅλον σε
αὐτοῖς ἀγροῖς καταπιοῦσα. So also Curc. 49 malus clandestinus est amor,
damnumst merum; cf. Aristoph. Achar. 737 τίς δ' οὕτως ἄνους ὃς ὑμέ κα πρίαιτο, φανερὰν
ζημίαν.

to the Latin sermo.   Extravagance in a lover is rarely emphasized in the
Greek sermo, and, where mentioned, is referred to by some such neutral
term as δαπάνη (sumptus) or ἀνάλωμα: cf. Timocles 23K. παμπολλ' ἀναλίσ-
κων ἐφ' ἑκάστῳ (coitu), Alciph. I.18.3 πέπαυσο εἰς ταῦτα δαπανώμενος μή
σε ἀντὶ τῆς θαλάττης ἡ γῆ ναυαγὸν ἀποφήνῃ ψιλώσασα τῶν χρημάτων,
ibid. III.8 δαπανᾶται οὐκ ὀλίγα μάτην: ibid. III.50, Diph. 32K. ἐὰν δ' ὑπὲρ τὴν
οὐσίαν δαπανῶν τύχῃ, Men. ap. Stob. Flor. XV.1 τοὺς τὸν ἴδιον δαπανῶντας
ἀλογίστως βίον.   (The last two cases are possibly not in erotic contexts.)
So far as we may judge from the existing fragments, Greek Comedy
had much less to say on this topic of extravagance than Latin imitations,
nor was it regarded as particularly vicious from the moral angle, i. e.
δαπάνη did not entail βλάβη, at least to any appreciable degree.

In Plautus and Terence we find a very different situation.   Damnum,
extended to mean wasteful or ruinous expenditures, is consistently
employed instead of the weaker sumptus.   More significant still is the
fact that in erotic contexts, and sometimes elsewhere, damnum is habitu-
ally paired with flagitia, dedecus, and the like: cf. Bacch. 376 tua flagitia
aut damna aut desidiabula, 380-1 tuom patrem meque una amicos, adfines
tuos tua infamia fecisti gerulifigulos flagiti, ibid. 1032, Merc. 784, Pseud.
440.   All Plautine examples of damnum with flagitium (dedecus) [cf.
Lodge I.349 c.] are in erotic contexts, with one exception, Asin. 571
dedecus.   Note also Horace Sat. II.2.96, Cicero phil. frag. V.81 quod
turpe damnum quod dedecus, quod non avocetur atque eliciatur volup-
tate.   Interesting in this connection is the gloss damnum=βλάβη (Corp.
Gloss. II.257.51).

The wastrel hero of Greek Comedy was something quite foreign to
Roman ideas of thrift and economy.   The idea suggests itself that in
damna (-um) flagitia, etc., in the sermo amatorius of Roman Comedy
we have a Roman reaction against the dissoluteness and particularly
the extravagance of the Hellenistic Greek.   There is involved an idea
of the interdependence of property and reputation; as damnum affects
res(property) it involves dedecus or flagitium (the reverse process is
also recognized).   This may perhaps be best illustrated by a few pas-
sages: cf. Most. 144 nunc simul res fides et fama, virtus, decus deseruerunt,
ibid. 227 ut fama est homini, exin solet pecuniam invenire, Phorm. 271
si est, patrue, culpam ut Antipho in se admiserit, ex qua re minus rei
foret aut famae temperans, and notably Livy XXXIX.9.6 sq. huic
(libertinae) consuetudo iuxta vicinitatem cum Aebutio fuit, minume
adulescentis aut rei aut famae damnosa; ultro enim amatus adpetitusque
erat, et maligne omnia praebentibus suis, meretriculae munificentia

sustentabatur. In this passage, emphasizing, as it does, the view that the reputation suffers only as the pocketbook, and ignoring altogether what seems to us most ignominious in the situation, we have, it seems to me, an explicit statement of the Roman gospel of thrift, as it appears in the use of res, fama vs. damnum, flagitium in Comedy.

The same idea appears in some other usages in Comedy: cf. the verbs pergraecari (Truc. 87b, Most. 22 with context. ibid. 64) congraecare (Bacch. 743), graecari (Horace Sat. II.2.11). Nequam = dissolute and frugi = continent (cf. p. 39) show the same development from Roman ideas of thrift as the paramount virtue.

The plural damna is more frequent than the singular in erotic contexts: cf. Truc. 950 stultus atque insanus damnis certant, Bacch. 66 palaestra ubi damnis desudascitur, ibid. 375-6 ut celem patrem, Pistoclere, †ua flagitia aut damna aut desidiabula. With the adjective damnigeruli Truc. 551 mulierei damnigeruli cf. Pseud. 181 amatores munigeruli; the idea in damnigeruli appears to be in effect "bearing the wasteful presents of their master." Cf. also the later use of damna with reference to foolish or extravagant conduct in erotic relations, Martial X.58 sed non solus amat, qui nocte dieque frequentat limina, nec vatem talia dámna decent.

The adjective damnosus takes its coloring from damnum. In accordance with the legal and common derived meanings of damnum (cf. pp. 20, 21) the adjective is glossed by ἐπιζήμιος and πολυζήμιος (Corp. Gloss. II.37.31; II.37.19). This covers such cases as Bacch. 117 quid tibi commercist cum dis damnosissumis i. e. qui damna inferunt, Hor. epist. I.18.21 quem damnosa Venus nudat, Juv. XIV.4 damnosa . . . . . alea. Cf. also Livy loc. cit. (p. 21) consuetudo . . . . . rei aut famae damnosa. The word is used, of extravagant giving, with the connotations peculiar to damna: Pseud. 415 si de damnosis aut si de amatoribus dictator fiat, Truc. 82 postquam alium repperit qui plus daret damnosiorem meo exinde immovit loco. A doubtful case is Epid. 319 argentum accipio ab damnoso sene (T. L. L. V.20.82 "qui invitus damnosus est cf. 309", ibid. 22.21 "passivo sensu i. e. qui damnum patitur Epid. 319 [?v. p. 20.82]"; so Lodge). The rarity of this usage suggests that the word is better taken in the sense of foolishly, harmfully wasteful; the old man is none the less wasteful because he does not know that he is wasteful.

A natural consequence of the extravagant lover, amator damnosus, is the amator egens (πένης): Asin. 684 da mi istas viginti minas: vides me amantem egere, Curc. 142 qui amat si eget misera adficitur aerumna,

Pseud. 273, Persa 1, Pseud. 695 (egestas)[40].   Inopia (argentaria) is a common complaint of lovers: cf. Pseud. 300, Caec. Stat. 199 Rib. (cited p. 14), Asin. 724.   Compare in general Callim. Epigr. 46. 5-6 τοῦτο, δοκέω, χἀ λιμὸς ἔχει μόνον ἐς τὰ πονηρὰ τὠγαθόν, ἐκκόπτει τὰν φιλόπαιδα νόσον, A. P. V.113 Ἡράσθης πλουτῶν Σωσίκρατες ἀλλὰ πένης ὢν οὐκέτ' ἐρᾷς. λιμὸς φάρμακον οἷον ἔχει . . . . . ὡς οὐδεὶς οὐδὲν ἔχοντι φίλος.   For σπάνις = inopia argentaria cf. Men. mon. 156 ἔρωτα παύει λιμὸς ἢ χαλκοῦ σπάνις.

The words so far discussed relate chiefly to the quaestus or ἐργασία of the meretrix.   It ranked also as an art, τέχνη, (Leo Plaut. Forsch.[2] p. 146, n. 1): Ter. Haut. 226 habet bene et pudice eductam, ignaram artis meretriciae, ibid. 366-7 haec arte tractabat virum, etc., Alexis 98K. ·καινὰς ἑταίρας πρωτοπείρους τῆς τέχνης (with πρωτοπείρους, cf. Latin rudis Prop. I.9.8 and Rothstein note ad loc.).   Considered in this light the profession of the meretrix is more complex, and the wiles of the courtesan are a favorite subject for literary expansion and development.   However, most of the terms used in this connection were doubtless common property before their adoption as literary motifs, and so would belong, in outline, at least, under the head of realistic material.

The stock epithet of the meretrix in Comedy is blanda (πιθανός, ἐπαγωγός).   She is constantly represented as wheedling or cajoling (κολακεύω) and her wiles or seductions are referred to as blanditiae (κολακεύματα): Casina 584 vitium tibi istuc maxumumst: blanda's parum—non matronarum officiumst sed meretricium, Men. 566K. χαλεπὸν . . . . . πρὸς πόρνην μάχη· πλείονα κακουργεῖ, πλείον' οἶδ', αἰσχύνεται οὐδέν, κολακεύει μᾶλλον, Men. Thais frag. 217K. θρασεῖαν, ὡραίαν δὲ καὶ πιθανὴν ἅμα, Petr. 127 illa risit tam blandum, Aristaen. I.1 μειδιᾷ πάνυ ἐπαγωγόν. For blanditiae (κολακεύματα), perhaps the most technical of these expressions, cf. Ps. Ascon. Verr. p. 138 blanditiae "feminis ac maxime meretricibus conveniunt," Corp. Gloss. II.352. 10 κολακίαι, 357. 54 κωτιλίαι—"blanditiae, singulare non habet."   In general, Truc. 318 blandimentis oramentis ceteris meretriciis, Men. 193, 262, Bacch. 50, 517, 1173, Cas. 586. Most. 221, Cist. 302, Pomp. 164 Rib. blanda fallax, Caec. 66 Rib., A. P. V.21, 186, etc., T. L. L. II.2034. 15 sq., 2034. 40 sq., 2030. 76 sq., Lodge s. v. blandus, blandior, blanditiae.

The blanditiae (κολακεύματα) of the meretrix (cf. Hoelzer p. 84 sq., p. 29) include, of course, the more general varieties of flattery, and, as a

---

[40]Leo Plaut. Forsch.[2] p. 151 n. 4 "auch der pauper amator der Elegie stammt aus der Komödie."

type, the courtesan has much in common with the parasite (Leo Plaut. Forsch.[2] p. 148, n. 2). These general aspects of the κόλαξ have been discussed by Ribbeck.[41] Erotic blanditiae include firstly endearments and caresses, for example the pet names[42] that are so frequent in Plautus: cf. Asin. 693 sq. dic igitur me(d) aniticulam, columbulam, catellum, etc. Mart. XI.29. 3-5 nam cum me murem, cum me tua lumina dicis . . . . . blanditias nescis, ibid. X.68, 9-10, cf. Aristoph. Plutus 1010-1011 καὶ νὴ Δί' εἰ λυπουμένην αἴσθοιτό με νηττάριον ἂν καὶ βάτιον ὑπεκορίζετο.

The lectus is frequently mentioned with reference to such blanditiae: Bacch. 54 quid metuis? ne tibi lectus malitiam apud me suadeat? Philiscus 1K. εἰς τὸ μεταπεῖσαι ῥᾳδίως ἃ βούλεται πιθανοὺς ἔχειν εἴωθεν ἡ κλίνη λόγους, Casina 883 conloco fulcio mollio blandior[43], Aristaen. II.7 ἀγνοοῦσα τὴν ἐπὶ τῆς εὐνῆς κολακείαν. For the general idea cf. Ach. Tat. I.5 ὑπέκκαυμα γὰρ ἐπιθυμίας λόγος ἐρωτικός and Catul. LV.20 verbosa gaudet venus loquella; cf. also Aristaen. II.14, A. P. V.262 (λάλημα), Theocr. Id. XX.6.

Other allurements are mentioned as illecebrae Men. 355 munditia illecebra animost amantium, Casina 887 inlecebram stupri principio eam savium posco, cf. ὑπέκκαυμα (L. fomes) Men. 237K. πολλοῖς ὑπέκκαυμ' ἔστ' ἔρωτος μουσική, Xen. Symp. IV.25, Ach. Tat. I.5 (cited above). The verbs illicio and pellicio are used of the meretrix: Asin. 206 quom inliciebas me ad te blande ac benedice, Truc. 298, cf. προτρέπω and προσάγομαι Aristaen. II.1 ἑταῖραι προτρέπουσαι πιθανῶς, ibid. II.10 καὶ ὁμιλεῖν ἐρωτικῶς προτρέπω τὴν κόρην, Parthen. 14 ἐρασθεῖσα πολλὰ ἐμηχανᾶτο εἰς τὸ προσαγαγέσθαι τὸν παῖδα. In this connection may be mentioned the Plautine word elecebra Bacch. 944, Men. 377 nam ita sunt hic meretrices: omnes elecebrae argentariae, cf. Festus p. 76, 5 M. elecebrae argentariae meretrices ab eliciendo argento dictae.

Among the blanditiae of the meretrix were tears: cf. Ter. Eunuch. 67 una mehercule falsa lacrimula, etc., And. 558, A. P. V.186 Μή με δόκει πιθανοῖς ἀπατᾶν δάκρυσσι Φιλαινί, Lucian Tox. 13 p. 520, 15 p. 522 κολακείᾳ . . . . καὶ ἐν καιρῷ δακρῦσαι καὶ μεταξὺ τῶν λόγων ἐλεεινῶς ὑποστενάξαι. Rebuffs and forced separation (cf. Hoelzer op. cit. p. 15) served to increase the eagerness of the lover: Haut. 366-7 haec arte tractabat virum ut illius animum cupidum inopia incenderet, Alciph. II.

---

[41]Abh. d. kgl. sächs. Gesellsch. d. Wiss. IX.1884 p. 1 ff.

[42]Cf. G. Fridberg Die Schmeichelworte der antiken Literatur, Bonn, 1912. Also Ramsay Mostellaria Excursus.

[43]"Fulcio mollio (lectum)" Lambinus ad loc.; an odd misunderstanding cf. fultus toro Juv. III.82, pulvino fultus Lucil. ap. Serv. in Verg. Ecl. 6. 53 (Marx 138).

1 (Hoelzer p. 83) διὸ καὶ μέγα τῶν ἑταιρουσῶν ἐστι σόφισμα ἀεὶ τὸ παρὸν τῆς ἀπολαύσεως ὑπερτιθεμένας ταῖς ἐλπίσι διακρατεῖν τοὺς ἐραστάς; cf. also Merc. 650, and, on inopia in general, p.14 n. 27.

From the point of view of the amator such treatment was contumelia (ὕβρις). In the list of vitia amoris, Merc. 30, we have the combination inopia (but cf. my interpretation, p. 14 and note) contumelia, and in Ter. Eunuch. 48, where the lover is denied access to his mistress, the expression non perpeti meretricum contumelias is used. Cf. also And. 557 denique eius libido occlusast contumeliis. According to Nonius (430. 15 cited p. 13 n. 25) contumelia is a stronger word than iniuria, but, as I have already remarked, (p. 13), this seems to be only in the sense of adding insult to injury. Iniuria is the word generally used of an actual breach of obligation: cf. Miles 438 meo ero facis iniuriam, and general usage outside the sermo. ὕβρις and ὑβρίζω are to be compared with contumelia: Theocr. Id. XIV.8 ἐμὲ δ' ἀ χαρίεσσα Κυνίσκα ὑβρίσδει, Ach. Tat.I.2 τοσαύτας ὕβρεις ἐξ ἔρωτος παθών, ibid. VII.1 Ὠργίζετο μὲν ὡς ὑβρισμένος ἤχθετο δὲ ὡς ἀποτυχών, Lucian Dial. meretr. III.3 ad f.

The most frequent form of contumelia is exclusio. A favored lover of course enjoyed the pas: Asin. 236 nec . . . . . alium admittat . . . . . quam me ad se virum, cf. also intromitto Truc. 944, Asin. 756, Ter. Hec. 743 (recepto), Eunuch. 485, cf. Greek δέχομαι εἰς(προσ-) δέχομαι[44], Theocr. Id. XIV.47 Λύκῳ καὶ νυκτὸς ἀνῷκται, Terence Eunuch. 89 sane quia haec mihi patent semper fores, Alciph. I.6.2 ἡ δὲ εἰσδέχεται καὶ ἀναλοῖ χαρύβδεως δίκην, ibid. I.34, Parthen. 34, Ach. Tat. II.19, Aristoph. Thesm. 346. On the other hand it was common for the meretrix to deny access: excludo, extrudo (ἀποκλείω, ἐκβάλλω, διωθέω) Eun. 49 exclusit, revocat; redeam? Menaech. 698 nunc ego sum exclussisimus, cf. Timocl. 23K. ἀλλ' ἔγωγ' ὁ δυστυχὴς Φρύνης ἐρασθείς . . . . . τῆς θύρας ἀπεκλήσμην, Aristaen. II.16 ὅτι μὴ ἀπέκλεισα ἐλθόντα "ἔνδον ἕτερος" εἰποῦσα ἀλλ' εἰσεδεχόμην ἀπροφασίστως,[45] Truc. 86 me extrudat foras, Cist. 530,

[44]Cf. Aristoph. Equites 737-8 σὺ γὰρ ὅμοιος εἶ τοῖς παισὶ τοῖς ἐρωμένοις. τοὺς μὲν καλούς τε κἀγαθοὺς οὐ προσδέχει (admitto), with Neil's note ad loc.

[45]With reference to ἀπροφασίστως, the excuses that might be used to put off a lover are illustrated by Miles 250 sq. (although the connection is slightly different) facilest, trecentae possunt· causae colligi "non domist: abit ambulatum: dormit: ornatur; lavat: prandet: potat: occupatast: operae non est: non potest." On lavat cf. Truc. 322 piscis ego credo, qui usque dum vivunt lavant, minus diu lavare quam haec lavat Phronesium. Some such connection is possible for the cryptic fragment Antiph. 148K. ἔρχεται μετέρχετ' αὖ, προσέρχετ' αὖ, μετέρχεται ἥκει, πάρεστι ῥύπτεται, προσέρχεται, σμῆται κτενίζετ' ἐκβέβηκ' ἐντρίβεται λοῦται, σκοπεῖται, στέλλεται μυρίζεται κοσμεῖτ', ἀλείφετ' ἂν δ' ἔχῃ τι ἀπάγχεται.

A. P. V.41 τίς γυμνὴν οὕτω σε καὶ ἐξέβαλεν καὶ ἔδειρεν, A. P. V.161, Alciph. I.37 ἀποκλείσειν καὶ διώσασθαι.

The doors (fores) of the loved one are frequently apostrophized by the excluded lover, and the serenade addressed to the doors (fores occentare) is a commonplace of Comedy and Elegy: Merc. 408, Persa 569, Curc. 145, quid si adeam ad fores atque occentem . . . . . pessuli, heus pessuli, vos saluto lubens, etc. Such a song is technically known as παρακλαυσίθυρον[46]: A. P. V.103 Μέχρι τίνος Προδίκη παρακλαύσομαι. So also προσᾴδειν, Aristaen. II.19 παρίτω πάλιν προσᾴδων; θυραυλῶ, properly to wait at the door, is used occasionally for fores occentare: Aristaen. II.20. For the latter word in the sermo cf. Philostr. Epist. 53.8 εἰς δὲ θητείαν ὑπήχθη πικρὰν, ἧς ἔργα θυραυλίαι καὶ χαμαικοιτίαι καὶ ἡ πρὸς θάλπος καὶ χειμῶνα ἀντίταξις. The impatient lover would often attack the door with "torch or crowbar": Persa 569 fores exurent, Turp. 200 Rib., Ter. Adelph. 88 fores ecfregit. Cf. θυροκοπῶ (θυροκοπία) Antiph. 239K., Diph. 128K., (Hoelzer p. 64-5, 63).

In connection with the excluded lover and the παρακλαυσίθυρον should be mentioned another convention of a somewhat similar character, the μωρολογία (Latin stultiloquentia); this expression may be used to denote extravagant or incoherent tirades of lovers, whether they be uttered as soliloquies or to some person. Often they were addressed to the sun, moon, stars, day, night, or air: cf. Merc. 4-5 vi amoris facere qui aut nocti aut dii aut soli aut lunae miserias narrant suas, Persa 49 amoris vitio non meo nunc tibi morologus (stultiloquos) fio, Poen. 435 sq., Cist. 283 sq., 512 sq.[47]

The words so far considered have dealt directly with the art or trade of the courtesan, and their connection with the sermo meretricius has been obvious. There remains a group of words and phrases, drawn from the vocabulary of everyday life, less obviously, perhaps, but no less certainly, a part of the same sermo. I refer particularly to the large

[46]For a general discussion cf. De la Villé de Mirmont "Le παρακλαυσίθυρον dans la littérature Latine" Philologie et Linguistique, Mélanges Havet pp. 57 sq. and Leo Gö. Gel. A. 1898 p. 748 "die lebendige Thür die die Menschen nach Willen einlässt oder ausschliesst ist altgriechische Vorstellung (Solon 4. 28, Aristoph. Ach. 127, Eurip. Androm. 924, Alc. 566); daraus erst erklärt sich der Typus des παρακλαυσίθυρον, wie ihn die neue Komödie entwickelt hat (Curculio); in der Ekklesiazusen heisst es noch (961) σύ μοι καταδραμοῦσα τὴν θύραν ἄνοιξον." Cf. also Hoelzer p. 60 sq.

[47]For Greek references cf. Leo Gö. Gel. A. 1898 p. 747, Plaut. Forsch.[2] p. 151 n. 1. Of the examples cited in these places note particularly Call. frag. 67, Alciph. I.8.1 and add A. P. V.166, 191, Men. 739K. Compare also Hoelzer pp. 46-7 (cites Ach. Tat. VI.18.2). On μωρολογία (stultiloquium) and the adj. μωρολόγος (morologus) cf. Brix-Niemeyer on Miles G. 296.

number of ordinary verbs and nouns which recur in erotic contexts with specialized meanings; the technical character of many of these words is further emphasized by the fact that they appear repeatedly in stereotyped combinations. Some words of this class, and many of less frequent occurrence, have a picturesqueness, and a colloquial quality, which seem to suggest that they were part of the argot, or slang, of the meretrix and the amator. Although it is somewhat difficult to differentiate this slang, I will attempt to do so, dealing first with those words and expressions that seem to have been in good and general usage. Such a classification must, in the nature of things, be more or less arbitrary, and the results are, therefore, open to criticism; it should be remembered that my object has been to suggest, as a working basis, what seems to be a valid distinction, without attempting to be dogmatic in its application.

It is interesting to find that, both in Greek and Latin, those "qui amant a lenone" are referred to by a class appellation, and seem almost to be thought of as a sort of Corinthian guild. For example, compare Aristaen. II.11 ἐβουλόμην . . . . . . τοὺς ἐρωτικοὺς ἅπαντας διερωτῆσαι, Philostr. Epist. XXXVIII.8, with the cruder Latin expressions homines voluptarii Menaech. 259, Rud. 54, and amatores mulierum Menaech. 268; the Greek, as in the example from Aristaenetus, seems to apply to "initiates" i. e. those who were more or less versed in the ars amatoria. Such Latin expressions as those noted above seem closer to the primary significance of ἐρωτικὸς amorous, libidinous: cf. Alciph. I. 29 ἐρωτικὸς γάρ ἐστι δαιμονίως. Very commonly used of lovers in Comedy are the adjectives venustus and invenustus, compared ordinarily with Greek ἐπαφρόδιτος and ἀναφρόδιτος. Like Latin venustus, ἐπαφρόδιτος is a standing epithet for the ἑταῖραι: cf. Herod. II.135 κάρτα ἐπαφρόδιτος γενομένη (Rhodopis) μεγάλα ἐκτήσατο χρήματα, ibid. φιλέουσι δέ κως ἐν τῇ Ναυκράτι ἐπαφρόδιτοι γίνεσθαι αἱ ἑταῖραι. Invenustus may be merely the opposite of venustus, i. e., lacking in charm: so Catull. X.4 (scortillum) non sane illepidum neque invenustum, or may have the special sense of unlucky in love: cf. Ter. And. 245, Luc. D. Deorum 15.2. For the former meaning in the case of ἀναφρόδιτος cf. Hortens. apud Aul. Gell. I.5.13 Ἄμουσος ἀναφρόδιτος ἀπροσδιόνυσος, Plutarch Mor. p. 57 D τὰς μονολεχεῖς καὶ φιλάνδρους, ἀναφροδίτους καὶ ἀγροίκους ἀποκαλοῦντες.[48]

[48]It may be worth noting that ἐρωτικός in its pleasant sense and combined with various other adjectives seems not far removed from Latin venustus. So Antiph. 80K. (of a parasite) ἐρωτικὸς γελοῖος ἱλαρὸς τῷ τρόπῳ (Meineke: ἐρωτικός esse videtur amabilis ut apud Theocritum XIV.61), cf. also Aristaen. II.19 παρίτω πάλιν προσᾴδων κἂν ἐρωτικός μοι δοκῇ χαριοῦμαι τῷ μειρακίῳ, Theocr. XIV.61 εὐγνώμων

In the parlance of the meretrix and the amator the verbs placeo (ἀρέσκω) and odi (μισῶ) are of considerable importance. The former is used of the lover who finds favor with his mistress: Casina 227 unguor ut illi placeam et placeo ut videor, Menaech. 670 si tibi displiceo, patiundum: at placuero huic Erotio, Asin. 183, Epid. 133, Most. 293, etc. Cf. Men. Perikeir. 241 ἤρεσκες αὐτῇ τάχα τέως νῦν δ' οὐκέτι, Alciphron I.33.5, etc. Odi is the antithesis of amare, as μισῶ of φιλῶ. Both verbs may express feelings ranging from hate to mere indifference, more often, in the sermo, the latter: cf. Ter. Eunuch. 40 amare, odisse, suspicari, Miles 1269 induxi in animum ne oderim item ut alias, Turp. 100 Rib., cf. Aristophanes Plut. 1072 οὐκ ἐῶ τὴν μείρακα μισεῖν σε ταύτην, Ach. Tat. V.25 ἡ καὶ μισουμένη τὸν μισοῦντα φιλῶ καὶ ὀδυνωμένη τὸν ὀδυνῶντα ἐλεῶ καὶ οὐδὲ ὕβρις τὸν ἔρωτα παύει. For stronger feelings cf. Merc. 761 uxor tua . . . . . quam dudum deixeras te odisse atque angues, Menaech. 189, Miles 128, 970, 1392; similarly μισῶ used in combination with ἐχθαίρω and σικχαίνω Call. Epigr. XXVIII (and compare Horace Odes III.1.1, I.8.4). Cf. also μισηταί, technical, Crat. 316 K. with notes.

Before passing to the euphemisms, perhaps the largest and most significant class of words in the erotic diction of Comedy, I wish to mention a few verbs which have something in common with euphemisms, in that they imply rather more than might appear on the surface. Sector is used regularly of the "love chase" with the meaning "pursue or press unwelcome attentions"; in this sense it is equivalent to διώκω[49] and is coupled or contrasted with fugio (φεύγω) in an antithesis common to both Greek and Latin: Merc. 669 ut illum persequar qui me fugit, Casina 466, Bacch. 28, Miles 91, 778, 1113, Sex. Turp. 100 Rib. quem olim oderat sectatur ultro ac detinet, Catull. VIII. 10 nec quae fugit sectare, Theocr. Id. VI.17 καὶ φεύγει φιλέοντα καὶ οὐ φιλέοντα διώκει, ibid. XI.75, Aristaen. II.16 ἐκείνην διώκεις ὅτι σε πόρρωθεν ἀποφεύγει, Call. Epigr. 31 (cf. Leo Plaut. Forsch.[2] p. 156). A stronger verb than sector is subigito (πειρῶ), which implies personal liberties and is used generally of improper advances: Miles 652 neque ego umquam alienum scortum subigito in

---

φιλόμουσος ἐρωτικός, εἰς ἄκρον ἀδύς, cf. Catull. XXII.2 homo est venustus et dicax et urbanus, Philostr. Epist. XXXI.2 καὶ γὰρ ἐστιν ἐρωτικὰ (ῥόδα) καὶ πανοῦργα καὶ κάλλει χρῆσθαι εἰδότα. The word seems to suggest a definite quality, and amabilis does not seem to me an adequate substitute in any example. Cf. the use of ἀνέραστος Philostr. Epist. XXXVII.1 Αἰτιᾷ με, ὅτι σοι ῥόδα οὐκ ἔπεμψα· Ἐγὼ δὲ οὔτε ὡς ὀλίγωρος τοῦτο ἐποίησα οὔτε ὡς ἀνέραστος ἄνθρωπος; does not ἀνέραστος here=invenustus?

[49] Sometimes sector = ἀκολουθῶ, which properly = sequor, consequor, cf. Phorm. 86, Cist. 91 (with Men. 558K.).

convivio (cf. Luc. Dial. meretr. III.1), Aristoph. Plut. 1068 πειρᾷ . . .
. . σε καὶ τῶν τιτθίων ἐφάπτεταί σου, ibid. 150 ὅταν μὲν αὐτάς (ἑταίρας)
τις πένης πειρῶν τύχῃ, Equites 517[50] πολλῶν γὰρ δὴ πειρασάντων αὐτὴν
ὀλίγοις χαρίσασθαι, Alciph. II.1. Subigitatio Capt. 1030 is paralleled by
πεῖρα: cf. lexicon, and Persa 227 ne me attrecta, subigitatrix further
illustrates the idea of the verb. Tento is similarly used in elegy: cf.
Prop. I.3.15 leviter positam tentare lacerto.

A more refined vehicle for the same idea is supplied by audeo (τολμῶ)
in its technical sense. The force of τολμῶ is clearly defined A. P. V.75
αὐτή μοι προσέπαιζε καὶ εἴ ποτε καιρὸς ἐτόλμων : ἠρυθρία . . . . .
ἤνυσα πολλὰ καμών, A. P. V.275 τολμήσας δ' ἐπέβην λεχέων ὕπερ, Longus I.
21 ὑπό τ'ἀπειρίας ἐρωτικῶν τολμημάτων. Audeo is not positively technical
in this sense in Comedy[51] (i. e., it is not used without a defining infini-
tive), but may be said to be on the way: cf. Aul. 755 ergo quia sum
tangere ausus haud causificor quin eam ego habeam potissimum, Bacch.
1163, Poen. 1310, Eunuch. 884. For later usage cf. Pichon s. v., and the
phrases auso (rapto, cupito) potiri: Verg. Aen. VI.624, IV.217, Apul. met.
IX.18(cited by Norden, Vergil Aeneis Buch VI, p. 286). Another word
with equal claim to be considered technical is ἐλπίς, ἐλπίζω (spes, spero):
A. P. V.101 'Ελπίζειν ἔξεστι ; (B) Ζητεῖς δὲ τί ; Νύκτα (B) φέρεις τί ; A. P.
V:267 ἐλπίζεις δὲ τυχεῖν, V.241, Ach. Tat. II.10 οἶνος, ἔρως, ἐλπίς, ἐρημία,
Aristaen. I.2 οὐδὲ καταβαλεῖς ἡμᾶς ἀπ' ἐλπίδος μεγάλης, ibid. I.4, Philemon
138K. cf. Miles 1051 sit necne sit spes in te unost, Ovid Ars Amat. I.719
nec semper Veneris spes est profitenda roganti. Answering to spes,
sensu venereo, is copia: Miles 1040-1 multae aliae idem istuc cupiunt
quibus copia non est, ibid. 1229, Ter. Phorm. 113, Casina 842, (cf. Lodge
s. v.). Opposed to copia in this sense is inopia (cf. p. 14, also p. 24);
for the two words in combination cf. Trin. 671 quom inopiast cupias
quando eius copiast, tum non velis with T. L. L. IV.902. 35; 900. 79.
Besides copia in various combinations (with esse, habere, etc.), potior
(cf. Norden Aeneis Buch VI, p. 286) is common in this sense: cf. Ter.
Haut. 322 vis amare, vis potiri, Curc. 170 ipsus se excruciat qui homo

[50]Van Leeuwen notes that the active πείρω was used in good Attic only in an erotic
sense. Cf. also Neil, note on Eq. 517, where Moeris s. v. and Eustath. on Il. 338.31
are cited as authority for this restriction. For other cases cf. Aristoph. Pax 763,
Theopomp. 32K. with Kock's note, Aristophont. 4K., Menand. 524K., Lys. I.12, Eur.
Cycl. 581 (V. Leeuwen).

[51]Audeo can hardly be said to be the equivalent of τολμῶ in general usage outside
the sermo, in Comedy, as the meaning "dare" is not as yet firmly established. Cf.
Brix, note on Trin. 244. On the other hand, audere does not have the technical force of
velle in the sermo.

quod amat videt nec potitur dum licet. In these and similar passages the verb has the distinctly technical force for which τυγχάνω or ἀνύω and sometimes εὐτυχῶ are used in Greek. The climactic sequence of the terms subigito (audeo), spero, potior is illustrated by such examples as Luc. Amores 3 πειράσας μὲν γὰρ ἐλπίζεις, τυχὼν δ' ἀπολέλαυκας, A. P. V.267 ἐλπίζεις δὲ τυχεῖν, cf. also Ach. Tat. I.9 πῶς ἄν τύχοιμι τῆς ἐρωμένης, A. P. V.75 ἤνυσα πολλὰ καμών. It is suggestive that in Greek verbs and phrases employed for this idea, the thought is merely one of success in hitting a mark or reaching a goal proposed. The Latin idiom employs, in a weakened sense, it is true, a verb implying complete, if temporary, possession.

Occasionally, as in Eunuch. 614 et de istac simul, quo pacto porro possim potiri, consilium volo capere tecum, potior has the meaning "use" or "enjoy", for which utor (χρῶμαι) and fruor (ἀπολαύω) are more general. These two verbs are practically interchangeable, as are their Greek equivalents, though in the case of fruor and ἀπολαύω more zest is perhaps implied. Utor is in effect rather neutral, formal, and reminiscent of legal phraseology: Persa 128 numquam edepol quoiquam etiam utendam dedi, Ter. Phorm. 413 item ut meretricem ubi abusus sis, mercedem dare lex iubet ei atque amittere? cf. χρῶμαι Ach. Tat. VI.15 ὑπονοεῖν μοι δοκεῖ σε χρησάμενον ἅπαξ, ἀφήσειν καὶ ὀκνεῖ τὴν ὕβριν, Heliod. I.15 'Αρσινόην ἀκούεις που πάντως τὴν αὐλητρίδα, ταύτῃ ἐκέχρητο; cf. also the expression uxor usuraria Amph. 498, 980. For fruor in a less explicit sense cf. Ter. Phorm. 165 ut mi liceat tam diu quod amo frui, but the noun fructus "use" or "enjoyment" is not on a high plane: Casina 839 meast haec. scio sed meus fructus est prior. Similarly Asin. 918 alternas cum illo noctes hac frui; cf. ἀπολαύω, ἀπόλαυσις Luc. Amores 3 πειράσας μὲν γὰρ ἐλπίζεις, τυχὼν δ˟ ἀπολέλαυκας, Aristaen. I.10 ὁ δὲ οὖν τῇ παρθένῳ βραχέα νυκτομαχήσας ἐρωτικῶς τό γε λοιπὸν εἰρηναίων ἀπέλαυεν ἡδονῶν, Alciph. II.1 ἀεὶ τὸ παρὸν τῆς ἀπολαύσεως ὑπερτιθεμένας, Heliod. I.15.

There remain to be considered the more pronounced euphemisms of the sermo meretricius in Comedy, i. e., such words as tracto, tango, ludo, amo, quiesco, dormio, accumbo, and the like. All these expressions are frequently employed, not only in their surface meanings, but to take the place of bolder or more vulgar terms. Tango and attingo may be explicit: Poen. 269 quas adeo hau quisquam umquam liber tetigit neque duxit domum ("tangere mulierem pro rem cum muliere habere dicunt Latini" Lamb.), Aul. 740 cur id ausu's facere ut id quod non tuom esset tangeres cf. also tactio infra l. 744), ibid. 755, Poen. 98, Ter. Phorm. 1018, Hec. 136, Catull. XXI.8. For the less drastic use, cf.

Rud. 426 non licet te sic placide bellam belle tangere, Eunuch. 373 adsis tangas ludas, Casina 458, Poen. 281, Miles 1092. Attrecto and contrecto, like subigito (the more general term), are used of caresses: Rudens 421 Ah, nimium familiariter me attrectas, Asin. 523, Casina 851, Poen. 698, cf. θιγγάνω (tango), ψαύω (tracto) A. P. XII. 209 Ἔστω προύνεικα πρῶτα θιγήματα καὶ τὰ πρὸ ἔργων παίγνια (Eunuchus 373 tangas ludas), Ach. Tat. IV.7 ἀκοῦσαι θέλω φωνῆς χειρὸς θιγεῖν, Ach. Tat. IV.7 χειρὸς θιγεῖν ψαῦσαι σώματος. For ψαύω (drastic) cf. A. P. XII.173 καὶ τῆς μὲν ψαύω· τῆς δ' οὐ θέμις cf. θιγγάνω Eur. Hipp. 1044, El. 51. Parallel with Latin intactus (-a) or integer is Greek ἄψαυστος: Cas. 832 integrae atque imperitae huic impercito, A. P. V.217 χρύσεος ἀψαύστοιο διέτμαγεν ἄμμα κορείας Ζεύς.[52]

The verb amo is on rather a low plane in Comedy, and it may be noted that when the emphasis is on pure affection diligo is preferred (cf. Friedr. Catull. p. 486). It is hardly necessary to indicate the common use of amo for meretricious relations; characteristic examples are Poen. 176 (dicit) se amare velle atque obsequi animo suo, ibid. 603 liberum . . . . . locum et voluptarium ubi ames, potes, pergraecere, Pseud. 203 qui amant a lenone (iuvenes), Ter. Andr. 87 ei tres tum simul eam amabant (in general cf. T. L.L. I.1951.80, 1952.60 inclus., Lodge s. v.). As used above, amo translates ἐρῶ, cf. amator (ἐραστής). It is used also of kisses or caresses, like φιλῶ Bacch. 1192b tecum accumbam, te amabo et te amplexabor, Aristoph. Equites 1341 ἐραστής τ' εἰμὶ σὸς φιλῶ τέ σε, Aristoph. Ach. 1200 φιλήσατόν με μαλθακῶς.

To be classed with amo is ludo (παίζω), to dally or toy amorously. In Eunuch. 373 cibum una capias, adsis, tangas, ludas, propter dormias, we have a sequence, in which the verbs increase in boldness. Ludo is not so definite here as in later Latin. Catullus has, LXI.211, ludite ut libet et brevi liberos date, Petr. 11 invenit me cum fratre ludentem, Mart. XI.39.7 ludere nec nobis nec tu permittis amare, Prop. I.10.9 and Rothstein ad loc.; cf. παίζειν and its compounds Aristaen. I.7 τῇ ποθουμένῃ, προσπαίζων ἅμα καὶ πειρώμενος τῆς καλῆς, A. P. V.158 Ἑρμιόνῃ πιθανῇ ποτ' ἐγὼ συνέπαιζον, ibid. V.245 παῖζε μόνη τὸ φίλημα. The noun ludus is used of dalliance, frequently in combination with iocus, and sometimes with other nouns: Pseud. 65 iocus ludus, sermo, suavisaviatio, Bacch. 116 (same personified), Rudens 429 otium ubi erit, tum tibi

---

[52] The opposite of tango is abstineo, to refrain from touching, Curc. 37 dum ted abstineas nupta, vidua, virgine, Ter. Hec. 139, 411, Poen. 282 (opposed to tango). Figuratively Miles 1309, cf. ἀπέχομαι Aristoph. Lysis. 124, 153, 771, 765, Men. Epitrep. 521 (447) τοιαυτησὶ γὰρ οὐκ ἀπέσχετ' ἂν ἐκεῖνος, εὖ τοῦτ' οἶδ,' ἐγὼ δ' ἀφέξομαι, A. P. V.242, Alciphr. I.29.3.

operam ludo et deliciae dabo, Hor. Ep. I.6.66, Catull. LXI.210. The
combination ludus iocusque, or either word used separately, seems to re-
present Greek παίγνια: A. P. XII.209 θιγήματα καὶ τὰ πρὸ ἔργων παίγνια,
Ephip. 7K. τοῖς ἡμετέροισι παιγνίοις, A. P. V.166 νέα παίγνια, ibid. V.197
'Ιλιάδος φίλα παίγνια.   Compare also iocus (Pichon s. v.) and Catull.
VIII.6, with Friedrich's note (p. 114). Paegnium (Παίγνιον), in the Persa,
is named advisedly, as the context shows: cf. lines 204 (deliciae), 284.
Compare also Aristoph. Eccl. 921 and Latin deliciae passim.

The very common verbs cubo, cubito, accumbo, and decumbo, are
perhaps adequately treated in the lexica, but a few remarks may be in
order. The two former are distinctly used sensu venereo in many
passages in Comedy, as, for example, Bacch. 860, 896, 1009, Truc. 547,
Miles 65, Amph. 132, Curc. 56.   The comic coinage cubitura = coitus
Cist. 379, and cubitus Amph. 1122 are to be cited in the same connec-
tion.   Accumbo and decumbo are, however, frequently without such
significance, even in erotic passages.   The contrary may be true in such
cases as Bacch. 1192a, Menaech. 476, 1142.   Even here such an inter-
pretation can hardly be insisted on, though Greek usage for κατάκειμαι
and κατακλίνω supports it: cf. Aristoph. Pax 1331 χὥπως μετ' ἐμοῦ καλὴ
καλῶς κατακείσει, Lysis. 904 σὺ δ' ἀλλὰ κατακλίνηθι μετ' ἐμοῦ διὰ χρόνου,
Eccl. 614. In the case of quiesco and dormio the amatory sense is
rather clearly established.   In Asin. 519 sq. we find the words quin
pol si reposivi remum, sola ego in casteria ubi quiesco, omnis familiae
causa consistit mihi.   The whole simile is rather suggestive, owing to the
many nautical comparisons of an erotic nature current in Greek Comedy:
cf. ἐλαύνω Aristoph. Eccl. 39 (Von Leeuwen ad loc.), Plato com. 3K.,
the extended simile Theophilus 6K., Theogn. 457, etc., but it is not neces-
sary to press an erotic interpretation for the entire passage.   The
meaning of quiesco, however, turning, as it does, upon that of sola,
becomes quite clear by a comparison with Cist. 44-5 numquam ego hanc
viduam cubare sivi, nam si haec non nubat, lugubri fame familia pereat.
Equally in point is the recurrence of μόνη in Greek, in such phrases as
A. P. V.184 ταῦτ' ἦν ταῦτ', ἐπίορκε; μόνη σὺ πάλιν μόνη ὑπνοῖς, A. P. V.
213, Alciph. I.38 κείσεται λοιπὸν μόνη, and the verb μονοκοιτῶ Aristoph.
Lysis. 592 cf. secubo in Latin.   Another variant is ἡσυχάζω A. P. V.133
δύο νύκτας ἀφ' 'Ηδυλίου . . . . . ἡσυχάσειν. Dormio apparently pos-
sesses an amatory sense, by way of double entendre, in Eunuch. 373
adsis, tangas, ludas, propter dormias.   Aside from the fact that climactic
effect would be expected, this sense for dormio is common in Elegy
(cf. Pichon) and follows naturally from the erotic significance of συγ-

καταδαρθάνω, συγκατάκειμαι, etc., Aristoph. Eccl. 613, 622, 628, Alciph. I.38; cf. also Caec. 96 Rib. with Ribbeck's note ad loc.—dormitum ut eam suadet "de meretricis illecebris, ni fallor, agitur" Rib.[53]

Euphemistic also is the use of volo: Miles 972 cupio hercle equidem si illa volt, ibid. 1149 et illa volt et ille autem cupit, Catull. VIII.9 Nunc iam illa non volt: tu quoque impotens noli, Pichon s. v. velle, cf. A. P. V.42 Μισῶ τὴν ἀφελῆ, μισῶ τὴν σώφρονα λίαν. ἡ μὲν γὰρ βραδέως, ἡ δὲ θέλει ταχέως, Philostr. Epist. 43.3 σύρεις μὴ θέλοντα, Theocr. XXIX.7. It will be noted that in these examples the idea of volo (θέλω) is practically "consent." The verb is often closer to βούλημαι: Asin. 542 sine me amare unum Argyrippum animi causa, quem volo; cf. Philostr. Epist. 66.1 ἦν αὐτὸς ἐβούλετο. For other examples cf. Boissonade on Aristaen. pp. 303, 308, 551 and Mart. VI.40 tempora quid faciunt? hanc volo te volui. The expressions morem gerere, morigerari, morigerus, though common in erotic contexts and in a broad sense equivalent to χαρίζεσθαι, are, in general, much less explicit than the Greek verb[54] and often refer to other than physical compliance, cf. Most. 189, 226 (Ramsay, note ad loc. and exc. p. 126), 398, Menaech. 202, Stich. 742, Cas. 896, Amph. 842, Ter. And. 294. With Amph. 131 pater nunc intus suo animo morem gerit (cf. ibid. 981) compare χαρίζεσθαι θύμῳ Soph. Elec. 331 et al. A more drastic case is supplied by the punning passage Ter. Adel. 214-5 adulescenti morem gestum oportuit. qui potui melius, qui hodie usque os praebui (obscene, Donatus with the approval of Spengel and others). Compare παρέχω Philostr. Epist. 68. 9-10 καὶ γεωργοῖς παρέχεις σεαυτὴν (= corpus volgare?) and passim.

Some euphemistic expressions which the Greek shares with later Latin erotic poetry are missing in Plautus and Terence: so opus (erotic = ἔργον) for which cf. Pichon and such cases as A. P. V.275 ἀνύσσαμεν ἔργον ἔρωτος, Ach. Tat. I.10 τὸ δ' ἔργον ζήτει πῶς γένηται σιωπῇ. It is not unlikely that Stat. Caec. 167 Rib. is a case in point: properatim in tenebris istuc confectum est opus. Possum is apparently not among verba nequiora in Comedy, despite δύναμαι A. P. XII.11, 213 and later Latin: cf. Mart. III.32.1, 76.4, XI.97.1. For facio = coeo, no cases from Plautus are recognized by the Thesaurus (T. L. L. VI.121. 40 sq.); cf.

[53]Some significance may be attached to Curc. 184 at meo more dormio; hic somnust mihi, but the force of hic somnust mihi is probably "this is (as good as) sleep to me."

[54]Cf. Schol. Pind. Pyth. 2.75 χαρίζεσθαι κυρίως τὸ συνουσιάζειν λέγεται, Alexis. 165K. ἐρρέτω μέλαιν' Ὀπώρα· πᾶσι γὰρ χαρίζεται, Aristoph. Equites 517, πολλῶν γὰρ δὴ πειρασάντων αὐτὴν ὀλίγοις χαρίσασθαι, ibid. Ach. 883-4, A. P. V.2, ibid. 233, 269, Aristaen. II.19 (p. 27 n. 48), Philostr. Epist. 68. 9-10, Theop. 29K. (1).

also T. L. L. VI.140.22 for factor (Curc. 297) where the word is cited as auctor facti, with reference to Leo's note ad loc. Outside of Comedy the use is well attested: cf. Catull. 110.2 with Friedrich's note ad loc. and T. L. L. loc. cit.[55] Friedrich compares πράττειν, with references to Aeschin. in Timarch. 160, Paus. 104; cf. also δρῶ Aristoph. Vesp. 1381, Thesm. 398, Eccl. 704, ἐνεργεῖν Theocr. IV.61, Alciph. III.55(19).9.

Do (dato) is technical in Plautus. The two noteworthy examples of dare=διδόναι are in paederastic passages, but the usage is one that belongs to the sermo meretricius in general: cf. Catull. 110.4 with Friedrich's note, Afranius 63 Rib. virosa (φίλανδρος) non sum, et si sum, non desunt mihi qui ultro dent, Naev. 75 Rib. quae in choro ludens datatim dat se (cf. also Isidore Orig. I.25 where this is cited with the comment "Ennius de quadam impudica"). For the Greek cf. Aristoph. Equit. 738-40 τοὺς μὲν καλοὺς . . . . . οὐ προσδέχει σαυτὸν δὲ . . . . . βυρσοπώλαισιν δίδως (cf. Van Leeuwen, note ad loc.), Theocr. XXVII.61 (Prescott, Class. Phil. 1909 p. 322). In Plautus, Aul. 637 pone id quidem pol te datare credo consuetum senex seems a clear example[56], as does Casina 362 comprime istunc. Immo istunc qui didicit dare (Lodge "in m. p."). Much less evident is the old interpretation for Curc. 296-7 isti qui ludunt datatim servi scurrarum in via et datores et factores omnes subdam sub solum. Lambinus and Taubmann interpret this in malam partem, comparing Naev. 75. Support for this view can be found in the fact that scurrae occurs in an objectionable passage Poen. 612, and also in the fact that examples of datatim are mostly in erotic relations. Datatim, properly=vicissim (invicem dare), cf. Nonius p. 96, is used de re venerea Afran. 222 Rib.[1], Naev. 75 (cited above), Pompon. Atell. 1 (cf. T. L. L. V.39. 35-45); without such meaning, only Nov. 22 Rib. (cf. Turnebus Adv. VI.5), though this is doubtful, and Curc. 296, the example under consideration. Waiving questions of usage, there is nothing in the passage that can not be satisfactorily explained on the theory of a ball game, adopted T. L. L. V.39.37, 42-9 (datores). Ribbeck explains the passage as referring to the game harpastum, a game of "sides" (Sitzungsb. sächs. Akad. 1879 p. 88).

Periphrases and ellipses are comparatively rare, and are limited to a few expressions like Pseud. 780 neque illud possum quod illi qui possunt

[55]Lambinus on Truc. 966 romabo siquis animatust facere, etc., reading the MSS si quid, adds "puto hanc cohortationem ad opus venereum pertinere." This seems reasonable. Note also that in Pseud. 780 neque ego illud possum, quod illi qui possunt solent, the omitted verb would appear to be facere. Similarly Rudens 1216 omnian licet (Lamb.).

[56]Cf. Taub. ad loc. and particularly Buecheler Rh. Mus. 35. 398.

solent (cf. ἐκεῖνος, δεῖνα); cf. hoc Most. 328 (Lamb.), Pseud. 1178
etiamne facere solitus es, scin quod loquar? Miles 1092 neque te
tago neque te—taceo, Persa 227 habes nescioquid, Bacch. 897 neque
ausculatur neque illud quod dici solet, Pseud. 216 ubi usque ad lang-
uorem—:

The peculiarly colloquial, or slang element of the sermo meretricius
is an elusive quantity, and, for present purposes, the term has been
given a rather broad acceptation. I have thought it reasonable to
include under this head all homely metaphors and proverbial expres-
sions, colloquial exaggerations, and a number of technical or quasi-
technical uses of verbs, nouns, and adjectives which do not appear in
later Latin outside of those authors that professedly exhibit the sermo
cotidianus. For most of the diction thus far discussed Elegy offers
numerous parallels, as it does for the distinctly literary element that
remains to be considered. That part of the sermo amatorius in Comedy
that has least in common with Elegy may most plausibly be assigned to
the argot of the meretrix and the amator. I do not, however, wish to
maintain that all that follows is argot; convenience has, to some extent,
influenced the grouping.

Certain colloquial phrases have to do directly with the business of the
meretrix. Thus rem (commercium) habere is used of intercourse:Truc.
94 cum ea quoque etiam mihi fuit commercium, Bacch. 563-4 tibi non
erat meretricum aliarum Athenis copia, quibuscum haberes rem? Merc.
535 rem habet, ibid. 533 mecum rem coepit. Similarly est res Ter.
Haut. 388[57], Eunuch. 119, Hec. 718.

The bankrupt lover is called inanis Bacch. 517, 531, or sterilis Truc.
241, instead of the usual inops Bacch. 517; cf. Greek κενός: Call. Epigr.
XXXII.1 οἶδ' ὅτι μου πλούτου κενεαὶ χέρες et al. So Greek αὖος is used in
the same connection (of a penniless lover) Luc. dial. meretr. XIV.1
ἐπεὶ δ' ἐγὼ μὲν αὖος ἀκριβῶς, σὺ δὲ τὸν Βιθυνὸν ἔμπορον εὕρηκας ἐραστήν,
ἀποκλείομαι μὲν ἐγώ (quoted by Leo Plaut. Forsch.[2] p. 149, Hoelzer

---

[57]For res in plural used euphemistically for res venereae cf. Heraeus Petr. u. die
Glossen p. 34 on Petr. 77 tu dominam tuam de illis rebus fecisti, Corp. Gloss. Lat.
V.462.1 irquitallus puer cum primum ad res accedit, Auson. technop. 14. 7 imperium
litem venerem cur una notat . . . . . res? Arnob. adv. nat. 3. 10,
Plautus Most. 897 (Rohde JHB. 1879, 847, from whom Heraeus draws most of the
foregoing examples) quaeso hercle abstine iam sermonem de istis rebus; this seems
forced; surely the meaning "topics" suffices for rebus in this passage. Add to these
examples Friedrich on Catullus 107. 7, particularly Miles 1437 magis metuant
(moechi) minus has res studeant. Res (pl.) as in the above examples, is, of course, a
different idiom from rem (commercium) habere.

p. 65). Compare Latin aridus=pauper (T. L. L. II.568) Mart. X.87.5 absit cereus aridi clientis. Again the bankrupt is stigmatized as a "dead one": Truc. 163 dum vivit, hominem noveris; ubi mortuost quiescat;[58] for mortuos as used here cf. (possibly) Men. Kolax 49 (Koerte) ἄνθρωπ[ε π]έ[ρυσι]ν πτωχὸς ἦσθα καὶ νεκρός νυν[ὶ] δὲ πλου[τεῖς]. It is possible also that inermus Caec. 67 Rib. should be classed with such expressions—sine blanditie nihil agit in amore inermus.

A variety of picturesque expressions is used of the meretrix and her abode. The former is a navis praedatoria (Menaech. 344), stabulum flagiti (Truc. 587), lupa (Epid. 403),[59] fera (Asin. 145), and her ancilla is a celox or "cruiser" (Miles 986) cf. celocula (a doubtful reading, cf. Lodge s. v.) ibid. 1006 and λέμβος Anaxand. 34K. The home of the meretrix or leno is referred to as latebrosa loca (Bacch. 430) cf. Trin. 240 (amor) latebricolarum hominum corrumptor, Bacch. 56 latebrosus locus, Poen. 835 tenebrae, latebrae; we have also the expressions damni conciliabulum (Trin. 314), conciliabulum[60] (Bacch. 80), desidiabula (Bacch. 376), lustra (Bacch. 743, Casina 243, Asin. 867, Curc. 508, Pseud. 1107 (lustrari); cf. the epithets fera, lupa, and the common term lupanar (Bacch. 454). In general the scortum (πόρνη) and the meretrix (ἑταίρα) are carefully differentiated, although the former term is habitually used of the meretrix in general observations of a moral character, or fixed idioms such as scortum ducere (scortari); for the caste distinction cf. Nonius p. 423 M. The scortum is referred to as a prostibulum (-a, -e?) Nonius loc. cit. prostibula, quod ante stabulum stent quaestus

[58]Noveris in this passage is apparently technical in the sense of ὁμιλεῖν or γιγνώσκειν cf. Pichon s. v. cognosco and T. L. L. III.1504. 1 sq. Examples in Comedy are Turp. 42 Rib. mulier meretrix, quae me quaesti causa cognovit sui, and Plautus Most. 894 novit erus me (noted by Taubmann). Similarly γιγνώσκω Men. 558K. ἔπειτα φοιτῶν καὶ κολακεύων ἐμέ τε καὶ τὴν μητέρ' ἔγνω μ' and elsewhere. In this case quiescat supports the double ɩntendre (supra p. 32, discussion of Asin. 519); ἡσυχάζω (=quiesco?) is quite technical. Quiescas (MSS and Ussing) lends even more point to this passage. For ἡσυχάζω cf. A. P. V.133, 167.

[59]Cf. Λύκα as name of a courtesan Amphis 23K., Tim. 25K., with Horace's Lyce Carm. IV.13 and III.10. Also the names Λυκαίνιον, Λυκαινίς in Pape (Griechische Eigennamen). Similarly, we have a procurer Lycus (Λύκος) in the Poenulus. The wolf was proverbial for rapacity (Otto Sprichwörter p. 198 sq.), cf. the hprase λύκου βίον ζῆν Polyb. XVI.24.4. Cf. also Bechtel Att. Frauennamen p. 95.

[60]According to Goldmann (Die Poetische Personifikation in der Sprache der alten Komödiendichter) p. 19, conciliabulum=σύλλογος. So also Brix-Niemeyer on Trin. 314, citing as parallels Menaech. 988 saltus damni, Truc. 551 damni via. σύλλογος occurs only once in the comic fragments (Plato 90K) and is there used in a good sense. For the meaning of conciliabulum cf. Lambinus on Trin. 314 (apparently a mistaken idea), T. L. L. IV.38. 43-52.

diurni et nocturni causa, Stich. 765 Prostibules(t) tandem? stantem stanti savium dare amicum amicae? Cist. ap. Non. p. 423 M., Persa 837, Aul. 285, Pomp. 148 Rib. Compare also the verb prostare (stare) Curc. 507, Stich. 765, Publil. Syr. 18 Rib., Pomp. 156 Rib., Juv. X.239, XI.172, III.65, Greek προΐστημι, Hesych. κεραμεικός. τόπος 'Αθήνησιν, ἔνθα αἱ πόρναι προεστήκασαν, ibid. s. v. Δημιάσι πύλαις . . . . . πρὸς γὰρ αὐτάς φασιν ἑστάναι τὰς πόρνας, Eubul. 67K. Like prostibulum is proseda: Poen. 266, cf. Paulus 226. 2: prosedas meretices Plautus appellat quae ante stabula sedeant: eaedem et prostibulae. In the same context other opprobrious epithets for the scortum occur: cf. pistorum amicas (Poen. 266), and Pseud. 188 Hedylium . . . . . . quae amica es frumentariis[61]. Reliquias alicarias (Poen. 266) is explained Paulus p. 717 after the analogy of the foregoing: "alicariae" meretrices dicebantur in Campania solitae ante pistrina alicariorum versari quaesti gratia."[62] For status cf. stare, prostare (supra). Stabulum (Poen. 268) used for fornix, recalls Truc. 587 stabulum flagiti, Cas. 160-um nequitiae (epithets in both cases); cf. also Persa 418 and Suet. Iul. 49. Pergula in the meaning lupanar (fornix) occurs Pseud. 213; cf. more-over Catull. XXXVII salax taberna, vosque contubernales. In connec-tion with prosedas (Poen. 266) note sella and sessibulum, and compare

[61]This passage is interesting as harping on the idea of guild preferences for a particu-lar meretrix, cf. 197-8 tu quae amicos tibi habes . . . . . lanios, 210 Xystilis, ... quoius amatores olivi dynamin domi habent maxumam. For a localized clientèle cf. Alciphr. I.6.2 κωμάζουσι γὰρ εἰς αὐτὴν ἡ πρὸς θάλατταν νεολαία καὶ ἄλλος ἄλλο δῶρον ἀποφέρει. (Leo Plaut. Forsch.² p. 150).

[62]Ussing rejects this too plausible explanation, interpreting the phrase reliquias alicarias as useless residue, "riffraff." Lindsay reads reginas, from the codex Turne-bus (not, however, among the readings known to Lambin or Taubmann). "Reginae" "queens" would be a natural expression for the sermo, but aside from the fact that it would be rather milder than the other epithets in this passage, I find no parallels in Greek or Latin Comedy. Ussing likewise departs from the traditional interpretation for line 267 schoeno delibutas servicolas sordidas cf. schoenicolae Cist. 407 ap. Varro L. L. VII.64 "ab schoeno nugatorio unguento" and Festus 329 b 32. Ussing (following Meursius) rejects this schoenus, as an ointment, and interprets the phrase as "who reek of the mat," citing Aristoph. Plut. 541 ἀντὶ δὲ κλίνης στιβάδα σχοίνων. Ussing comments "et schoenicolae appellantur meretrices talibus cubilibus consuetae." For the teges or rush mat made of the iuncus (σχοῖνος) cf. Mayor on Juvenal IV.8. In defense of the traditional interpretation it may be said that delibutus is properly used of liquids, particularly perfumes, cf. Thes. L. L. V.442.47 where this passage is cited "Plaut. Poen. 267 schoeno-utas (i. unguento cf. Titius or. frg. Macr. sat. III.16.14 delibuti unguentis, etc.)." Compare also Cato De re rust. 113.1, in directions for imparting a bouquet to wine, suffito serta et schoeno et palma, quam habent unguen-tarii, ibid. 105.2. The fragrance of the calamus was well known.

Juv. III.136 et dubitas alta Chionen deducere sella (Ussing), with May-
or's note ad loc.   Similar in tone to Poen. 266 sq. is Cist.405-8
= Plaut. ap. Varro de l. l. VII.64 non quasi nunc haec sunt hic limaces
lividae febriculosae, miserae amicae osseae diobolares, schoeniculae,
miraculae, cum extritis talis, cum todillis crusculis.   On limaces Varro
loc. cit. says: limax ab limo quod ibi vivit,[63] but, for modern ideas cf.
Walde s. v. Ussing, on Bacchides 13, limaces viri, derives the word from
lima, explaining the phrase, "viri alterum atterentes, quales v. c. para-
siti."   The other epithets offer little room for discussion.   For diobolares
cf. Poen. 270 and supra p. 19.

A number of adjectives have peculiar meanings, perhaps colloquial,
in erotic contexts.   Turpis (αἰσχρός) = ugly Most. 288 turpi mulieri
is perhaps too common to require comment; for ὡραῖος contrasted with
αἰσχρός cf. Anaxand. 52K.9 ἀλλ' ἔλαβεν αἰσχράν . . . . . ἀλλ'
ἔλαβεν ὡραίαν τις, Philemon 170K. σαπρὰν γυναῖκα δ' ὁ τρόπος εὔμορφον
ποιεῖ.   It is possible that malus bears the same meaning Bacch.
1161 haud malast mulier, but this is open to question; the older com-
mentators (Lamb., Taub.) explain "non invenusta," as does Ussing, in
double entendre.   But whatever mala means in Bacch. 1161, it certainly
does not refer to appearance in the next line, where it balances nihili,
pol vero ista mala et tu nihili.   In Bacch. 1139 b we have with reference
to the old men (as oves), stultae atque (haud) malae videntur (haud
solus B in marg. omittit Ussing).   The negative is supported by 1131
sine omni malitia, which might also have accounted for its insertion;
malitia can hardly mean anything but cunning, duplicity, with a bad
connotation: cf. Persa 238 malitia tecum certare miseriast, Epid. 546
muliebris adhibenda . . . . . malitia est, Miles 880 mala esse et
fraudulenta, ibid. 887 male atque malitiose with Lorenz' note, Truc. 131,
Ter. Hec. 203 (Hoelzer p. 76).   Then in Bacch. 1139 b, reading the nega-
tive, haud malae should mean guileless or innocent.   In default of
evidence for the meaning "not bad looking" in Bacch. 1161 we should
perhaps understand the phrase as meaning "she looks harmless."   The
idea of slyness is sometimes transferred from the words malus, malitia,
to the proverbial mala merx[64], originally commercial and opposed to
proba merx, cf. Poen. 342 proba mers facile emptorem reperit (cf. 341
invendibili merci); of a leno, as a "bad lot" Pseud. 954; of age Menaech.

[63]Note, in this connection, Meursius' emendation of Poen. 267 schoeno delibutas
to coeno delibutas (cf. caeno conlitus 835).

[64]Cf. Brix on Miles 895 "sprichwörtlich und plebejisch, 'eine leichte Ware.' " Otto
op. cit. p. 200 n. 2 "mala merx braucht Plautus von Leuten die wenig taugen."

758; of women, with slyness or deceit emphasized Cist. 727 mala mers, era, haec et callidast, Miles 894, Persa 238, Truc. 409, Casina 754 b; cf. simple merces Miles 1023 pedetemptim tu has scis tractari solitas esse huiusmodi merces. The phrase mala (nequam) bestia, proverbial (Otto p. 55), can hardly be classed in the sermo, as it is used outside of erotic contexts as a term of abuse for both men and women: cf. Thes. L. L. II.1939. 81 sq. In Plautus the term is used of women Bacch. 55 mala tu's bestia (of a meretrix), Cist. 728 imitatur nequam bestiam et damnificam; cf. κακὸν θηρίον Bion IV.13 κακόν ἐντι τὸ θηρίον, Anaxilas 22K. ἐξωλέστερον (ἑταίρα), Men. 488K. μέγιστόν ἐστι θηρίον γ·ινή.

Nequam (nequitia) seems to be the colloquial word for lewdness or wantonness: Bacch. 111-12 Lycurgus mihi quidem videtur posse hic ad nequitiam adducier, ibid. 1180 Vidi ego nequam homines verum te neminem deteriorem, Pomp. 131 Rib. In later Latin cf. Pichon s. v. and Mart. III.69.5 nequam iuvenes facilesque puellae, III.91.4. insignis forma nequitiaque puer, IV.42.4. Frugi, in erotic contexts, is the opposite of nequam, i. e., "continent" cf. Poen. 721 (720) ut frugi sies. quid si animus esse non sinit, with Ussing ad loc., similarly Asin. 857 siccum, frugi, continentem, amantem uxoris maxime, and, in contrast ibid. 859 madidum, nihili, incontinentem atque osorem uxoris suae, Asin. 856 virum frugi rata, Mart. VI.21.8 tam frugi Iuno vellet habere Iovem. In Poen. 178, nequam facere apparently resumes amare velle atque obsequi animo suo (176) and is synonymous with stulte facere Bacch. 57 apud me si quid stulte facere cupias prohibeam; cf. supra 54 quid metuis? ne tibi lectus malitiam (=nequitia?) apud me suadeat. The choice of these expressions instead of stronger terms to express licentious conduct does not originate in an effort to be euphemistic; ideas of thrift and discretion were apparently stronger than the purely moral sense, and it is this sort of commercial morality that accounts for the erotic meaning of frugi, nequam, etc., (cf. supra p. 21, on damna).

The adjective putidus is used like Greek σαπρός of age and impotence: Bacch. 1163 tun, homo putide, amator istac fieri aetate audes, cf. Aristoph. Vesp. 1380-1 νομίσας σ' εἶναι σαπρὸν κοὐδὲν δύνασθαι δρᾶν, Pax 698. With Bacch. 1163 (homo putide) cf. nihili esse ibid. 1188, 1207, Persa 179 certo is quidem nilist qui nil amat; the phrase is an elusive one, but in these examples the idea of lack of virility seems consistently present: cf. Eupolis 221K. ὡς μόλις ἀνήρρησ'· οὐδέν ἐσμεν οἱ σαπροί, also V. Leeuwen on Vesp. 1343.

Fortis in Bacch. 216 sed Bacchis etiam fortis tibi visast and Miles 1106 ecquid fortis visa est, invites comment. According to the ancients

fortis=formosa, so Serv. on Verg. Aen. IV.149 Quidnam fortis est? id
est pulchra, Nonius 306 M. Fortis rursum formosa Plautus Milite (quoting
Miles 1106, cf. supra)[65]. Modern commentators (cf. Brix, Lorenz on
Miles 1106) seem to be justified in regarding fortis as meaning rather
strong, robust, cf. such adjectives as "strapping," "buxom," "husky."
This meaning is more consistent with the transferred meanings of fortis
in Plautus and elsewhere: cf. Trin. 1133 tam fortem familiam, Nonius
p. 306 divitem et copiosam. In Bacch. 216 sq. the comparison to Juno
(217) ni nanctus Venerem essem, hanc Iunonem dicerem seems to
suggest stately proportions for Bacchis. In the Afranius passage
cited by Lorenz (156 Rib.) formosa virgost . . . . . praeterea
fortis, the meaning of the adjective is debatable, but it is certainly not
the same as formosa. Fortis is applicable also to men: Miles 1111
Quid is? ecqui fortis? Lodge submits as possible examples of fortis
"de corporis forma" Rudens 314 and Miles 10; the former seems to be a
possible case, but the latter, where the word is coupled with fortunatus,
is apparently out of the question. There is hardly ground for saying,
as Lodge does, that fortis when used of appearance is sometimes in
malam partem, apart from the fact that a query like Miles 1111 would
doubtless be pronounced with a leer.[66]

Proverbial expressions are comparatively rare in the sermo ama-
torius of Comedy, and popular metaphor is infrequent, and limited to a
few stock figures. Clearly proverbial is the expression Asin. 874 alienum
fundum arat, cf. Theogn. 582 ἀλλοτρίην ἀροῦν ἄρουραν; for numerous
other examples cf. Lid. and Scott on ἄρουρα, Men. Perikeir. 436 γνησίων
παίδων ἐπ' ἀρότῳ, Aristaen. I.19. The transfer of agricultural activities
to res venereae has been a prolific source of imagery, at all times. For
other examples in Plautus cf. Epid. 557 Qui per voluptatem tuam in me
aerumnam obsevisti gravem, Truc. 145 sq. (discussed p. 54). In the
above proverb (Asin. 874), the word to be stressed is fundus.[67]

[65]Lambinus on Bacch. 216 is worth quoting for its own sake. Accepting formosa,
he says: fortassis . . . . . quia formosa mulier quovis viro, quantumvis
robusto ac valido, potentior atque validior est (quotes Anacreon to this effect).

[66]On Persa 846 hicinest, qui fuit quondam fortis Leo (crit. note ad loc.) quotes,
aptly enough, πάλαι ποτ' ἦσαν ἄλκιμοι. If the Greek adage suggested the Plautine
phrase, as seems likely, the Latin here would mean "who has seen better days."

[67]Hortus Miles 194 is wrongly suspected, as it seems, by the older commentators,
but with fundus (ἄρουρα) cf. hortus (κῆπος) Priap. V.4, κῆπος Diog. L. II.116, μανιόκηπος
Anacr., 156. Similarly saltus, Casina 922 saepit veste id qui estis (see Lamb. ad, loc.)
ubi illum *saltum* video obsaeptum, and also Taub. on Curc. 56 pandit saltum (wrongly
suspected). Additional material on this sort of popular metaphor may be found in
Lamb. and Taub. on the Plautine passages mentioned, as also in Thes. L. L. II.627.
55-64 (aro), and Latin lexica s. v. sulcus.

With this passage compare Curc. 35, where the prostitute is compared
to a public highway, as in Callimachus and Propertius; Curc. 35 nemo
ire quemquam publica prohibet via, dum ne per fundum saeptum facias
semitam, cf. Prop. II.23.1 sq. cui fuit indocti fugienda haec semita
vulgi, ipsa petita lacu nunc mihi dulcis aqua est, Callim. ep. 28
(also involving the public well) οὐδὲ κελεύθῳ χαίρω τίς πολλοὺς ὧδε καὶ
ὧδε φέρει, μισῶ καὶ περίφοιτον ἐρώμενον οὐδ' ἀπὸ κρήνης πίνω. Akin to this
is the Pythagorean maxim τὰς λεωφόρους μὴ βαδίζειν cited Diog. Laer.
VIII.1.17 (Cobet), Arist. frg. 192, though this σύμβολον had not appar-
ently a direct erotic application. The πόρνη is called λεωφόρος and
πανδοσία cf. Anacr. 157, Suidas s. v. Μυσάχνη.

Proverbial also is the phrase Curc. 50 iamne fert iugum? The
young girl was popularly compared to an unbroken filly or heifer (πῶλος,
δάμαλις, etc.) cf. Epicr. 9K. ὡς δάμαλις, ὡς παρθένος ὡς πῶλος ἀδμής, A. P.
V.292, Eur. Hipp. 546, with Harry's note, Petr. 25 posse taurum tollere
qui vitulum sustulerit with Greek adj. ἀταύρωτος and Aesch. Ag. 1126
ἄπεχε τῆς βοὸς τὸν ταῦρον, Call. Epigr. 45 τῇ δεκάτῃ ἦλθεν ὁ βοῦς ὑπ' ἄροτρον
ἑκούσιος. Similarly Miles 304 quam mox horsum ad stabulum
iuvenix recipiat se a pabulo, Cist. 308 quamquam vetus cantherius sum,
etiam nunc, ut opinor, adhinnire equolam possum ego hanc, si detur
sola soli; with equola compare Eubul. 84K. πώλους Κύπριδος (of courtesans).
The verb inruo Cas. 891 should perhaps be referred to this form of
comparison, as the noun admissarius Miles 1112 ad equas fuisti scitus
admissarius (cf. Casina 811 edepol ne tu, si equos esses, esses
indomabilis, etc.). This latter form of comparison is employed, grossly,
Miles 1059 nisi huic verri adfertur merces, etc.

In addition to these expressions a few others of a metaphorical
nature occur. Some are mere suggestions: Miles 625 nil amas, umbra's
amantum magis quam amator, Pleusicles, cf. Men. Incert. 554K. ἂν
ἔχῃ φίλου σκιάν. Umor (sucus), exaresco, are used of res venereae: Miles
640 Et ego amoris aliquantum habeo umorisque etiam in corpore,
nequedum exarui ex amoenis rebus et voluptariis, ibid. 787 lautam vis
an quae nondum sit lauta? Sic consucidam. Cf. the opposite siccus,
used of bodily soundness, the result of temperate living (cf. Catull.
23.12, with Friedrich's note) or of austere habits, as in Asin. 857 siccum,
frugi, continentem, Afran. 61 Rib. sicca, sana, sobria, virosa non sum,
cf. Gr. ξηρός Aristoph. Vesp. 1452 ξηροὶ τρόποι. With Miles 641
(exarui) cf. αὐαίνω Aristoph. 612K. ἐνταῦθα δὴ παιδάριον ἐξαυαίνεται ὥστ'
ἔγωγ' ηὐαινόμην θεώμενος. For siccus cf. also Lucil. 239 Marx and
note, Ter. Eun. 318, Priap. 32 B. The comparison of old age to death

is a commonplace in Comedy, as well as elsewhere: Bacch. 1152 quam odiosumst mortem amplexari, Miles 627-8 tam tibi ego videor oppido Acherunticus? Tam capularis? Cf. A. P. V.21 (spoken of the old age of the courtesan) ὡς δὲ τάφον νῦν σε παρερχόμεθα, also Aristoph. Eccl. 996, sq., 1030-1036. Divortium is used of separation from the meretrix (cf. supra p. 18 on duco) Truc. 420; similarly nubo=coeo Cist. 45 numquam ego hanc viduam cubare sivi, nam si haec non nubat, etc., cf. Verg. Ecl. VIII.18 coniugis indigno Nisae deceptus amore, where coniunx =puella amata (γυναῖκα Theocr. VI.26) ibid. 66 where coniunx=iuvenis amatus, Aen. VII.189, cf. also ἄνδρα Theocr. II.3,42, νυμφεύω Eubul. 67K. ὅστις λέχη γὰρ σκότια νυμφεύει λάθρᾳ,[68] Luc. Asin. c. 32, Call. H. in Del. 240, A. P. V.94. Sororcula as applied to the meretrix Cist. 451 germana mea sororcula. repudio te fraterculum, suggests, at least, the later use of soror and frater as verba nequiora cf. Mart. II.4, X.65, XII.20, Petr. 127. A colloquial expression is suggested by Bacch. 1015 ego animo cupido atque oculis indomitis fui, cf. Alciphr. I.6.2 ῥᾴδιος ὢν τὼ ὀφθαλμὼ καὶ πρὸς πᾶσαν ἡδονὴν ἀφροδίσιον κεχυμένος (quasi qui oculos emissicios habeat nec possit irretortis spectare formosas, Bergl.), cf. also A. P. XII.106 ἕν μοι μόνον οἶδε τὸ λίχνον ὄμμα, Μυίσκον ὀρᾶν.

The sermo meretricius, so called, is not devoid of a certain refinement, but, with its numerous euphemisms, it combines a few drastic expressions, apparently colloquial, which, by their candor, seem to claim a somewhat lower origin than most of the terms so far discussed. Paederastic terms will be omitted from this discussion, but some others should be mentioned, as offering a field for interpretation. Cado (Persa 656 libera eris actutum, si crebro cades) is apparently after the Greek πίπτω used as the passive of βάλλω in a drastic erotic sense, cf. Aristoph. Ach. 275 καταβαλόντα καταγιγαρτίσαι ("tumble" Starkie).[69] No other case of cado in this sense occurs, cf. T. L. L. III. 22. 73-5. conturbare (Casina 465) is paederastic; Lamb. ad loc. discusses similar phrases. On inclinabo (Persa 737 inclinabo me cum liberta tua) cf. Leo n. ad loc. "verbum ambigue ductum a κλίνη cf. 765 quin lectis nos actutum commendamus?"; not necessarily in mal. part. here but

---

[68]Cf. also Eub. 67K. καὶ μὴ λαθραίαν κύπριν αἰσχίστην νόσων πασῶν διώκειν and Men. 535K., apparently different versions of a proverbial sentiment against illicit love, cf. Curc. 49 malus clandestinus est amor, damnum est merum.

[69]Professor Prescott, who suggests this possible Greek background, i. e., πεσοῦσα πολλάκις εἰς ἐλευθερίαν πεσῇ, or the like, adds that Plautus' rather pointless verse may be due to the fact that in libertatem cadere was not yet good Latin, cf. T. L. L. s. v. cadere. For the use of πίπτω cf. Alexis 293K. μετὰ ταῦτ' ἀναπεσεῖν ἐκέλευον αὐτὴν παρ' ἐμέ.

cf. Juv. IX.26, X.2.24. Ferio (Bacch. 1173) non metuo ne quid mihi doleat quod ferias, is certainly among verba nequiora, cf. the preceding line 1172 b Malum tibi magnum dabo iam. patiar (Gr. πείσομαι tech.); with ferio cf. τύπτω (χαμαιτύπη), παίω Aristoph. Pax 874, ibid. fr. 967K., κρούω Anec. Bek. 101, Aristoph. Eccl. 990; so κρούειν πέπλον (tunicam pertundere) Eur. Cycl. 328. With tero (Capt. 888) cf. τρίβω used literally Herodas V.61-2 (sc. we will see you) τὰs 'Αχαικὰs κεινὰs ἃs πρῶν ἔθηκas τοῖs σφυροῖσι τρίβοντα: in double entendre, Aristoph. Vespae 1343 w. scholia, Ach. 1149 (ἀνατρίβω); so, in Latin Prop. III. 11.30 Petr. 87. In the phrase caput limare, the origin of the verb is somewhat uncertain, cf. Walde s. v. limax, and supra p. 38; the relation to limus is supported by Poen. 292-3 At vide sis; cum illac numquam limavi caput . . . . . limum petam (ex piscina), ... ut illi et tibi limem caput; but, as the verb is generally used, it seems to be synonymous with copulare, iungere, etc., in the sense of "join" cf. Nonius p. 334. 11 limare etiam dicitur coniungere (cf. ibid. 333 limare exquirere et delenire . . . . . a lima dicitur). Coniungo, copulo, conduplico, etc., are used in phrases with caput and corpus in the sermo: Poen. 343 caput et corpus copulas? Pseud. 1261 corpora conduplicant, Miles 1334 capita inter se nimis nexa hisce habent. Limare caput, to join, "rub" heads=osculari is similar to the above examples. The meaning osculari fits the phrase in every occurrence, cf. T. L. L. III.387, 1-7, Liv. Andr. trag. 28, Caec. 140,Turp. 112 Rib., Plaut. Bacch. frg. XVII. Poen. 292, Merc. 537, Scem. frg. 1, cf. particularly Merc. 537 neuter stupri causa caput limaret, and Cas. 887 inlecebram stupri principio eam savium posco.

Another debatable phrase is caput prurit Bacch. 1193; the context suggests a special erotic application, which Plautine usage hardly confirms. Other phrases with prurio are Amph. 295 dentes pruriunt (anticipation of physical violence), Persa 32a scapulae pruriunt (application as above), Miles 397 dorsus prurit (same force), Poen. 1315 num tibi, adulescens, malae aut dentes pruriunt qui huic es molestus, an malam rem quaeritas? The apparent meaning in this last is "you must lack instinct to warn you of approaching danger, or are you actually looking for trouble?" The verb prurio apparently suggests the retort 1317-18 qur non adhibuisti, dum istaec loquere, tympanum? Nam te cinaedum esse arbitror magis quam virum, cf. Stich. 760-1 lepidam et suavem cantionem aliquam occipito cinaedicam, ubi perpruriscamus usque ex unguiculis. Otto, s. v. dorsus, quotes all four examples, referring also to supercilium; Pseud. 107 supercilium salit, Theocr. III.37. If I have not

inferred too much from cinaedus (Poen. 1318), Poen. 1315 belongs with
the examples under digitus in Otto (p. 116) where we note that an itching
head apparently was taken as a sign of impudicitia; in all Otto's examples
digitus (unus) is emphasized; he therefore concludes that an extreme
sollicitude for coiffures was the sign of the cinaedus, following in this the
(mistaken?) scholiast on Juv. IX. 133 qui digito scalpunt uno caput
cinaedi cum muliebri more componunt caput. For the correct idea cf.
T. L. L. III.390. 20-31: "Plaut. Bacch. 1193 -t prurit (senis libidinosi),
Lucil. 883 -t scabit, pedes legit (Hor. Sat. I.10.71) inde scalpere caput
proverbialiter fere proprium impudicorum". Ussing (after Taub.)
seems mistaken in taking Bacch. 1193 merely of hesitation, uncertainty.
Marx on Lucilius 883 has additional illustrations for Ussing's idea, but
his examples would hardly bear on the Plautine passage. Prurio
Bacch. 1193, Poen. 1315 sq. in double entendre, perprurisco (Stich.
761), are parallel to Greek κνησιῶ: Aristoph. Eccl. 919 Ἤδη τὸν ἀπ'
Ἰονίας τρόπον τάλαινα κνησιᾷς (cf. Blaydes, V. Leeuwen ad loc.).

The lingua duplex is another recurring phrase: Asin. 695 fac proser-
pentem bestiam me duplicem ut habeam linguam, Pseud. 1260 bilingui
manifesto, cf. Aristoph. Ach. 1201 (φίλημα) ἐπιμανδαλωτόν, Thesm.
132 the kiss with bolt shot, i. e., with protruding tongue; the Latin
phrasing is different. The lingua duplex occurs also Persa 299 tamquam
proserpens bestiast bilinguis et scelestus, Poen. 1034 bisulci lingua,
quasi proserpens bestia, of glibness and deceit; on the basis of these
examples we may regard Asin. 695 and Pseud. 1260 as punning pas-
sages. For proserpens bestia cf. also Stich. 724.

Certain common nouns have, or are said to have, indecent meanings,
for the most part in punning passages. So vasa = testes (for the latter
used in a pun cf. Curc. 32) Poen. 862 facio quod manufesti moechi hau
ferme solent. Quid id est? refero vasa salva. Cf. Gr. σκεῦος (medical)
Ael. N. A. 17. 11, Anth. Plan. 243, Taub. on Pseud. IV.7.92, Burmann on
Petr. 24, Lipsius Antiq. lect. lib. I.8; with Poen. 862 cf. Anax. 22K.10-11
εἷς μόνος δ'ἱππεύς τις αὐτῆς τὸν βίον παρείλετο. πάντα τὰ σκεύη γὰρ
ἕλκων ᾤχετ' ἐκ τῆς οἰκίας[70]; cf. also Priapeia LXVIII.24 grandia Dulichii
vasa petisse viri.

A number of false interpretations center about the word peculium,
alleged to mean membrum virile in Plautus. The most plausible case
for this meaning is afforded by Pseud. 1187-1190 quid somniatis? mea

---

[70]I do not find this interpretation suggested for the Anaxilas passage, but it seems
to fit the context; for ἱππεύς cf. Pomp. Prostibulum 155 Rib. quae peditibus nubere
poterant, equites sperant spurcae.

quidem haec habeo omnia meo peculio empta. nempe quod femina summa sustinent (cf. Lamb. Taub. ad loc.). Ussing rejects these lines, on the ground that this meaning for peculium is later than Plautus.[71] The other alleged occurrences are not convincing. In Most. 253 dabo aliquid hodie peculi—tibi, Philematium, the ordinary meaning of peculium is quite adequate, "I will hand over a little something to salt away—to you, Philematium"; the tone of the passage and the entire context forbid obscenity. The adj. peculiaris carries no bad connotation, cf. its use in a sentimental passage Asin. 540- 1 etiam opilio qui pascit, mater, alienas oves aliquam habet peculiarem, qui spem soletur suam, Merc. 524-5 ovem tibi...dabo....peculiarem, Aul. 466 (gallus gallinaceus) anu peculiaris, Persa 201 (ancilla) peculiaris. The verb peculio is used in m. p. Persa 192 scelus tu pueri's atque ob istanc rem ego aliqui te peculiabo, cf. impudicitia in 193, also 284-6, but the suggestion is innate in the context rather than the verb. Cf. also Poen 843 expeculiatus. Even later usage for peculium is doubtful. Petr. 8 peculio prolato, has been absurdly misinterpreted; it can hardly mean anything but pecunia prolata. Auct. Priap. LII.7 pulcre pensilibus peculiati has no significance, as the phrase would be equally pointed with praediti used in place of peculiati. Retia (Ep. 216) has been suspected, but the meaning seems to be as Naudet states it "Retia haec profecto fuere quae secum gerebant lenocinia voluptarii pulchrique corporis (cf. also literal interpretation there suggested); cf. Aristoph. ap. Phrynich. Bekk. p. 18, 22 αἱ τῶν γυναικῶν παγίδες—τοὺς κόσμους καὶ τὰς ἐσθῆτας αἷς χρῶνται αἱ γυναῖκες, Luc. Dial. meretr. 11 τὴν ἑτέραν (ἑταίραν), ἣν Παγίδα ἐπικαλοῦσιν.

In Poen. 690 (hospitium quaeritare) a muscis, the joke, if one is intended, is not apparent. Leo compares Truc. 64, Merc. 361 (Truc. 284), referring also to Lindsay, Archiv. f. L. L. VIII.442 (where Lindsay postulates a slang form ἀμύξεις L. amussis, used sensu obsceno). Lindsay also compares (Class. R. X.333) Hesych. s. v. μύσχον—τὸ ἀνδρεῖον καὶ γυναικεῖον μόριον. These suggestions are hardly convincing, and the passage remains obscure. It is perhaps more to the point to compare the name Μυῖα, used for an Attic hetaira, Luc. Μυίας ἐγκ· 11, and also (perhaps) on a black figured lekuthos in the British Museum (Bechtel,

---

[71]Peculium may perhaps be taken in its ordinary meaning here, thus making it unnecessary to reject the lines. Why not understand sustinent=alunt (merentur)? i. e., peculium quod per stuprum alitur, cf. corpus corpore alere ἐργάζεσθαι τῷ σώματι, etc.; for this meaning of sustinet cf. Poen. prol. 90 quantum hominum terra sustinet (cf. Il. VI.142 εἰ δέ τίς ἐσσι βροτῶν οἳ ἀρούρης καρπὸν ἔδουσιν).

Die attischen Frauennamen p. 94). For the idea in this name Bechtel compares Curc. 499 sq. item genus est lenonium inter homines meo quidem animo ut muscae, culices, cimices pedesque pulicesque: odio et malo et molestiae, bono usui estis nulli. Cf. Bechtel, loc. cit., where other similar names are mentioned.

For the pun on concha Rudens 702 sq. cf. Bechtel op. cit. p. 91. So Jahn (Bericht d. sächs. Ges. 1853 p. 18). Ussing contra.

A possible double entendre is contained in Bacch. 73 sq. ah nimium ferus es. †Mihi sum. †Malacissandus es. Equidem tibi do hanc operam. †Ah, nimium pretiosa's operaria. Ferus may translate ὠμός, used of temperament Xen. Anab. II-6-12 χαλεπὸς καὶ ὠμός, Mem. III.16, Luc. Dial. meretr. IV.4, etc.; in a literal sense, of leather, Xen. Anab. IV.7.22 γέρρα δασειῶν βοῶν ὠμοβόεια; cf. ὠμοδέψητος Suidas s. v. Σεμίραμις, ὠμοβύρσος Plut. Crass. 25. With malacissandus cf. μαλάσσω figuratively = mollio Eur. Or. 1201, Alc. 771; of working leather Schol. Plat. Conv. p. 221 E βυρσοδέψας τοὺς τὰς βύρσας ἐργαζαμένους καὶ μαλάττοντας, cf. δερματομαλάκτης Phot. s. v. σκυτοδέψης; of administering a beating Aristoph. Eq. 388. Operaria, opera, etc., suggest the δημιουργός. For the pun cf. lex. s. v. δέφω.

Less ambiguous than the foregoing are Pseud. 24 scando (ἀναβαίνω), Men. Perikeir. 234, Aristoph. 329K., dirumpo Cas. 326, cf. διαμηρίζω Aristoph. Aves 669, 706, 1254, moveri (= crisso) Asin. 788, Catull. XV.11, cf. κινῶ, βινῶ Aristoph. Nubes 1103, 1371, Pax 867, 903, Lysis. 227, etc. Pernoctare, not in itself particularly suggestive (cf. Ter. Hec. 539) occurs in the coarse combination Truc. 278 cumque ea noctem in stramentis pernoctare perpetim, cf. Aristoph. Nubes 1069 ἐν τοῖς στρώμασιν τὴν νύκτα παννυχίζειν, ibid. fr. 695K. The Greek verb is frequent in an erotic sense; cf. also the name Παννυχίς Luc. Dial. meretr. IX (Bechtel op. cit. p. 125).

III

In discussing what I have termed the sermo meretricius, I have been concerned with the realistic and colloquial elements of the sermo amatorius in Comedy. Under this head I have included some metaphors and similes which seemed distinctly popular or proverbial. There remain to be considered the more elaborate metaphor and simile of Comedy, that which shows most points of contact with poetry, and would appear more distinctly literary in origin. Much, in fact, of this imagery, was a manifest legacy from the lyric and tragic poets, and was destined to be handed down, in turn, to Elegy. Such imagery is naturally rather familiar, and many of these commonplaces have already been discussed by Leo, Hoelzer, and others. Some of this material I have felt obliged to include, because of its relation to other topics, or in the interest of completeness. My intention has been to include all that has special significance in regard to the erotic diction of Comedy, and to omit such passages as contribute nothing from this point of view.

The conventional Cupido (Amor), with his wings, bow and arrows, his paramount power, and his blind vindictiveness, pervades Comedy (cf. Hoelzer p. 10 sq.). The ingenuity of the Comic poets makes him a torturer: Cist. 203 sq. credo ego amorem primum apud homines carnuficinam commentum (Hoelzer p. 55-6); his functions as carnufex are described in the same context: cf. cruciabilitatibus animi (205) and 206 sq. iactor, crucior, agitor, stimulor, vorsor in amoris rota, etc.; cf. also (on carnuficina) Capt. 597 pix atra agitet apud carnuficem tuoque capiti inluceat. Incidentally Cupido is a εὑρέτης, i. e., (amorem) primum apud homines carnuficinam commentum; for the εὑρήματα in general cf. Leo Plaut. Forsch.[2] 151 sq. The comparison versor in amoris rota (Cist. 207) is apparently Greek: cf. for the literal idea Aristoph. Plutus 875-6 ἐπὶ τοῦ τροχοῦ γὰρ δεῖ σ' ἐκεῖ στρεβλούμενον εἰπεῖν ἃ πεπανούργηκας, Lysis. 845-6 (a debased comparison), Ranae 615 sq. For στρέβλη used figuratively cf. Diphil. 88K. λύπας, μερίμνας, ἀρπαγάς, στρέβλας. Stimulor (Cist. 207) suggests the κέντρον; cf. also Bacch. 1159 cor stimulo foditur, and stimulatrix, a temptress, Most. 203-219. For Gr. κέντρον cf. A. P. V.220 καὶ τὸ θαλυκρὸν κεῖνο κατημβλύνθη κέντρον ἐρωμανίης, ibid. V.247 κεντρομανὲς δ' ἄγκιστρον ἔφυ στόμα, cf. also Eur.Hipp.39 κέντροις ἔρωτος, Plat. Republ. 573 A, (other examples in Hoelzer p. 55). Similarly used is ἀκίς Timoth. 2K. ἔρως . . . . . ἡ φρενῶν ἀκίς, A. P. XII.76 πόθων ἀκίδες. The idea in such comparisons is sometimes a sting: cf. Theocr. XIX, where Cupid and the bee are com-

48 STUDIES IN THE DICTION OF THE

pared.[72] A weaker comparison is involved in the verb κνίζω: Luc. Dial. meretr. X.4 κέκνισται γὰρ κἀκεῖνος τῆς Νεβρίδος, Theocr. IV.59.[73]

Love is apparently personified as a poisoner Cist. 298 video ego te Amoris valde tactum toxico[74]; the idea is probably a philtre: cf. Eur. Hipp. 509 ἐστιν... φίλτρα μοι θελκτήρια ἔρωτος, Alciph. I.37.5 ἀλλ' ἀμφιβάλλειν εἴωθε τὰ φίλτρα καὶ ἀποσκήπτειν εἰς ὄλεθρον. Love is a malignant caupo Trin. 673 insanum malumst hospitio devorti ad Cupidinem, a comparison not paralleled in Greek, so far as I can discover. The speed of love is compared to the flight of a missile from a ballista Trin. 668 itast amor ballista ut iacitur: nil sic celerest neque volat; possibly a Latin comparison, although the swiftness of love is a Greek common-place (cf. Hoelzer p. 14). We have a rain of love Most. 142, in a simile perhaps suggested by the Zeus and Danae myth, so familiar in Greek and Latin erotic poetry[76]; love as a stain Poen. 198 inest amoris macula huic homini in pectore, cf. eluere (amorem) Prop. III.24.10, and love as a disease Cist. 71, etc. (Hoelzer pp. 43-4). The familiar bow and arrows occur Persa 25 sagitta Cupido cor meum transfixit (cf. Hoelzer p. 55). Less trite is the spike of Love Asin. 156 fixus clavo Cupidinis, on which compare Leo Plaut. Forsch.[2] p. 154 n. 4. Love is referred to as a sauce Casina 220 sq., and the loved one is the food of the lover Bacch. 23, Merc. 744, Curc. 186.

The combination of joy and pain in love which the Greek expressed by γλυκύπικρον is developed in Latin by the gall and honey figure. The Latin passages for this dulce (mel) and amarum (fel) oxymoron, with adequate Greek comparisons, are cited by Hoelzer p. 41.

The heart is regularly the seat of the affections: Miles 1088 cor . . . . . saliat (cor is perhaps merely physical here, and the

[73]For aculeus, outside of an erotic context, cf. Trin. 1000 iam dudum meum ille pectus pungit aculeus, Bacch. 63 aculeata. For stimulus Truc. 853 ne ista stimulum longum habet.

[73]Apropos of the tortures of love, the fires of love are as trite a figure in Comedy as elsewhere, cf. Asin. 919 ex amore tantum est homini incendium, Merc. 590 (cf. Trin. 675 facis incendium, Lamb., Prescott Class. Phil. V.103-4), Ter. And. 308, Haut. 367. So πῦρ A. P. V.50 πῦρ δὲ φέρειν κύπριδος οὐ δύναμαι, ibid. V.6 ὁ μὲν ἀρσενικῷ θέρεται πυρί. The loved one is sometimes regarded as the flame: Eun. 85 accede ad ignem hunc, iam calesces plus satis. The lover burns with passion: Merc. 600 pectus ardet, ibid. 591. So καίω A. P. V.5 ἄμφω καιόμεθα, Alciphron I.13 φλέγομαι, A. P. V.10 καταφλέγω, Aristoph. Lysis. 221 ἐπιτύφομαι.

[74]For the personification cf. ibid. 300 cave sis cum Amore tu umquam bellum sumpseris. On amor vs. Amor in Elegy cf. Pichon p. 66.

[75]Cf. also στάζω Eur. Hipp. 525 sq. Ἔρως, Ἔρως, ὁ κατ' ὀμμάτων στάζεις πόθον, A. P. V.13.

throb the actual result of excitement: cf. T. L. L. IV. 931. 45-50), Merc. 204, Bacch. 1159 (cf. T. L. L. IV.932. 5 sq., 932. 40 sq., 934. 31 sq.). From this idea develop the stereotyped phrases amat corde Truc. 177, cordist Cist. 109, Ter. Phorm. 800, and the noun cordolium (heartache) Cist. 65. Pectus is synonymous with cor, and about equally common as the seat of the affections, cf. Bacch. 628 multa mala mi in pectore nunc atque acerba eveniunt, Epid. 555, Merc. 590, 600, Most. 164, Rud. 221. It is not, however, found in stereotyped phrases, excepting as the seat of reason (cf. cor Miles 786, Cist. 509, etc., T. L. L. IV.935.79 sq.) in the phrase pectus qui sapiat Bacch. 659, Miles 786. καρδία is used frequently as the seat of the affections: Aristoph. Ranae 54 πόθος τὴν καρδίαν ἐπάταξε, A. P. V. 235 καὶ τρομέω κραδίη τε βυθῷ πελεμίζεται οἴστρῳ, A. P. V.10 ἐπ' ἐμὴν ἰοβολεῖ κραδίην ('Ἔρως), Aristaen. II.5 πυκνὰ παλλομένης ἐφάπτομαι τῆς καρδίας καὶ δεινῶς ἐκπηδᾷ καὶ φλέγεσθαί μοι δοκεῖ, A. P. XII.49. Love is responsible not only for the heart throbs but for pallor and emaciation (Hoelzer pp. 48, 55). The unhappy lover languishes and pines away: Ter. Ad. 603, cor contabescit Merc. 205, Pseud. 21, cf. τήκομαι A. P. V.210 τήκομαι ὡς κηρὸς πὰρ πυρὶ κάλλος ὁρῶν, ibid. V.259, ἔρωτι κατατετηκώς Eubulus 104K. and τρύχομαι Aristoph. Pax 989 οἱ σου τρυχόμεθα ἤδη τρία καὶ δέκα ἔτη (cf. Blaydes, critical note and commentary ad locum, and compare κνίζω (κέκνισται) etc., p. 48). For Latin references on pallor, etc., cf. Hoelzer p. 48 and compare A. P. V.242 ὡς εἶδον Μελίτην ὤχρος μ'ἔλε, A. P. V.259, Ach. Tat. I.8. ὡς οὖν ταῦτ' ἤκουσεν ὁ Κλεινίας ὠχρίασεν.

The surge or tide of love is suggested Asin. 158 quam magis te in altum capessis tam aestus te in portum refert. Cf. Catull. 68.107. So also κῦμα A. P. V.235 ψυχῆς πνιγομένης κύματι κυπριδίῳ, A. P.V.190 κῦμα τὸ πικρὸν Ἔρωτος. Cf. fluctuat Merc. 890 quid si mi animus fluctuat (Hoelzer p. 50), aestuo Catull. 25. 12 aestues velut . . . . . magno deprensa navis in mari, Varro Men. 204 (T. L. L. I.1113. 77 sq.), Mart. IX.22.11 aestuet ut nostro madidus conviva ministro. The paths of love figure in Trin. 667 atque ipse Amoris teneo omnis vias, Persa 1ff. qui amans egens ingressus est princeps in Amoris vias superavit aerumnis suis aerumnas Herculi. The idea in the two passages is different; in Persa 1, the thought is the course of trials and tribulations which love imposes on the needy lover; in Trin. 667 viae=artes, i. e., the wiles of love; cf. Prop. I.1.17 in me tardus Amor non ullas cogitat artes, nec meminit notas ut prius ire vias. Leo compares aptly enough (Pl. F.² p. 154) Plato Symposium 203 D, the description of Love as the son of Πόρος, hence πόριμος, ἀεί τινας πλέκων μηχανάς; as for his statement

50 STUDIES IN THE DICTION OF THE

(Gött. Gel. Anz. 1898, 748) "viae amoris aus dem Symposium in die Erotik gekommen wird" cf. the very just criticism of Rothstein, Philologus 59 p. 457 and note 1, where the danger of positing sources on slight resemblances is pointed out.[76]

Comparisons of love and war are equally frequent in both Greek and Latin: Persa 24 saucius factus sum in Veneris proelio, is used of himself by a disheartened lover; cf. A. P. XII.100.4 ἔτρωσε. The service of the meretrix is called militia Truc. 230 ubi nil det, pro infrequenti eum mittat militia domum (cf. Lamb., Taub., ad loc.). Cf. Horace Odes 3.26.2 militavi non sine gloria, Persa 231-2 at confidentia illa militia militatur multo magis quam pondere, Caec. 67 Rib., militia Prop. I.6.30. Lovers' quarrels are bellum, and reconciliation pax: Ter. Eun. 52 ubi pati non poteris, quom nemo expetet infecta pace ultro ad eum venies, ibid. 61 (vitia amoris) indutiae bellum pax rursum. Cf. σπονδαί Aristaen. II.14 ὑμᾶς ἐχώριζον ἀπ' ἀλλήλων · ἄσπονδος μάχη καὶ ἀδιάλλακτος ἔρις, ibid. II.2 τοίνυν καὶ προσάξω τὸν νέον πλουσίως ἐπικηρυκευόμενον δι' ἐμοῦ· τὸ γὰρ πρὸς ἑταίρας κηρύκειον κτλ., Lucian Dial. meretr. XII.5 ἤδη καὶ Πυθιὰς μεθ' ἡμῶν· ἄξιον γὰρ αὐτὴν παρεῖναι ταῖς σπονδαῖς (libations and truce). Seduction is governed by military tactics: Curc. 56 qui volt cubare pandit saltum saviis (for literal idea cf. Casina 887 inlecebram stupri principio savium posco, and examples under caput limare p. 43). Cf. πορθῶ A. P. V.294 ναὶ τάχα πορθήσω τείχεα παρθενίης, ibid. V.58, ἐξαλαπάζω V.294 οὔπω δ' ἐξαλάπαξα φίλης πύργωμα κορείης ἀλλ' ἔτ' ἀδηρίτῳ σφίγγεται ἀμβολίῃ. Cf. Truc. 169 sq. amator similist oppidi hostilis. †Quo argumento (st)? †Quam primum expugnari potis (est), tam id optumumst amicae. For another form of comparison cf. νυκτομαχῶ Aristaen. I.10 ὁ δὲ οὖν τῇ παρθένῳ βραχέα νυκτομαχήσας ἐρωτικῶς τό γε λοιπὸν εἰρηναίων ἀπέλαυεν ἡδονῶν. So in Latin elegy, arma Prop. I.3.16, bella ibid. III.8.32.

Plautus sometimes employs legal phraseology of the lover who is bound hand and foot. Instead of the simple servus, servio (δουλεύω) the lover is said to be addictus: Bacch. 1205 ducite nos quolibet tamquam quidem addictos. Sometimes it is merely that he is under bonds: Bacch. 180 ita me vadatum amore vinctumque attines, Curc. 162 ubi tu's qui me convadatu's Veneriis vadimoniis. This, at least, appears to be a

[76]Greek ὁδός, κέλευθος, δόλιχος, are also used figuratively, but with the same definite suggestion found in such phrases as εἰς τέλος ἔρχεσθαι, ἀνύω, ἔργον ἔρωτος ἀνῦσαι. Cf. ὁδός Ach. Tat. I.9.7 πῶς ἂν τύχοιμι τῆς ἐρωμένης; οὐκ οἶδα γὰρ τοὺς ὁδούς, Longus, I, 17 ἀπέδραμε ζητῶν ἄλλην ὁδὸν ἔρωτος, A. P. V.275 Ὡς δὲ κελεύθου ἥμισυ κυπριδίης ἥνυσον ἀσπασίως, ibid. V.55 ἥνυσεν ἀκλινέως τὸν κύπριδος δόλιχον. With these expressions compare Prop. II.33.22 noctibus his vacui ter faciamus iter. The Plautine use of viae=artes appears Prop. I.1.18. Prop. I.8.30 is perhaps midway between the two.

SERMO AMATORIUS IN ROMAN COMEDY

characteristically Roman turn of phrase, though merely a substitute for
the familiar vincula amoris, as Bacch. 180 (supra) suggests, cf. also
Trin. 658 vi veneris vinctus, Ter. And. 561, Hec. 168. On the vincula
amoris cf. Leo Gött. G. A. 1898 pp. 748-9 and Rothstein Philologus 59
pp. 454-5.

Another common class of figures is taken from the palaestra. Erotic
figures from this source are favored in Greek, and occur as frequently
as military comparisons in Latin. For example, in the Fotis episode,
Apuleius Metam. 2. 17, Lucian (Asinus c. 8 p. 576) uses palaestra
figures where Apuleius has figures drawn from warfare; the girl in the
Ὄνος is appropriately named Παλαίστρα and this name turns up else-
where also (Bechtel Attische Frauennamen p. 124). The prevalence
of such comparisons in Greek may be explained by the fact that the
wrestling schools were actually notorious as sources of corruption for
young boys (cf. Aristoph. Nubes 973 sq., Becker Charikles (Berlin 1877)
II.p. 260 sq.), and by the ease with which the various athletic exercises
suggested erotic comparisons. It seems probable, then, that the elab-
orate comparison Bacch. 66 sq. was found in much the same form in the
Greek original. In Plautus it stands as follows: Bacch. 66-72 penetrem
me huius modi in palaestram ubi damnis desudascitur? Ubi pro disco
damnum capiam, pro cursura dedecus . . . . . ubi ego capiam
pro machaera turturem, (ubique imponat in manum alius mihi pro
cestu cantharum:) pro galea scaphium, pro insigni sit corolla plectilis,
pro hasta talos, pro lorica malacum capiam pallium: ubi mi pro equo
lectus detur, scortum pro scuto accubet? Palaestra is the key word
that suggests the detailed simile. There is some evidence of free hand-
ling by the Latin poet. The antitheses pro disco damnum, pro cursura
dedecus, containing, as they do, the favorite Latin (and Plautine) com-
bination damnum dedecus, seem to show Plautine originality, partly
for the sake of alliteration, in the second members; but for discus and
cursura in such comparisons cf. A. P. V.19 νῦν δὲ καλοῦμαι θηλυμανὴς, καὶ
νῦν δίσκος ἐμοὶ κρόταλον, ibid. V.55 ἤνυσεν ἀκλινέως τὴν κύπριδος δόλιχον.
Scortum pro scuto (72) is likewise Plautine alliteration. The other
pairs show, for the most part, neat contrasts between the nouns opposed
to one another, and the implied verbs fit either member; for example
ἐπιβαίνω, ἀναβαίνω (ascendere) is equally applicable to ἵππος (equos) or
κλίνη (lectus). This does not hold good of one pair, i. e., machaera,
turturem, and the line has been questioned for this reason. It should
be remembered that we are considering a series of contrasts between the
accoutrements of the athlete or soldier, and the paraphernalia of the

reveler; in this series turtur serves as well as the next thing for a representative dainty, cf. Most. 46. Whether it be taken as a live pet (Lamb.) or a part of the menu, there seems to be a particular erotic significance to the dove: cf. Artem. II.20 Φάσσαι δὲ καὶ περιστεραὶ γυναῖκας σημαίνουσι. φάσσαι μὲν πάντως πορνικάς. περιστεραὶ δὲ ἐστιν ὅτε καὶ κοσμίας καὶ οἰκοδεσποίνας, Photius Lex. τρυγών· τὸ ζῷον· παίζεται δὲ εἰς τὴν τῶν γυναικῶν συνουσίαν, Hesychius τρυγών· ἰχθύς θαλάσσιος . . . . . καὶ ὄρνις καὶ ἡ τῶν γυναικῶν μῖξις. καὶ σύντροφος.[77] These passages go to show that the dove, as the bird of Aphrodite, was not without an esoteric significance for the initiate. In the very similar passage Aristoph. Ach. 1118-1142 ΛΑΜ.—παῖ. παῖ καθελών μοι τὸ δόρυ δεῦρ' ἔξω φέρε. ΔΙΚ. παῖ παῖ, σὺ δ' ἀφελὼν δεῦρο τὴν χορδὴν φέρε κτλ. most of the contrasts are as startling as machaera turturem. For comparisons of a more exact type cf. Bacch. 70 pro galea scaphium with Antiph. 109K. τὸ μὲν ἐφίππιον στρῶμ' ἐστὶν ἡμῖν, ὁ δὲ καλὸς πῖλος κάδος and Aristoph. Thesm. 633, Lysis. 751 with Van Leeuwen's note ad loc. The Bacchides passage need contain nothing more than the surface meanings. For a somewhat similar Latin comparison cf. Ovid Her. III.117 tutius est iacuisse toro, tenuisse puellam—quam manibus clupeos et acutae cuspidis hastam et galeam pressa sustinuisse coma (Leo Plaut. Forsch.[2] p. 55). Figures from the gymnasium are also current: cf. the verb exercere Amph. 288 haec nox scita est exercendo scorto conducto (male), Bacch. 429 saliendo sese exercebant magis quam scorto aut saviis, cf. Eup. 158K. οὐκ' οἴκαδ' ἐλθὼν τὴν σεαυτοῦ γυμνάσεις δάμαρτα, and Gymnasium as the name of a meretrix Plaut. Cist. (Bechtel Die attische Frauennamen p. 124). The wrestling figure is a common one in Greek: Aristoph. Pax 896 ἐπὶ γῆς παλαίειν, Ach. 275 μέσην λαβόντ' ἄραντα καταβαλόντα κτλ. Ach. Tat. V.3 παλαίων πάλην 'Αφροδισίαν, Longus III.19 Χλόη δὲ συμπαλαίουσα σοὶ ταύτην τὴν πάλην, A. P. XII.206 παίδων

[77]Buecheler A. L. L. II.116 cites these three passages (the Artemidorus passages had already been compared by Gruter) and adds (from Gruter?) Isidore glosses p. 697. 14 Vulc. turturilla ita dictus locus in quo corruptelae fiebant, quod ibi turturi opera daretur i. panem. Adopting the emendation penem, B. concludes that turtur here = penis (following Douza, Gruter). As additional support B., following Gruter, cites Sen. ep. 96 where turturillae is an epithet for weaklings. B. refers also to the anonymous glossarium eroticum, Paris, 1826. I am inclined to think that Gruter, who was in possession of practically all of Buecheler's material, and some additional passages (cf. Taub. on Bacch. 68) was correct in his doubt "hoc scio, non inepte molliorem sensum tueri Douzam: nisi tam pudentis videretur iste Pistoclerus verecundiae, ut tale quid usurpare metuerit. Certe tota narratione nihil promit spurci, nihil ambigui." The Greek contributes nothing toward the proposed meaning for turtur (τρυγών) and the Latin parallels are not convincing.

δ' ἡ πάλη ἔσθ' ἑτέρα, ibid. XII.90. Cf. Apuleius II.17 his et huius modi conluctationibus. For παλαίστρα in this sense cf. A. P. V.259 κ' ἐν μὲν παννυχίησιν ὁμιλήσασα παλαίστραις, Theocr. Id. VII.125, Antiph. 332K. Similarly Mart. X.55.4 idem post opus et suas palaestras. On Phormio 484 Eccum ab sua palaestra exit foras Dziatzko-Hauler compare Bacch. 66 and Mart. X.55.4. To these we may add Mart. IV.55 aut libidinosae Ledaeas Lacedaemonos palaestras. In all these cases the word is, apparently, somewhat more drastic than in the Phormio passage.

The ingenuity of the Comic poets was largely occupied with inventing new comparisons for the meretrix and her rapacity. The home of the courtesan is a mire or morass: Bacch. 384 ut eum ex lutulento caeno propere hinc eliciat foras; in Bacch. 368 her gates are the gates of an upper world Hell and those who enter there all hope abandon of being thrifty, pandite atque aperite propere ianuam hanc Orci. The meretrix herself has the prescience of a bird of carrion in anticipating spoils: Truc. 337 quasi volturii triduo prius praedivinant quo die essuri sient, cf. Epicr. 28K. πεπονθέναι δὲ ταὐτά μοι δοκεῖ τοῖς ἀετοῖς· οὗτοι γὰρ ὅταν ὦσιν νέοι ἐκ τῶν ὀρῶν πρόβατ' ἐσθίουσι καὶ λαγὼς μετέωρ' ἀναρπάζοντες ὑπὸ τῆς ἰσχύος κτλ. Again, she is a leech, or, less probably, a vampire, Bacch. 372 apage istas a me sorores quae hominum sorbent sanguinem, Curc. 152 quae mihi misero amanti ebibit sanguinem, but compare Epid. 188 me convortam in hirudinem atque eorum exsugebo sanguinem; for the leech idea cf. Theocr. Id. II.55.6 αἰαῖ ἔρως ἀνιηρέ, τί μευ μέλαν ἐκ χροὸς αἷμα ἐμφὺς ὡς λιμνᾶτις ἅπαν ἐκ βδέλλα πέπωκας; cf. also A. P. V.151 αἵματος ἀνδρῶν σίφωνες. The destructive effect of the courtesan is compared to that of a tempest: Most. 162 haec illa'st tempestas mea mihi quae modestiam omnem detexit, tectus qua fui; she is a torrent: Bacch. 85 rapidus fluvius est hic: non hac temere transiri potest, and presents to her greed are like water running into the sea: Truc. 565 nam hoc in mare abit misereque perit sine bona omni gratia, Asin. 135 nam mare haud est mare: vos mare acerrimum: nam in mari repperi, hic elavi bonis. In the same vein are comparisons to an eddy or whirlpool: cf. Hoelzer p. 72, Leo Plaut. Forsch.[2] p. 150, and note 3, Bacch. 470-1 meretricem indigne deperit . . . . . atque acerrume aestuosam: absorbet ubi quemque attigit, of doors of meretrix Truc. 350, cf. Alciph. I.6.3, Anaxilas 22K. ἡ δὲ Φρύνη τὴν χάρυβδιν οὐχὶ πόρρω που ποιεῖ τὸν δὲ ναύκληρον λαβοῦσα καταπέπωκ·' αὐτῷ σκάφει. The Anaxilas fragment includes also comparisons of the courtesan to Scylla, Sphinx, and Chimaera; cf. the Horatian "triformi Chimaera" and Bechtel,

Attische Frauennamen p. 83. Most of the other similes used in Plautus
of the meretrix could probably have been paralleled in Greek Comedy,
if the remains were more extensive.

There is more prose than poetry about those figures in which the
meretrix is likened to a custom house officer, portitor, or a tax collector,
publicanus (τελώνης). The former comparison is suggested Asin. 159
tam aestus te in portum refert. †Ego pol istum portitorem[78] privabo
portorio, and developed ibid. 241 portitorum simillimae sunt ianuae
lenoniae: si adfers, tum patent: si non est quod des, aedes non patent.
For the general idea compare Aristophon 3K. αἱ τῶν ἑταιρῶν γὰρ διοπετεῖς
οἰκίαι γεγόνασιν ἄβατοι τοῖς ἔχουσι μηδὲ ἕν. The Plautine simile may
perhaps be fixed as Greek by comparison with Eupolis 48K. ἐλλιμένιον
δοῦναι πρὶν εἰσβῆναι σε δεῖ. Kock suggests that this passage has to do
with admission to a lupanar, but fails to compare it directly with the
Asinaria passage.

The extended simile Truc. 141 sq. tu te Veneris publicum aut Amoris
alia lege habere posse postulas, etc., can hardly be claimed as definitely
Latin, or Greek, on existing evidence, though I am inclined to believe it
Plautine in the main. The possible Greek background for such words as
publicanus (τελώνης), publicum (τελωνία) is obvious, but hardly con-
tributes anything definite. On the other hand line 144 Nam advorsum
legem meam ob meam scripturam pecudem cepit, seems to require the
definite Latin background supplied by Varro R.R.II.1.16 ad publica-
num profitentur, ne, si inscriptum pecus paverint, lege censoria com-
mittant. On the basis of this passage Ussing construes, "Contra legem,
ait Diniarchus, Phronesium meum pecus cepit quasi non scriptum esset
aut quasi scriptura non soluta esset"; this seems far more likely than "per-
egrinum pecus in id quod mihi adscriptum est, recepit" (Taub.). I take
the phrase cepit pecudem to mean, she has confiscated my property,"closed
me out," cf. dedistis otium (138), negotium abstulistis (139). For res
pecuaria (147), aratiuncula (148), aratio (149) cf. Cic. Tull. 19 deinde
iste pater familias Asiaticus beatus, novus arator et idem pecuarius,
Verr. II.188 qui sit iste Verrucius, mercator . . . . . an arator
an pecuarius, Deiot. 27 agricola et pecuarius. With reference to
Veneris publicum habere (141-2), habuit publicum (143), I do not find
that δημόσιον = τελωνία; the Latin phrase corpus publicare should be

---

[78]Cf. Nonius p. 24, 13 portitores dicuntur telonarii qui portum obsidentes omnia
sciscitentur, ut ex eo vectigal accipiant.

quoted in connection with publicum habere.[79] Apparently the only
things to suggest Greek influence on this passage are the punning on
aro (aratiuncula) and the comparison between girl and boy love (150
sq.), which was rather a Greek than a Latin commonplace, at least in
Plautus' time.

There is clearer evidence of a Greek background for the somewhat
obscure lines beginning Mercator 518 possin tu, sei ussus venerit, sub-
temen tenue nere.   The phrase subtemen tenue is the Greek στήμων
ἐξεσμένος (ἰσχνός, ἀραιός) cf. Blümner Technologie² I.p. 128.   For the
full phrase subtemen tenue nere cf. Hom. Batrach. 181 (Blümner I.142
n. 2). πέπλον . . . . . ὃν ἐξύφηνα καμοῦσα ἐκ ῥοδάνης λεπτῆς
καὶ στήμονα λεπτὸν ἔνησα. For the opposite, i. e., the filum (subte-
men) crassum, the Greek is στήμων πυκνός, στερεός (Blümner loc.
cit.), cf. Merc. 519 scio te uberius posse nere. Uberius nere is apparently
a translation of πυκνότερον νεῖν, (νήθειν). The difficulty of the lines
consists in the fact that the poets seem to be developing some
flagitious jest, as is made almost certain by 523 operam accusari non
sinam meam. None, however, of the words involved, in Greek or
Latin, save only operam (523) seems to be used elsewhere in erotic
meanings, and it may be that the whole passage simply leads up to
ovis (524): ovem tibi millam dabo, natam annos sexaginta. Ovis as a
simile for the senex amator (Leo Plaut. Forsch.² p. 156) occurs of the
two old men Bacch. 1121 sq., and, in this passage, of the old dotard
who is to be sheared or exploited, cf. the Greek use of πρόβατα for "good
for nothings" (Lamb.). The expression ovis peculiaris (Merc. 524)
is used sentimentally of the one true lover of the meretrix, Asin. 540-1
etiam opilio qui pascit, mater, alienas ovis aliquam habet peculiarem
qui spem soletur suam. The lover is referred to as a dog, Poen. 1234
sq. etiam me meae latrant canes (cf. T. L. L. III.256.16), but not in
compliment (T. L. L. III.258.21 sq.).

Figures from hunting, fowling, and fishing, as parallel to the arts
of the meretrix, are very frequent, and are developed at unusual length.
Hoelzer (p. 73) has noted most of the passages for Comedy, and I need
add only a few more or less significant Greek parallels to what he has
collected. For piscatura cf. A. P. V.67 κάλλος ἄνευ χαρίτων τέρπει
μόνον, οὐ κατέχει δὲ ὡς ἄτερ ἀγκίστρου νηχόμενον δέλεαρ (esca), Nicophon 4K.,
Crat. 216K., where Kock refers to As. 221. Aristaen. I.17 συχνότερον οὖν
τὸ δέλεαρ αὐτῇ προσακτέον, κἂν αὖθις τὸ ἄγκιστρον καταπίῃ πάλιν ἀσπαλ-

ιεύσω. Cf. Truc. 34 sq., Asir. 178. For piscatus="catch," of the lover ensnared, cf. Bacch. 102 and Aristaen. I.7 ἑτέρα πολλῷ βελτίων τῆς προτέρας ἐμπέπτωκεν ἄγρα. For venatura Miles 990 viden tu illam oculis venaturam facere, cf. A. P. V.231 πάντοθεν ἀγρεύεις τλήμονας ἠιθέους, Aristaen. II.2 μὴ τρόπος ἀπειθὴς ἀποσοβήσῃ ὃν εὖ μάλα τεθήρακεν ἡ μορφή, A. P. V.193, XII.99. For aucupium (viscus, retia, etc.) Asin. 215 sq., Bacch. 50, 1158 (on rete cf. also Leo Plaut. Forsch.[2] p. 149), and Truc. 37 (fish nets), Epid. 216, and Amphis 23K. (discussed p. 45), A. P. V.100 θηρευτὴν ὄμμασιν ἰξὸν ἔχων, ibid. V.56 (γλῆναι) σπλάγχνων ἡμετέρων δίκτυα καὶ παγίδες, ibid. V.96. To be mentioned in the same connection are the Latin verbs capio and ·capto: Epid. 215, Ter. Hec. 73, particularly the use of captus (amore) Andria 82, cf. A. P. XII.99 Ἠγρεύθην ὑπ' Ἔρωτος.

IV

I have yet to consider a few terms that have to do with the senti-
mental side of the sermo amatorius in Comedy, and are, incidentally,
of considerable importance in the interpretation of numerous passages
in Elegy. It has already been remarked that what little sentiment
appears in Comedy is necessarily associated with the meretricious rela-
tionship. The Comic poets were obliged to look, for this sort of interest,
to those more lasting attachments between the meretrix and a single
lover which differed from the ordinary ὁμιλίαι (consuetudines) in per-
manence, and in the presence of real affection on both sides. However
rare such ideal relationships may have been in fact, they are fairly
numerous in Plautus and Terence, and in Greek Comedy as represented
by Lucian, Alciphron, and Aristaenetus. The best examples in Plautus
are Selenium and Alcesimarchus (Cist.), Philematium and Philolaches
(Most.). Selenium expresses her passion for her lover Cist. 76 sq.
misera maceror quom illum unum mi exoptavi, quicum aetatem degerem.
Philematium is warned against a similar attachment Most. 195-6 stulta's
plane quae illum tibi aeternum putes fore amicum et benevolentem.
Moneo ego te: te ille deseret aetate et satietate.[80] In such a relation
the girl was rated as pudica if she remained faithful to one lover: Cist.
88 nec pudicitiam imminuit meam mihi alius quisquam, Miles 508-9
quod concubinam erilem insimulare ausus es probri pudicam, cf.
σώφρων Men. Epitrep. 520. Beside the ties of intimacy and affec-
tion (consuetudo), (cf. p. 17), there were oaths to bind the lovers
together: Men. Samia 279 ὅρκος πόθος χρόνος συνήθει' οἷς ἐδουλούμην ἐγώ,
Ter. And. 277 sq. adeon me ignavom putas, adeon porro ingratum aut
inhumanum aut ferum, ut neque me consuetudo neque pudor commoveat
ut servem fidem? Such an oath-bound compact of fealty between
lovers was commonly termed a ὅρκος φιλίας. It is to be distinguished
from the formal contract, syngraphus[81] (Asin. 746), by which a courtesan
was legally bound to one lover for a prescribed space of time. The Latin
expression for the ὅρκος φιλίας was foedus.

[80]For satietas (amoris) cf. taedium in Elegy; κόρος in Greek, A. P. V.77 εἰ
τοίην χάριν εἶχε γυνὴ μετὰ Κύπριδος εὐνήν, οὐκ ἄν τοι κορον ἔσχεν ἀνὴρ ἀλόχοισιν ὁμιλῶν.
πᾶσαι γὰρ μετὰ Κύπριν ἀτερπέες εἰσὶ γυναῖκες, A. P. V.255 οὐ κόρον εἶχεν ἔρωτος
ἀφειδέος, Aristaen. II.1 τῶν ἀφροδισίων . . . . . τὸν κόρον, Aristoph. Pl.
190 πλησμονὴ ἔρωτος.

[81]Cf. Reitzenstein Sitzungsberichte der Heidelberger Akademie der Wissenschaf-
ten, Heidelberg, 1912, Zur Sprache der lateinischen Erotik p. 9 sq.

Though Comedy sheds but little light on the exact meaning of foedus in the sermo amatorius, examples are frequent in Catullus and in the elegiac poets. Starting with Leo's theory[82] that foedus in Elegy was used with special reference to the above mentioned contracts, the word has been much discussed. Reitzenstein, in the work cited, makes it tolerably clear that foedus, as used by Catullus and the elegiac poets, has nothing whatever to do with the syngraphs of Asin. 746, or similar contracts. His own conception of the foedus amicitiae as, in origin at least, a compact of friendship in the Roman sense, and consequently something "peculiar to Roman life and Roman feeling" is ingeniously supported by a deft comparison of numerous passages from Roman Comedy, Catullus, Cicero, and the elegiac poets. In these examples, the terms amicitia, inimicitia, culpa, benevolus, inimicus, officium, etc., are carefully analyzed and compared, with a view to determining their exact significance in the best Latin usage, and their precise relation to one another; the results are then applied to those passages in Roman erotic poetry where the foedus amicitiae is mentioned. The main objection to the conclusions reached is that they appear to rest upon a too rigid interpretation of the words considered. It is true that amicitia is rarely used as the exact equivalent of amor, but there is no doubt that it is sometimes so used (cf. Pseud. 1262), and consequently no obstacle to such an interpretation where it may seem otherwise indicated. Amicus is regularly a lover in Comedy, and the complement of amica: Most. 195, 247, Pseud. 196, 218, 228, Stich. 679, as ἑταῖρος in Greek: Eccl. 913 αἰαῖ τί ποτε πείσομαι; οὐχ ἥκει μοὐταῖρος and elsewhere. If the word amicus is used by Diniarchus, Truc. 171, in its proper sense (longe aliter est amicus and amator) it must be remembered that even ἑταίρα is sometimes correspondingly used in Greek: cf. Antiphanes 212 ἦθός τι χρυσοῦν πρὸς ἀρετὴν κεκτημένης, ὄντως ἑταίρας· αἱ μὲν ἄλλαι τοὔνομα βλάπτουσι τοῖς τρόποις γὰρ ὄντως ὂν καλόν. The terms benevolus, benevolentia, inimicitia, etc., to which Reitzenstein would give a hard and fast interpretation, are also frequent in Comedy in erotic contexts with no apparent indication of the idea that he attributes to them. Neither in Comedy nor in Catullus can any technical force be fastened upon the word iniuria or the phrase iniuriam facere, that is not amply covered by the verb ἀδικῶ as used in the Greek sermo amatorius. Just as iniuria and contumelia are, for most purposes, synonymous, so ἀδίκημα and ὕβρις show barely a shade of difference in general use: cf. A. P. XII.188 Εἴ σε φιλῶν ἀδικῶ καὶ τοῦτο δοκεῖς ὕβριν εἶναι τὴν αὐτὴν κόλασιν καὶ σὺ

[82] Plautinische Forschungen² p. 139, n. 2.

φίλει με λαβών. Ἀδίκημα may be a trivial offence, A. P. XII.118 ἐφίλησα τὴν Φλιήν, εἰ τοῦτ' ἔστ' ἀδίκημ' ἀδικῶ, or it may be actual unfaithfulness in the technical sense, Xen. Eph. II.4 οὐ γὰρ ἄν ποτε πεισθείην ἑκὼν Ἄνθειαν ἀδικῆσαι.

Reitzenstein (op. cit. p. 26) quotes Catullus 72. 7 quod amantem iniuria talis cogit amare magis sed bene velle minus. With reference to iniuria he says: "Weil es (iniuria) die formelhafte Beziehung der Verletzung der fides in der amicitia ist, wird durch sie das innerste Wesen derselben, das bene velle aufgehoben." Are we really justified in seeing more in this passage than the familiar paradox odi et amo? Cf. Ter. Eunuch. 70 sq. nunc ego et illam scelestam esse et me miserum sentio: et taedet et amore ardeo, et prudens sciens vivos vidensque pereo nec quid agam scio. The lover's grievance, in this case "exclusit," leads his slave to remark: "in amore haec omnia insunt vitia: iniuriae, etc." The state of mind provoked by these iniuriae is recognized by the courtesan Thais as inimicitia (174): potius quam te inimicum, etc.; yet the facts in this case absolutely preclude those over subtle distinctions which may be grafted on the same words by one who considers too curiously their use in Catullus.

The lover's oath or ὅρκος is a commonplace in the Greek sermo amatorius, as Reitzenstein recognizes p. 15, where he quotes a significant passage from Dioscorides, A. P. V.52 ὅρκον κοινὸν Ἔρωτ' ἀνεθήκαμεν, ὅρκος ὁ πιστὴν Ἀρσινόης θέμενος Σωσιπάτρῳ φιλίην. He fails only to remark that the high sentiment of Catullus, and his vehement protestations, may be easily paralleled from the same sources. With regard to the word foedus itself, Comedy supplies the link between the Greek and Catullus: cf. Cist. 460 qui frangant foedera; the meaning of foedus in this passage is explained by Cist. 472, similest ius iurandum amantum quasi ius confusicium. The terms of such a contract, or the leges amatoriae, may be illustrated from Longus II.39 ὅμοσον μὴ καταλιπεῖν Χλόην ἔστ' ἂν πιστή σοι μένῃ ἄδικον δ' εἰς σὲ καὶ τὰς Νύμφας γενομένην καὶ φεῦγε καὶ μίσει. Reitzenstein quotes (p.28) a passage from Catullus which seems to him to illustrate conclusively his friendship argument. The passage in question is Catullus 76:

> si qua recordanti bene facta priora voluptas
>   est homini, cum se cogitat esse pium,
> nec sanctum viclasse fidem, nec foedere in ullo
>   divum ad fallendos numine abusum homines.
> multa parata manent in longa aetate, Catulle,
>   ex hoc ingrato gaudia amore tibi.

> nam quaecumque homines bene cuiquam aut dicere possunt
> aut facere, haec a te dictaque factaque sunt;
> omnia quae ingratae perierunt credita menti.
> quare cur te iam amplius excrucies?
> quin tu animo offirmas atque istinc teque reducis
> et dis invitis desinis esse miser?

The whole tone and sentiment of this Catullan passage is amply illustrated by Aristaen. II.9, where the parties concerned are a young man and a girl of the courtesan class, περιφρονοῦσα τηλικοῦτον ὅρκον παρέβης ἀλλὰ τοὐμὸν μέρος ἀνυπεύθυνος μηδὲ συνθήκας ἔγνως ἐνωμότους φυλάττειν . . . . . ἢ τῆς σῆς διαπεπτωκέναι φιλίας . . . . . ἔρρωσω κἂν ἀδικῇς. With μηδὲ συνθήκας ἔγνως ἐνωμότους φυλάττειν compare nec sanctum violasse fidem (foedere in ullo); with ὀρκίοις θεοῖς compare divum numine abusum. The iniuria in this case is suggested in the words κἂν ἀδικῇς. The same idea appears in Horace Carm. II.8 ulla si iuris tibi peierati poena, Barine, nocuisset umquam, etc.

It is quite evident that a standing relationship ὁμιλία, or consuetudo with one of the courtesan class was frequently invested with an aura of sentiment, which made it fit subject for romantic literary treatment. Such relationships were frequently strengthened with oaths (ὅρκοι, foedera) in which the gods were called upon to witness the mutual obligations entailed. A certain dignity was thereby imparted to the relationship, which could appropriately be called a φιλία (amicitia). A significant passage in this connection is Apuleius Met. V.28, where such ties are mentioned, with marriages, as under the special patronage of Venus, non nuptiae coniugales, non amicitiae sociales, non liberum societates-squalentium foederum insuave fastidium. The woman was σώφρων (pudica) so long as she remained faithful to her lover. While, before, any slight or insult was merely ὕβρις (contumelia, iniuria) or ἀτιμία (Ach. Tat. V.26, Alciph. I.27.1, I.6.2), in this relationship a similar action became an ἀδίκημα (iniuria) and ἀδικεῖν (iniuriam facere) is the verb applied. The injured party might look for justice to the gods originally invoked, Luc. Dial. meretr. XII.2 ἔστι τις θεὸς ἡ Ἀδράστεια καὶ τὰ τοιαῦτα ὁρᾷ. The relationship had much in common with marriage, and, upon the death of a refractory parent, not uncommonly led up to it. So, while foedus in Latin Elegy should not be related to formal contracts for purely mercenary considerations, it may fairly be considered an echo of this somewhat more elevated relationship. There is undoubtedly an intensity of feeling in Catullus which is peculiar to him, but I see no need to look outside the Greek sermo amatorius to interpret his forms of expression.

abstineo, 31 n. 52.
accipio, 19-20.
accumbc, 32.
aculeus, 48 n. 72.
addictus, 50.
adduco, 18.
adeo, 16.
adhinnio, 41 (Cist. 308) cf. χρεμέτισμα in Greek index
admissarius, 41.
admitto, 25.
advenio, 16.
adventor, 16.
aegritudo, 5-8.
aegrotatio, 6.
aerumna, 11.
aestuosus, 53.
aestus, 49.
ago, (Cist. 311) cf. facio infra, and Friedr. on Catull. 64.145.
amator, 31.
amica, 37, 58.
amicitia, 58.
amicus, 58.
amo, 31.
amor, 48 n. 74, 58.
aratio, aratiuncula, 54.
ardor, 10 n. 17.
aridus, 36.
aro, 40.
ars (meretricia), 23.
artes (amoris), 49.
attingo, 30.
attrecto, 31.
aucupium, 56.
audeo, 29.
aviditas, 12.

bellum, 50
benevolus,-entia, 58.
bestia(mala), 39.
blandior, blanditiae, 23-24.
blandus, 23.

cado, 42.
caenum, 53.
canis, 55.
capio, 56.

capularis, 42.
caput(limare), 43; prurit, *ibid.*
carnuficina, 47.
celox, celocula, 36.
Chimaera, 53.
clandestinus, 42 n. 68.
clavus (Cupidinis), 48.
commercium (habere), 35.
concha, 46.
conciliabulum, 36 and n. 60.
condimentum, 46.
conduco, 18 n. 35.
congraeco, 22.
coniunx, 42.
conloco, 24; Afr. 143 Rib.
consuesco, 17,
consuetio, 17 r. 34.
consuetudo, 17, 57.
contabesco, 49.
contrecto, 31.
contumelia, 13, 25, 60.
conturbo (pedes), 42.
copia, 29.
cor, 48-9.
cordolium, 49.
cubitura, cubitus, 32.
cubo, cubito, 32.
culex, 46 cf. Cas. 239 and T. L. L. s. v.
cupido, 47.
cupiditas, 12.
cura, 7, 8, 11.
cursura, 51.

damnum (-a), 20, 21, 22, 51.
damnigeruli, 22.
damnosus, 22.
dato, datatim, 34.
decumbo, 21.
dedecus, 21, 51.
defero, 19.
degero, 19.
deliciae, 32.
desidia, 12, 13.
desidiabula, 21, 22.
diligo, 31.
diobolaris, 19, 38.
dirumpo, 46.
discus, 51.

divortium, 42.
do, dono, dona, 19.
do (obsc.), 34.
dormio, 32.
duco, 18, 36.
ducto, 18.

egens (amator), 22, 23.
elecebra, 24.
emo, 19.
eques, 44 n. 70.
equola, 41.
error, 10.
esca, 55.
exaresco, 41.
excludo, 25.
exclusio, 25.
exerceo, 52.
extrudo, 25.

facio, 33, 34, and n. 55.
factor, 34.
fama, 21, 22.
fel, 48.
fera, 36.
ferio, 43.
ferus, 46.
flagitium (-a), 21, 22.
fluctuo, 49.
fluvius, 53.
foedus, 57-60 cf. A. J. P. 1915, 182 n. 2,
    183 n. 1.
fores, 26.
formido, 6, 9.
formosus, 40 n. 65.
fortis, 39-40, cf. valens Catull. 89. 2.
frater, fraterculus, 42.
fructus, 30.
frugi, 22, 39 cf. Horace Sat. II. 5. 77.
fruor, 30.
fuga, 10.
fugio, 28.
fulcio, 24.

galea, 52.
gaudium, 6, 7.
graecor, 22.
Gymnasium, 52.

habeo, 19.
hirudo, 53.
hortus, 40 n. 67.
hospitium, 45, 48.

ianua, 53.
ignis, 48 n. 73.
illecebra, 24.
illicio, 24.
inanis, 35.
incendium, 48.
inclino, 42 cf. oquinisco Pomp. 149 Rib.
indignus, 15.
indomitus, 42.
ineptia, 9.
inermus, 36.
inimicitia, 58, 59.
iniuria, 13, 25, 58, 59, 60.
inopia, 14, 23, 24, 25, 29.
inops, 35.
inruo, 41.
insania, 8,9.
insomnia, 11.
intactus, 31.
integer, 31.
invenustus, 27.
invidia, 12.
iocus, 31.
iugum, 41.
labor, 11.
lacrima, 24.
lacus, 41.
laetitia, 6.
latebrae, latebrosus, 36.
lavo, 25 n. 45.
lectus, 24.
leges (amatoriae), 59.
limax, 38 (for limo vid. caput)
lingua (duplex), 44.
lubido, 12.
lucrum, 20.
ludo, 31.
ludus, 31.
lupa, lupanar, 36.
lustra, lustror, 36.

machaera, 51-2.
macula, 5, 48.

malacisso, 46.
malevolentia, 12.
malitia, 38.
malus, 38 (cf. merx).
mare, 53.
medicina, 7.
mel, 48.
merces, 19.
meretrix, 36.
merx (mala), 38.
metus, 9.
militia, 50.
mitto, 18.
morbus, 5.
morem gero, morigerus, 33.
morologia, 26, cf. multiloquium Merc. 37
   and Donatus on Ter. Eun. 207.
mortuos, 36.
moveo, 46.
munigerulus, 19.
musca, 45-6.

navis (praedatoria), 36 cf. λέμβος Greek
   index.
nequam, nequitia, 22, 39.
neo (uberius), 55.
nihili (nili), 39.
novi (gnosco), 36.
nubo, 42.

obducto, 18.
occento, 26.
odi, 28, 59.
officium, 16.
opera, 16 cf. Ter. Adelph. 532.
operaria, 16.
operatrix, 16.
opus, 33.
ovis, 55.

Paegnium, 32.
palaestra, 51, 53.
pallor, 49.
patior, 43 cf. Capt. 867.
pax, 50.
pectus, 49.
peculiaris, 45, 55.
pecuaria, 54.

peculio, 45.
peculium, 44, 45.
pecus, 54.
pellicio, 24.
pergraecor, 22.
pergula, 37.
pernocto, 46.
perprurisco, 44.
petulantia, 12.
piscatura, piscatus, 55, 56.
placeo, 28.
portitor, 54.
portorium, 54.
posco, 19.
possum, 33.
potior, 29, 30.
praedatoria (navis), 36.
pretiosus, 19, cf. πολυτελὴς ἑταίρα
   Men. 824 K.
proseda, 37.
prostibulum, 36.
prosto, 37.
prurio, 43, 44.
publico (corpus), 54.
publicum, 54.
pudicus, 57, 60.
putidus, 39.

quaero, 16 n. 31 (quaerito, 16, 45)
quaestus, 15, 16.
quiesco, 36 n. 58.

regina, 37 n. 62, cf. Petr. 128 'quaeso'
   inquam 'regina.'
reliquiae, 37.
res, sing. = property, 21; = commercium
   35; pl. = res veneriae 35 n. 37.
rete (retia), 45, 56.
rogo, 17 n. 31.
rota (amoris), 47.
rudis, 23.

saltus, 40 n. 67.
satietas, 57.
saucius, 50.
scando, 46.
scaphium, 52.

λαθραῖος, 42 n. 68.
λαμβάνω, 18, 20 cf. λῆμμα; A. P. VI. 285.
λέμβος, 36. cf. A. P. V. 44 Λέμβιον, ἡ δ'
     ἑτέρα Κερκούριον cf. also Turp. 98 Rib.
λεωφόρος, 41.
Λύκος, Λύκα, etc., 36.
λύπη, 5-8.

μαλακία, 13.
μαλάσσω, 46.
μέριμνα, 8.
μηχαναί, 49.
μισηταί, 28.
μισθοῦμαι, 18.
μίσθωμα, 19.
μισθωμάτιον, 19.
μισῶ, 28.
μόνος (-η), 32.
μονοκοιτῶ, 32.
Μυῖα, 45.
μύσχον, 45.
μωρολογία, 26.

νῶ (πυκνότερον), 55.
νεκρός, 36.
νόσημα, 5.
νυκτομαχῶ, 50.

ξηρός, 41.

ὀδός, 50 n. 76.
ὁμιλία, 17, 57, 60.
ὁμιλῶ, 17.
ὅρκος (φιλίας), 57, 59, 60.

παγίς (-δες), 45 cf. Nicophon 4K; 56.
παίγνια, 32.
παίζω, 31.
παίω, 43.
παλαίστρα, 51, 53.
παλαίω, 52.
πανδοσία, 41.
παννυχίζω, 46.
Παννυχίς, 46.
παρακλαυσίθυρον, 26.
παρέχω, 33.
πάσχω, 43.
πεῖρα, 29.

πειρῶ, 28.
πένης, 22.
πέριστερά, 52.
πιθανός, 23.
πίπτω, 42.
πλάνη, 10.
πολυξήμιος, 22.
πόνος, 11.
πορθῶ, 50.
πόρνη, 16, 36.
πράττω, 34.
πρίαμαι, 19.
πρόβατα, 55.
προΐστημι, 37.
προσάγω, 24.
προσᾴδω, 26.
προσφοιτῶ, 16.
προτρέπω, 24.
πρωτόπειρος, 23.
πῦρ, 48.
πῶλος, 41.

σαπρός, 39.
σίφων, 53.
σκεῦος, 44.
σπανίς, 14 and n. 27; σπανίς =inopia
     argentaria 23.
σπονδαί, 50.
στήμων ἐξεσμένος, 55 cf. Aristoph. 728 K.
στρέβλη, 47.
συγγραφή, 19.
συγκαταδαρθάνω, 33.
συγκατάκειμαι, 33.
συμφοραί, 5.
σύνειμι, 18 n. 34.
συνήθεια, 17.
συνουσία, 18 n. 34.
σχολή, 13 n. 24.
σώφρων, 60.

τελώνης, 54.
τελωνία, 54.
τέχνη, 23.
τήκομαι, 49.
τολμῶ, 29.
τρίβω (ἀνατρίβω), 43.
τρύγων, 52.
τρυφή, 13.

τύπτω, 43.
τυγχάνω, 30.

ὕβρις, 58, 60.
ὑβρίζω, 25.
ὑπέκκαυμα, 24.

φάρμακον, 7 n. 12.
φάσσα, 52.
φεύγω, 28.
φίλανδρος, 34.
φιλαργυρία, 12.
φιλία, 60.
φίλτρον, 48.
φιλῶ, 31.
φόβος, 6, 9.

φοιτῶ, 16.
φροντίς, 7, 8.

χαμαιτύπη, 43.
χαρίζομαι, 20, 33.
χάριτες, 20.
χρεμέτισμα, cf. adhinnio (Cist. 308) and
    A. P. V. 245 χρεμέτισμα γάμου προκέ-
    λευθον λεῖσα.
χρῶμαι, 30.

ψαύω, 31.

ὡραῖος, 38.
ὠμός, 46.

Militat omnis amans

Ein Beitrag zur Bildersprache der antiken Erotik

Inaugural-Dissertation

zur

Erlangung der Doktorwürde

einer

hohen philosophischen Fakultät

der

Universität zu Tübingen

vorgelegt von

Alfons Spies

aus Ertingen (Württbg.)

Tübingen 1930
Druck von H. Laupp jr.

Gedruckt mit Genehmigung der philosophischen Fakultät
Promotion: 25. Mai 1928
Referent: Professor Dr. Otto Weinreich.

Druck von H. Laupp jr in Tübingen.

Meiner lieben Braut

Inhaltsangabe.

Die Untersuchung von Bildern, Gemeinplätzen und literarischen Motiven ist, sofern sie nicht zu einseitig und mechanisch geschieht, nicht nur von großem Nutzen für die Analyse der Einzelwerke und für das Verständnis der einzelnen Autoren, sondern dient gleichzeitig in hohem Maße dazu, größere literarische Zusammenhänge zu erkennen. In den letzten Dezennien ist eine Reihe von Programmen und Dissertationen erschienen, die in mehr oder weniger fördernder Weise den Bilderschmuck der griechischen bzw. römischen Literatur zum Gegenstand ihrer Forschung machten. Meine Aufgabe soll darin bestehen, das Bild des „Liebeskriegs" eingehend zu verfolgen. Die Metaphern und Gleichnisse aus dem Kriegsleben sind ja überaus häufig. Ich brauche nur an die Rhetorik zu erinnern, wo die Kriegersprache eine große Rolle spielt [1]). Aehnlich ist die Diktion der Erotiker stark vom Soldatenleben beeinflußt. Diese Tatsache wird uns am greifbarsten in der römischen Elegie. Einzelne Dissertationen stellten sich bereits zur Aufgabe, die Tropen bei den augusteischen Elegikern zu behandeln. Sie alle berücksichtigen gar nicht oder nur unzulänglich unser Thema. Selbst eine Abhandlung wie die von A. W a s h i e t e l *De similitudinibus imaginibusque Ovidianis* (Diss. Vindobonae 1883) berührt nicht einmal unsere Metapher, die doch bei Ovid eine Hauptrolle spielt [2]). Die griechische Literatur ist, soweit ich sehe, selbst in neueren Kommentaren wie denen zu Ovids Liebespoesie von Brandt für meine engere Untersuchung nicht verwertet. Bei dieser Sachlage bedarf wohl die

---

1) Vgl. D. W o l l n e r, Die von der Beredtsamkeit aus der Krieger- und Fechtersprache entlehnten bildlichen Wendungen in den rhetorischen Schriften des Cicero, Quintilian und Tacitus. Gymn.-Progr. Landau 1886.

2) Ich erwähne außerdem M. H a n s e n *De tropis et figuris apud Tibullum* Diss. 1881; sie bietet für uns nichts. Das einschlägige Material bei Properz stellt tabellenmäßig zusammen G. M e u s e l *Curae Propertianae* Diss. 1902 p. 36 ff. Am meisten Berücksichtigung erfährt unser Thema bei R. P i c h o n *De sermone amatorio apud Latinos elegiarum scriptores* Diss. Paris 1902. Unter ‚*militia*', ‚*bellum*' u. a. Kriegsausdrücken ist das Material der römischen Elegie zum großen Teil gesammelt.

Themastellung keiner weiteren Rechtfertigung. Denn abgesehen davon, daß es nicht wenig Reiz hat, ein Bild durch die ganze griechische und römische Literatur hin zu verfolgen, zu sehen, wie es entstanden und geworden ist, und wie es von den einzelnen Autoren verschieden gehandhabt wird, ist die Arbeit ein Beitrag für das Verständis der römischen Elegie, deren Vorbilder und Nachahmungen.

Es liegt mir ob, über **Bedeutung und Wesen der Metapher** kurz das Wesentlichste vorauszuschicken. Unter den Tropen[1]) erfreut sich die Metapher der größten Beliebtheit. Gehört sie doch mit zum wichtigsten Bestandteil der Dichtersprache und zum vorzüglichsten Redeschmuck überhaupt. Diese Ansicht finden wir schon bei den Alten. **Aristoteles** sagt **rhet.** 1405a 4 ff.: ὅτι τοῦτο πλεῖστον δύναται καὶ ἐν ποιήσει καὶ ἐν λόγοις, αἱ μεταφοραί, εἴρηται, καθάπερ ἐλέγομεν, ἐν τοῖς περὶ ποιητικῆς. Damit stimmt das Urteil Quintilians überein *inst. or. VIII. 6. 4: Incipiamus igitur ab eo ⟨tropo⟩ qui cum frequentissimus est tum longe pulcherrimus, translationem dico, quae 'μεταφορά' Graece vocatur . . . .* und daselbst 2. 6: *Translatio quoque, in qua vel maximus est orationis ornatus, verba non suis rebus accomodat,* vgl. Cicero *or.* 94. Antike Stilkritiker betonen neben Farbe, Fülle und Stimmung, die durch den Gebrauch von Bildern erzeugt wird, den sich damit verbindenden Vorzug der **Deutlichkeit** und **Anschaulichkeit**, was den Inhalt anlangt. So urteilt Aristoteles rhet. 1405a 8/9: καὶ τὸ σαφὲς καὶ τὸ ἡδὺ καὶ τὸ ξενικὸν ἔχει μάλιστα ἡ μεταφορά . . vgl. Demetrius 'περὶ ἑρμηνείας' rhet. Gr. III. 281 (Spengel), ähnlich Cicero *de or.* III. 161: *unde enim simile duci potest — potest autem ex omnibus — indidem verbum unum, quod similitudinem continet, translatum lumen adferre orationi.*

Worin haben wir das Wesen der Metapher zu erblicken? Die Literatur über diesen Tropus ist sehr ausgedehnt[2]). — Die Sprache an und für sich stellt eine Summe von Bildern dar, die als solche freilich nicht empfunden werden. So sagt **Jean Paul** in der Vorschule zur Aesthetik § 50: „Daher ist jede Sprache in Rücksicht geistiger Beziehungen ein Wörterbuch erblaßter Metaphern“. Was

---

1) Die Zahl der Tropen ist unsicher, und ihre Abgrenzung gegen die „Figuren“ ist auch bei modernen Aesthetikern recht umstritten. Zu den Tropen rechnet man im allgemeinen Metonymie, Synekdoche und **Metapher** (vgl. R. M. Meyer, Deutsche Stilistik, München 1913 S. 110).

2) Ueber moderne Literatur siehe R. M. Meyer p. 119 Anm. 2.

wir unter Metapher verstehen, ist zumeist ein Kunstgewächs. Sie ist ein poetisch gefärbter Ausdruck irgend eines Gedankens oder einer Vorstellung; statt des gewöhnlichen Ausdrucks wird ein bildlicher verwendet. Dabei machen sich Beziehungsmerkmale von zwei Gefühls- oder Gedankensphären geltend. Aristoteles definiert *de art. poet. 1457* [b] *7: μεταφορὰ δ᾽ ἐστὶν ὀνόματος ἀλλοτρίου ἐπιφορὰ ἢ ἀπὸ τοῦ γένους ἐπὶ εἶδος . . . . . ἢ κατὰ τὸ ἀνάλογον.* Aehnlich sagt der *Auctor ad Herennium IV. 34: translatio est, cum verbum in quandam rem transferetur ex alia re, quod propter similitudinem recte videbitur posse transferri* vgl. Cicero *de or.* III. 38 § 155 ff. Dem psychologischen Moment wird etwa folgende Formulierung (R. M. Meyer S. 121) gerecht: „Die 'Metaphora', die Uebertragung (lat. *translatio*) dient dem persönlichen Anschauungsbedürfnis, das aus der weniger anschaulichen oder weniger bekannten Sphäre in die bekanntere überträgt."

In welchem Verhältnis stehen Gleichnis (Vergleich) und Allegorie zur Metapher? Der Unterschied ist im wesentlichen ein formaler. Der Vergleich setzt dem Sachbegriff den Bildbegriff an die Seite. Ur- und Bildbegriff sind getrennt und als solche erkennbar, während bei der Metapher die Uebertragung des Bildbegriffes in den Sachbegriff stattfindet. Bekannt ist das Beispiel des Aristoteles rhet. III 4, 1406 b. *ὅταν μὲν γὰρ εἴπῃ τὸν Ἀχιλλέα 'ὡς δὲ λέων ἐπόρουσεν' εἰκών ἐστιν, ͺὅταν δὲ 'λέων ἐπόρουσε' μεταφορά,* vgl. Quint. *inst. or.* VIII. 6. 8. Auch die Allegorie ist mit der Metapher verwandt. Nach Gerber „Die Sprache als Kunst" II. 1. 98 ff. ist die Allegorie eine gedehnte Metapher. Cicero hebt schon das Wesentliche hervor or. 27: *iam cum fluxerunt continuae plures translationes, alia plane fit oratio; itaque genus hoc Graeci appellant ἀλληγορίαν: nomine recte, genere melius illē* (Aristoteles), *qui ista omnia translationes vocat.* Eine passende Definition von Gerber möchte ich hier anführen (II. 1. 98): „Wenn der metaphorische Ausdruck weitere Glieder der Rede ergreift, so daß die aus dem fremden Gebiete übertragenen Bezeichnungen ganz an die Stelle der eigentlichen treten, und das Verständnis überhaupt nur aus der Anschauung des Gebietes gewonnen wird, in welchem die Metapher lebt, so hat man dies Allegorie genannt, begleitet dagegen die durch Ausführung einzelner Züge des Bildes entfaltete Metapher den eigentlichen Ausdruck in einer Nebenstellung, so hat man das Gleichnis." Metaphern sind jedoch nicht schlechtweg verkürzte Gleichnisse oder Allegorien. Scherer bemerkt (Poetik S. 267):

Die Metaphern entständen in der Regel durch Hervorhebung einer
einzelnen Eigenschaft oder Personifikation, ohne den Umweg über
das Bild.

Die Einteilung des Stoffes macht gewisse Schwierigkeiten. Die
Gefahr, Zitate aus Schriftstellern öfters anführen zu müssen, wird
kaum zu umgehen sein. Vorteilhaft ist die historische Anordnung,
weil so die Genesis der Metapher am klarsten zutage tritt. Näher
mit einander verwandte Beispiele werde ich womöglich zusammen-
rücken. Gelegentlich wird auch der eidologische Gesichtspunkt
Beachtung finden müssen.

Der erste Teil meiner Abhandlung soll uns mit dem Bild des
mit den Menschen kämpfenden Eros vertraut machen; dabei kann
es nicht meine Absicht sein, für diese Allegorie sämtliche Stellen
beizubringen; vielmehr sollen nur die auftretenden Typen unter
besonderer Berücksichtigung der Alexandriner und der römischen
Elegie herausgestellt und damit eine Gesamtübersicht gewonnen
werden. Der Hauptteil beschäftigt sich eingehend mit unserem
eigentlichen Thema, dem Bild des Liebenden als eines „Kriegers".
Die Frage nach der Abhängigkeit, sowie die ästhetisch-stilistische
Würdigung der Stellen mag jeweils im Vordergrund des Interesses
stehen.

Erstes Kapitel.

§ 1.

Vielfach wirken die Pfeile des Amor: einige ritzen,
Und vom schleichenden Gift kranket auf Jahre das Herz.
Aber mächtig befiedert, mit frisch geschliffener Schärfe,
Dringen die andern ins Mark, zünden behende das Blut.
Goethe „röm. Eleg." I. 3.

Der Gott Eros begegnet zum erstenmal in der griechischen Literatur bei Hesiod. Er ist hier das dritte der drei Urprinzipien. Daß er unter die Urgötter aufgenommen wurde, um ihm als alten Heimatgott, der nichts anderes als ein phallischer Fruchtbarkeitsgott war, eine Huldigung darzubringen, wurde mit Recht von vielen betont[1]). Wenngleich Eros in der Weltentwicklung und bei der Entstehung des Götterstaates keine Funktion erhält, so dürfen wir doch vermuten, daß bei Hesiod das Empfinden mitgeschwungen habe, daß Eros der Erreger des Liebestriebes ist. Dessen Macht charakterisiert er mit dem anschaulich-wuchtigen Attribut 'λυσιμελής'[2]). Im Hymnenstil preist ihn der Dichter von Askra als 'schönsten unter den unsterblichen Göttern, der aller Menschen Sinn bändigt in ihrer Brust und verständigen Rat überwältigt' (theog. 120 ff.)[3]). Indes werden letztere Verse von Jacoby als Interpolation erklärt[4]).

---

1) In Thespiä in Böotien war Eros seit alters unter einem ἄγαλμα παλαιότατον, das in einem unbehauenen Stein (ἀγρὸς λίθος) bestand, verehrt worden (vgl. Pausanias IX. 27. 1). Das schwierige Problem des Eros bei Hesiod behandelten in jüngster Zeit Jacoby, Hermes 1926, 157 ff. und O. Kern 'Religion der Griechen' I 1927.

2) Auch Archilochus (fr. 118 [Diehl]) und Sappho (fr. 137) nennen Eros 'λυσιμελής'.

3) Theog. 201 erscheint Eros neben Himeros als Begleiter der Aphrodite. Die Gestalten des Himeros und Pothos sind dem Eros analoge Personifikationen begehrenden Verlangens mit vielleicht größerem Intensitätswert.

4) Seine Argumente sind wenig stichhaltig. In überscharfsinniger Weise spürt er Widersprüche und sprachliche Ungereimtheiten auf, die kaum

Bei den Lyrikern ist Eros schlechthin zum Erreger der Liebe
zwischen Mann und Weib, bzw. Mann und Knaben, geworden. Er
ist vom Dichter nicht mehr bloß als eine unfaßbare, das Gemüt der
Menschen bezwingende Macht geschildert. Die Phantasie der äoli-
schen Sänger weiß ihn mit persönlichen Farben zu schmücken:
Sappho läßt Eros die Herzen erschüttern wie der Sturmwind im
Eichenhain wütet[1]). Mit goldenen Flügeln durchsaust er bei Ana-
kreon die Welt[2]). Der Dichter kämpft sogar mit ihm wie ein Faust-
kämpfer[3]). Eros tritt als Jäger auf (Ibyk. fr. 6, 7). Dabei handelt
es sich für die Dichter darum, des Eros absolutes Regiment her-
vorzuheben: alle Menschen und Götter[4]), ja sogar der Kriegsgott
Ares muß sich ihm beugen; hier wird öfters auf die schon bei
Homer (Od. ϑ 267 ff.) erzählte Liebesszene zwischen Ares und Aphro-
dite angespielt[5]). Bei vielen Dichtern wird selbst die oberste Welt-
regierung ein Opfer des Liebesgottes. Die Mythen von Zeus als
Liebhaber sterblicher Frauen finden in Kunst und Literatur[6]) ihren
Niederschlag. Im älteren Drama, bei Aeschylus und Sophokles,

vorhanden sind oder sich unschwer erklären lassen in einem so frühen Werk
wie die Theogonie Hesiods. Auch Kern hält in seinen vorzüglichen Aus-
führungen die Verse für echt.

1) Sappho fr. 50
. . . . . ἐτίναξεν ⟨ἔμας⟩ φρένας
Ἔρος ὡς ἄνεμος κατ᾿ ὄρος δρύσιν ἐμπέσων.

2) Anakr. fr. 53
. . . . . χρυσοφαέννων πτερύγων ἀήταις παραπέτεται.

3) Anakr. fr. 27
Φέρ᾿ ὕδωρ, φέρ᾿ οἶνον, ὦ παῖ, φέρε⟨δ᾿⟩ ἀνθεμόεντας ἡμῖν
στεφάνους, ἔνεικον, ὡς δὴ πρὸς Ἔρωτα πυκταλίζω.

4) Vgl. Eurip. Hipp. 538.
Ἔρωτα δέ, τὸν τύραννον τῶν ἀνδρῶν . . .
und Eurip. fr. 136 (N)
σὺ δ᾿ ὦ ϑεῶν τύραννε κἀνθρώπων Ἔρως.

5) Plato Symp. 196 d: καὶ μὴν εἴς γε ἀνδρείαν Ἔρωτι ᾿οὐδ᾿ Ἄρης ἀνθίσταται᾿
οὐ γὰρ ἔχει Ἔρωτα Ἄρης, ἀλλ᾿ Ἔρως Ἄρη — Ἀφροδίτης, ὡς λόγος — · κρείττων
δ᾿ ὁ ἔχων τοῦ ἐχομένου.

6) Ein Beispiel: Asklepiades, A. P. V. 63 (Stadtmüller)
ἕλκει γάρ μ᾿ ὁ κρατῶν καὶ σοῦ ϑεός, ᾧ ποτε πεισϑείς,
Ζεῦ, διὰ χαλκείων χρυσὸς ἔδυς ϑαλάμων.
Im ,Venusgärtlein', einem Liederbuch des 17. Jahrh., das ein Gemisch ge-
lehrter Kunst- und Popularlyrik darstellt und viele Motive der antiken Erotik
entlehnt hat, heißt es S. 139. 2 (hsg. v. M. Freih. von Waldberg 1890):
Jupiter, sampt seinen Plitzen, sampt der starken Donnersmacht, weicht dir
kleinem Bogenschützen, du hast ihn dahin gebracht, daß er muß, aus Liebes-
pein, in einen Schwan verwandelt sein usw.

ist Eros mehr noch Symbol allbesiegender Leidenschaft[1]). Bei Euripides, wo das Problem der Liebe zentralere Bedeutung im Drama gewinnt, ist er zum Teil persönlicher gedacht, mit menschlichen Eigenschaften bedacht. Allerdings, wenn Aeschylus oben vom ‚Geschoß' des ἵμερος spricht, so liegt hier schon das Bild des „Kriegers" oder „Jägers" Eros zugrunde. Sophokles preist zwar die das ganze All durchdringende und bezwingende Macht des „unbesiegbaren" Eros, stattet ihn aber nicht mit einzelnen Waffen aus, auch wenn er durch: ἀνίκατε μάχαν . . . implicite als Kriegsheld erscheint (Antig. 781 ff.: Ἔρως ἀνίκατε μάχαν, ὃς . . .). Euripides führt dieses Bild weiter aus. Er stattet Eros mit Pfeil und Bogen[2]) aus und läßt ihn gegen die Menschen zu Felde ziehen. Unserer fragmentarischen Kenntnis nach liegt diese Vorstellung zum erstenmal breiter ausgemalt in folgender Euripidesstelle vor (Hipp. 525 ff.):

Ἔρως Ἔρως, ὃ κατ' ὀμμάτων
στάζεις πόθον, εἰσάγων γλυκεῖαν
ψυχᾷ χάριν οὓς ἐπιστρατεύσῃ
μή μοί ποτε σὺν κακῷ φανείης
μηδ' ἄρρυθμος ἔλθοις.
οὔτε γὰρ πυρὸς οὔτ' ἄστρων ὑπέρτερον βέλος,
οἷον τὸ τᾶς Ἀφροδίτας
ἵησιν ἐκ χερῶν
Ἔρως, ὃ Διὸς παῖς.

Mit dem Geschoß also **verwundet** er die Herzen, vgl. Hipp. 392: ἐπεὶ μ' Ἔρως ἔτρωσεν.

Im Zeitalter des Hellenismus ist die Auffassung des Eros wie die der übrigen Gottheiten eine andere geworden. Der Umschwung in religiös-weltanschaulichen Dingen war z. T. in der alle bisherigen Normen zerstörenden Kritik der Sophistik begründet. Euripides hatte die neuen Ideen popularisiert. Künstler und Dichter stehen damals noch im Banne der Tradition, denken und fühlen aber anders über Gott und Welt als ihre Vorfahren[3]). Die Poesie ist Spiel geworden. Das Ernsthafte seines Wesens verliert Eros. Er wird

1) **Aeschylus** Prom. 649:
Ζεὺς γὰρ ἱμέρου βέλει πρὸς σοῦ τέθαλπται.
2) Interessant ist die Parallelerscheinung in der altindischen Literatur, wo der Wunschgott Kâma auch mit Pfeilen versehen ist (Macdonell: Vedic mythology [Grundriß der indo-ar. Philol. III. 1. A. 13 f. 120]).
3) Ich verweise auf die Ausführungen bei U. v. Wilamowitz-Moellendorff, Hellenist. Dicht. 1924 I. 68 ff.

analog der Darstellung in der Kunst aus dem attischen Epheben
zum spielenden Kind, zum frivolen Knaben. Münzen und Wandge-
mälde zeigen ihn als geflügelten Knaben, z. T. neben dem mit
Aphrodite kosenden Ares[1]). Bukoliker, Lyriker, besonders aber
die Dichter der palatinischen Anthologie schildern variierend Eros fast
bis zur Ermüdung. Sie schaffen das stereotype Bild, das bis zu den
spätesten griechischen Romanschriftstellern und bis ins Mittelalter,
ja bis in die jüngste Zeit hinein immer wiederkehrt. Aus der
Masse von Beispielen greife ich unter Berücksichtigung der ver-
schiedenen Epochen nur einzelne typische Fälle heraus.

Eros im Kampfe mit den Menschen finden wir in charakteristi-
scher Weise in den sog. Anakreonteen. Es sind tändelnde Spiele-
reien, die den alten Anakreon nachahmen. Daß die frühesten zu
Beginn des Hellenismus, die meisten von ihnen erst in der Kaiser-
zeit entstanden sind, ergab sich aus deren inhaltlicher und metri-
scher Interpretation[2]). Ein anmutiges und lebendiges Bildchen aus
dieser Sammlung möge die Reihe eröffnen. Eros, mit Köcher und
Pfeil bewaffnet, kämpft mit dem Dichter. Als ihm die Pfeile aus-
gehen, dringt Eros selbst als Pfeil in des Feindes Herz und er-
kämpft hier den vollen Sieg. Anakreontea fr. 13 (Preisendanz):

> Θέλω, θέλω φιλῆσαι,
> ἔπειθ' Ἔρως φιλεῖν με·
> ἐγὼ δ' ἔχων νόημα
> ἄβουλον οὐκ ἐπείσθην.
> ὁ δ' εὐθὺ τόξον ἄρας
> καὶ χρυσείην φαρέτρην
> μάχῃ με προὐκαλεῖτο.
> κἀγὼ λαβὼν ἐπ' ὤμων
> θώρηχ', ὅπως Ἀχιλλεύς,
> καὶ δοῦρα καὶ βοείην
> ἐμαρνάμην Ἔρωτι.
> ἔβαλλ', ἐγὼ δ' ἔφευγον.
> ὡς δ' οὐκέτ' εἶχ' ὀιστούς,
> ἤσχαλλεν, εἶθ' ἑαυτὸν
> ἀφῆκεν εἰς βέλεμνον·
> μέσος δὲ καρδίης μευ

---

1) Helbig 'Wandgemälde' 319 (324). Siehe die Literaturangaben bei C. Ro-
bert, Real-Enzykl. v. Pauly-Wissowa VI, 1. S. 498 ff.

2) O. Crusius Realenzykl. I. 2044 ff. u. Christ-Schmid Lit.Gesch. I⁶
203 f.

ἔδυνε καὶ μ'ἔλυσεν·
μάτην δ' ἔχω βοείην·
τί γὰρ βάλωμεν ἔξω
μάχης ἔσω μ' ἐχούσης;

Oft sieht der Dichter nicht nur e i n e n Eros, sondern eine ganze Schar von Eroten[1]): Anakreontea fr. 5. 14: *χάρασσ' Ἔρωτας ἀνόπλους.*

Auch die Fackel wird in alexandrinischer Zeit zu einem wichtigen Attribut des Eros. Als Kriegsgerät (etwa bei einer Stadtbelagerung) kann sie das Bild des Fackelträgers Eros hervorgerufen haben. Letzteres ist aber nicht wahrscheinlich. Denn, wenn vom 'Brennen' oder der 'Glut' der Liebe gesprochen wurde, lag der Gedanke des mit einer Fackel versehenen Amor nahe. Mit Feuer steckt dieser die Herzen in Brand. Meleager A. P. V. 138: .. *Ποῖ σε φύγω ... πυρὶ φλέγομαι.*

Sehr beliebt ist der Gedanke, daß der Liebesgott so viele Pfeile sendet, daß sein Opfer vernichtet werden m u ß. Ironisch fordert der Dichter die Eroten auf, ihn mit Pfeilen zu überschütten. Poseidipp A. P. XII. 45:

Ναὶ ναὶ βάλλετ', Ἔρωτες· ἐγὼ σκοπὸς εἷς ἅμα πολλοῖς
κεῖμαι· μὴ φείσησθ' ἄφρονες· ἢν γὰρ ἐμὲ
νικήσητ', ὀνομαστοὶ ἐν ἀθανάτοισιν ἔσεσθε
τοξόται, ὡς μεγάλης δεσπόται ἰοδόκης[2]).

Vgl. A. P. V. 57, 197, 214 u. a.

Am sorgfältigsten gezeichnet und am farbigsten gemalt ist Eros in den bekannten Meleagerepigrammen A. P. V. 176—178, von denen ich wenigstens eines hier anführen möchte: A. P. V. 176:

Κηρύσσω τὸν Ἔρωτα, τὸν ἄγριον· ἄρτι γάρ, ἄρτι
ὀρθρινὸς ἐκ κοίτας ᾤχετ' ἀποπτάμενος.
Ἔστι δ' ὁ παῖς γλυκύδακρυς, ἀείλαλος, ὠκύς, ἀθαμβής,
σιμὰ γελῶν, πτερόεις νῶτα, φαρετροφόρος.
Πατρὸς δ' οὐκέτ' ἔχω φράζειν τίνος· οὔτε γὰρ Αἰθήρ,
οὐ Χθών φησι τεκεῖν τὸν θρασύν, οὐ Πέλαγος·
πάντῃ γὰρ καὶ πᾶσιν ἀπέχθεται. Ἀλλ' ἐσορᾶτε
μή που νῦν ψυχαῖς ἄλλα τίθησι λίνα[3]).

---

1) Schon Euripides gebraucht den Plural.
2) P. S c h o t t 'Posidippi epigrammata collecta et illustrata' Diss. Berl. 1905 p. 60.
3) Das Bild des 'Jägers' Eros ist auch sehr beliebt s. o.

Καίτοι κεῖνος, ἰδού, περὶ φωλεόν. Οὔ με λέληθας,
τοξότα, Ζηνοφίλας ὄμμασι κρυπτόμενος.

Eros muß bisweilen auch auf 'Gegenkampf' gefaßt sein. Der Sieg aber bleibt ihm für gewöhnlich[1]). Ein Beispiel: T h e o k r. I. 97 f.:

... *τύ θην τὸν Ἔρωτα κατεύχεο, Δάφνι, λυγιξεῖν,*
ἦ ῥ᾽ οὐκ αὐτὸς Ἔρωτος ὑπ᾽ ἀργαλέω ἐλυγίχθης;

Sein Sieg ist in Frage gestellt, wenn er Bakchos nicht zum Bundesgenossen hat. Rufinus A. P. V. 92:

Ὥπλισμαι πρὸς Ἔρωτα περὶ στέρνοισι λογισμόν,
οὐδέ με νικήσει, μοῦνος ἐὼν πρὸς ἕνα.
θνατὸς δ᾽ ἀθανάτῳ συστήσομαι· ἢν δὲ βοηθὸν
Βάκχον ἔχῃ, τί μόνος πρὸς δύ᾽ ἐγὼ δύναμαι;

Seltener ist die Mutter des Eros, Kypris, bewaffnet gedacht. Die Römer allerdings sprechen, wie wir weiter unten sehen werden, mit Vorliebe von der bewaffneten Venus[2]). Bei E u r i p i d e s schon übernimmt Aphrodite die Funktion ihres Sohnes. Med. 631 ff.:

Κύπρις . . . .
μήποτ᾽, ὦ δέσποιν᾽, ἐπ᾽ ἐμοὶ χρυσέων τόξων ἐφείης
ἱμέρῳ χρίσασ᾽ ἄφυκτον ὀιστόν.

Ein *ἀδέσποτον* läßt in witziger Weise Athene sich mit Kypris unterhalten: A. P. XVI. 174:

Παλλὰς τὰν Κυθέρειαν ἔνοπλον ἔειπεν ἰδοῦσα·
'Κύπρι, θέλεις οὕτως ἐς κρίσιν ἐρχόμεθα᾽;
Ἡ δ᾽ ἀπαλὸν γελάσασα· 'Τί μοι σάκος ἀντίον αἴρειν;
εἰ γυμνὴ νικῶ, πῶς ὅταν ὅπλα λάβω;[3])

vgl. Leonidas A. P. XVI. 171 u. a.

---

1) Schon Euripides sagt fr. 430 (N.):
   ἔχω . . . . Ἔρωτα, πάντων δυσμαχώτατον θεόν.
2) Die armata Venus hatte in Sparta ihren Kult. Darüber berichtet Pausanias III. 15. 8, Quintilian II. 4. 26 u. Lactantius I. 76. 28 ff. Durch Marius u. Cäsar, die sie als Schutzpatronin wählten, hat sie für Rom besondere Bedeutung gewonnen. So übernimmt auch Martial diesen Typus (vgl. O t t o W e i n r e i c h, Studien zu Martial (Tübinger Beitr. zur Altertumsw. Heft 4) 1928) S. 35 f.
3) Ausonius übertrug dieses Epigramm (ep. 64 p. 336 Peiper, vgl. Ps. Aus. p. 423 no. 7); es lautet:
   Armatam vidit Venerem Lacedaemone Pallas:
   'nunc certemus' ait 'iudice vel Paride'.
   Cui Venus: 'armatam tu me, temeraria, temnis
   quae quo te vici tempore nuda fui'?

Die attische Komödie scheint, wie wir aus den erhaltenen Resten, besonders aber aus Plautus und Terenz schließen dürfen, sehr wenig mit der Allegorie vom pfeilsendenden Eros vertraut gewesen zu sein. Um so mehr beuteten sie die Alexandriner im Anschluß an Euripides aus. Spätere Autoren übernehmen diese Art, den Liebesgott zu kennzeichnen; insbesondere die Verfasser erotischer Briefe, Aristänetus und Philostratus, ebenso die Romanschriftsteller. Diese wie jene, die ihre Gedanken und Motive zum großen Teil der hellenistischen Literatur verdanken, können sich nicht genug tun, das Erosbild möglichst oft und bunt dem Leser vor Augen zu führen. Nur wenige Beispiele auch hievon: A r i s t ä n. *ἐπιστ. ἐρωτ.* I. 10: ὁ Ἔρως οὐ μετρίως ἐνέτεινε τὴν νευρὰν (ὅτε καὶ τερπνὴ πέφυκεν ἡ τοξεία), ἀλλ᾽ ὅσον εἶχεν ἰσχύος προσελκύσας τὰ τόξα, σφοδρότατα διαφῆκε τὸ βέλος[1]). — Eros im Kampfe mit einem spröden, die Liebe verschmähenden Jungen: X e n o p h o n E p h e s. I. 2. 1: καὶ γὰρ καὶ τῷ θεῷ δυσάλωτος ἐφαίνετο. Ἐξοπλίσας οὖν ἑαυτὸν καὶ πᾶσαν δύναμιν ἐρωτικῶν φαρμάκων περιβαλόμενος ἐστράτευεν ἐφ᾽ Ἀβροκόμην. Dazu I. 4. 1. Eros ist der 'στρατιώτης' schlechthin: A c h i l l. T a t. IV. 7. 3: ἔνδον μου τῆς ψυχῆς ἄλλος πόλεμος κάθηται· στρατιώτης με πορθεῖ τόξον ἔχων, βέλος ἔχων· νενίκημαι, πεπλήρωμαι βελῶν.... Gegenkampf: A c h i l l T a t. II. 5. 2: κάτωθεν δὲ ὥσπερ ἐκ τῆς καρδίας ὁ Ἔρως[2]) ἀντεφθέγγετο· 'ναὶ τολμηρέ, κατ᾽ ἐμοῦ στρατεύῃ καὶ ἀντιπαρατάττῃ; ἵπταμαι καὶ τοξεύω καὶ φλέγω' oder N i k e t a s E u g e n. II. 99 f.:

Ἦν, εὐσθενὴς ὢν ἐκ φιλήματος μόνου,
ἀντιστρατεύειν ταῖς Ἔρωτος σφενδόναις[3]).

Die Beispiele zeigen, wie die alten Bilder und Vorstellungen immer wieder auftauchen; diese hatten höchstens bei einem Dichter wie E u r i p i d e s individuelles Gepräge erhalten. Zu beachten ist, daß die Wortwahl dieser Epigonen nach größerer Anschaulichkeit und Bildkraft strebt. Eros ist von ihnen nicht so sehr als spielender

---

1) Dasselbe Motiv begegnete schon oben und wird in der römischen Literatur auch öfters vorkommen. Hier möchte ich noch eine L u k i a n stelle beifügen: Ἔρωτες 2. 3 ff.: ἐγὼ γοῦν ἅπασαν αὐτῶν κενὴν ἀπολελεῖφθαι φαρέτραν νομίζω, κἂν ἐπ᾽ ἄλλον τινὰ πτῆναι θελήσωσιν, ἄνοπλος αὐτῶν ἡ δεξιὰ γελασθήσεται. Vgl. Niketas Eugen. II. 127. Eustath. III. 2, 3. Paul. Silentiarius A. P. V. 57, 267.

2) Ἔρως ist bei Hercher *erot. script. Gr.* m. E. mit Unrecht klein geschrieben.

3) Vgl. P l u t a r c h 'ἐρωτικὸς' c. 3: εἰ καὶ Πρωτογένης Ἔρωτι πολεμήσων πάρεστιν.

Knabe, denn als mächtiger Kriegsheld dargestellt. Worte wie *πορ-θεῖν, ἀντιπαρατάττειν, στρατιώτης* u. a. sind bei den Alexandrinern für den Eroskrieg nicht zu finden. Im allgemeinen aber ist die präzise und pointierte Formulierung der hellenistischen Epigrammatik verlorengegangen. Die Allegorie ist öfters zur Karikatur verzerrt, andererseits geschmacklos weit ausgesponnen[1]). Außer den genannten Fällen mögen noch einige typische das Gesagte beleuchten: E u s t a t h. III. 2. 6: *πόλις ἐγώ, καὶ πόλις Διός· ἀλλ' "Ερως πολιορκεῖ με καὶ πρὸς ἑαυτὸν ὅλον μεθέλκεται.* Der Liebende ist also eine Stadt, die von Eros belagert wird[2]). Die Attribute und Funktionen des Liebesgottes: E u s t a t h. II. 11, 2. 3: *ὁ "Ερως γυμνός, ὁπλοφόρος, πυρφόρος, τοξότης, πτερωτός· ὅπλα φέρει κατ' ἀνδρῶν, πῦρ κατὰ γυναικῶν, τόξα κατὰ θηρῶν, κατὰ πτηνῶν τὸ πτερόν, τὴν γύμνωσιν κατὰ τῶν ἐν θαλάττῃ καὶ καθ' ὅλης αὐτῆς.*

Verfolgen wir dieses Erosbild kurz in der r ö m i s c h e n Literatur. Auch hier spielt es in der erotischen Dichtung, speziell in der Elegie eine große Rolle. Literarische Vorlagen, dazu die vielen Erosdarstellungen auf Gemälden[3]), Tafeln und Münzen ließen dem Dichter dauernd das Bild vor Augen schweben. Zunächst einige Beispiele aus älterer Zeit: Plautus Persa 27:

sagitta Cupido[4]) *cor meum transfixit* — Plautus und Terenz gebrauchen überaus selten das Bild[5]). — Venus sendet auch Geschosse:
L u k r e z IV. 1052:

---

1) Der Einfluß der Rhetorik ist bei den meisten Romanschreibern unverkennbar.

2) Bei Plautus (Truc. 170) wird der *amans* mit einem „*oppidum hostile*" verglichen, das vom Mädchen erobert werden soll (s. u.).

3) Vgl. J a h n Arch. Studien S. 184.

4) Amor und Cupido werden im allgemeinen ganz willkürlich gebraucht. Ein Afraniusfragment zwar belehrt uns (Ribb. scaen. II. p. 198): . . . *alius est Amor . . alius Cupido.*

5) Sehr charakteristisch ist, daß der Komiker gewöhnlich das Bild des Rades und Kreuzes wählt, wenn er Amors Tyrannei kennzeichnet. Drängt sich doch die strenge S k l a v e n s t r a f e dem Römer vor. (Vgl. F r ä n k e l Plaut. i. Pl. c. VIII. u. sonst). Vgl. Plaut. Cist. 203 ff.:

> *Credo ego Amorem primum apud homines carunficinam commentum*
> . . . . . .
> *iactor, crucior, agitor,*
> *stimulor, vorsor,*
> *in Amori' rota, miser exanimor,*
> *feror, differor, distrahor, diripior. . .*

Sic igitur Veneris qui telis accipit ictus vgl. IV. 1278. Charakteristisch für die Behandlung griechischer τόποι seitens der Römer ist die **Horazstelle** Od. II. 8. 14 ff.:

> *ridet .... ferus et Cupido,*
> *semper ardentis acuens sagittas*
> *cote cruenta.*

Der Römer sucht das griechische Bild vom bewaffneten Eros gleichsam zu übertrumpfen, wenn er Amor die Waffen mit dem Wetzstein schärfen läßt. Wenigstens läßt sich dafür bei den Griechen keine Parallelstelle auffinden.

Wie in der Epigrammatik der Alexandriner, ist der kämpfende Eros auch in der römischen Elegie ein τόπος geworden. Noch nicht ausgesprochenermaßen bei **Catull**; er sieht ihn anthropomorph als Despoten, dessen Sklaven wir arme Menschen sind, die er entflammt (Cat. 45. 14. oder 64. 93 ff.), aber er deutet nicht auf die Fackel als seine Waffe. Aber **Tibull** beschreibt das 'Wüten' des Regenten Amor: I. 6. 3 ff.:

> *Quid tibi saevitiae mecum est? an gloria magna est*
> *Insidias homini composuisse deum[1]?*

Dazu Tib. I. 8. 49; Ovid Am. II. 9. 6. Den mit Bogen, Pfeilen und Fackeln versehenen Amor treffen wir bei Tibull in folgenden Stellen an: **Tib.** II. 1. 69 f.:

> *Illic indocto primum se exercuit arcu:*
> *Ei mihi, quam doctas nunc habet ille manus!*

vgl. Tib. II. 1. 71 f.; II. 1. 81 f.; II. 5. 105 f.; II. 6. 15 f.

Dieselbe Manier, Amors Macht Ausdruck zu verleihen, können wir bei Properz und Ovid feststellen. Bei Properz ist das Bild sehr lebendig und mit an Poseidipp erinnerndem Temperament geformt:

Originell ist der Gedanke, daß die Herkulesarbeiten dem Kampf mit Amor vorzuziehen seien. Plaut. 'Persa' 3 ff.:

> *cum lenone . . .*
> *cum Antaeo deluctari mavelim*
> *quam cum Amore.*

Hier haben wir das Ringerbild vgl. Anakreon fr. 27 u. Soph. Trach. 441 f.

1) Formell und inhaltlich verwandt mit dem Epigramm des Alkäus A. P. V. 9:

> . . . . .
> Τί πλέον, εἰ θεὸς ἄνδρα καταφλέγει; ἢ τί τὸ σεμνὸν
> δρώσας ἀπ' ἐμῆς ἆθλον ἔχει κεφαλῆς;

2*

Ovid würzt es mit dem ihm eigenen Witz und mit Anmut (s. unten).
Prop. II. 13. 2:

> *Spicula quot nostro pectore fixit Amor*

vgl. Prop. I. 7. 15. Ov. Am. I. 1. 25. Wie Properz (II. 9. 38 f.) vom
Amorschuß 'tela figere' sagt, so auch M a r t i a l: Ep. IX. 56, 2 f.:

> *Quae puero dones tela, Cupido, para,*
> *Illa quibus iuvenes figis mollesque puellas*

Prop. II. 12. 13 ff.:

> *In me tela manent, manet et puerilis imago:*
> . . . . .
> *assiduusque meo sanguine bella gerit[1]).*

Prop. II. 9. 38 ff.:

> *tela, precor, pueri, promite acuta magis.*
> *figite certantes atque hanc mihi solvite vitam:*
> *sanguis erit vobis maxima palma meus[2]).*

Eindrucksvoll schildert Properz seine Gefangennahme durch die
Eroten: Prop. II. 29. 3 ff.:

> *Obvia nescio quot pueri mihi, turba minuta,*
> *venerat (hos vetuit me numerare timor),*
> *quorum alii faculas, alii retinere sagittas,*
> *pars etiam visa est vincla parare mihi.*

Zu bemerken ist, daß in diesem Zusammenhang Catull und Tibull
nur von e i n e m Amor (Cupido) sprechen, Properz, Ovid u. a. da-
gegen des öfteren auch von Amores (oder pueri) wie die Alexandriner.

Der Sieger und Triumphator Amor ist von O v i d in der bekann-
ten Elegie Am. I. 2 glänzend dargestellt. — Noch einige Stellen,
die so recht ovidisch sind, mögen zitiert werden. Ars am.I. 261 f.:

> *Illa quod est virgo, quod tela Cupidinis odit,*
> *Multa dedit populo vulnera, multa dabit.*

---

1) Einen näheren Vergleich dazu bietet Meleager A. P. V. 214:

> Ναὶ γὰρ δὴ τὰ σὰ τόξα τὰ μὴ δεδιδαγμένα βάλλειν
> ἄλλον, ἀεὶ δ' ἐπ' ἐμοὶ πτανὰ χέοντα βέλη,
> εἰ καὶ ἐμὲ κτείναις, λείψω φωνὴν προϊέντα
> γράμματ'· Ἔρωτος ὅρα, ξεῖνε, μιαιφονίαν'.

Dazu A. P. V. 211.

2) Nicht so kraftvoll bringt Meleager den Gedanken zum Ausdruck
A. P. V. 138:

> Ποῖ σε φύγω; πάντῃ με περιστείχουσιν Ἔρωτες,
> οὐδ' ὅσον ἀμπνεῦσαι βαιὸν ἐῶσι χρόνον.

Ars I. 169:

> *Saucius ingemuit telumque volatile sensit*

vgl. a r s I. 261; II. 708; III. 515 ff. Venus als Kämpferin: ars
II. 397 f.:

> *Laesa Venus iusta arma movet telumque remittit*
> *Et, modo quod questast, ipse querare, facit.*

Der Dichter ist unwillig über Amors Geschosse, er will Rache
nehmen: ars I. 21 ff.

> *Et mihi cedit Amor, quamvis mea vulneret arcu*
> *Pectora iactatas excutiatque faces:*
> *Quo me fixit Amor, quo me violentius ussit,*
> *Hoc melior facti vulneris ultor ero.*

Amor soll ein „*molle regnum*“ ausüben: spielen soll er, nicht
kämpfen. Rem. 24 ff.:

> *lude! decent annos mollia regna tuos.*
> *Nam poteras uti nudis ad bella sagittis,*
> *sed tua mortifero sanguine tela carent.*
> *Vitricus et gladiis et acuta dimicet husta,*
> *et victor multa caede cruentus eat.*

Das Spielerische der Allegorie ist bei Ovid auf die Spitze ge-
trieben. Bei Properz und Tibull haben wir noch mehr den Eindruck
des Ernsthaften und Erlebten, wenn sie Amors Wille und Macht
charakterisieren.

Nach den Elegikern ist der „Krieger“ Amor besonders originell,
zum Teil mit an Ovid erinnerndem Witz von A p u l e i u s darge-
stellt. Met. IV. 30: Venus ruft ihren Sohn zu Hilfe . . . . *et vocat
confestim puerum suum pinnatum illum et satis temerarium, qui malis
suis moribus contempta disciplina publica, flammis et sagittis arma-
tus, per alienas domos nocte discurrens et omnium matrimonia cor-
rumpens impune committit tanta flagitia et nihil prorsus boni facit.
. . . . ʻper ego teʼ, inquit, ʻmaternae caritatis foedera deprecor, per tuae
sagittae dulcia vulnera, per flammae istius mellitas uredines, . . .*
Noch ein Beispiel: Met. X. 2: *at ubi completis igne vaesano totis
praecordiis inmodice bacchatus Amor exaestuabat, saevienti deo iam
succubuit, et languore simulato vulnus animi*[1]*) mentitur in corporis
valetudine.* Dazu Met. VI. 22; II. 16; V. 23; V. 25.

---

1) Vgl. Vergil Aen. IV. 1 f.:

> *At regina gravi iamdudum saucia cura*
> *volnus alit venis et caeco carpitur igni.*

Daß der Elegiker Maximian den Gemeinplatz auch verwertet, ist
bei seiner sonstigen Abhängigkeit von der angusteischen Elegie
wohl begreiflich. Ein Beispiel genügt auch hier: el. III, 89 f.:

> Arma tibi Veneris ceduntque Cupidinis arcus,
> cedit et armipotens ipsa Minerva tibi.

Venus' und Cupidos Kriegsrüstung also nebeneinander; die Ver-
bindung mit der wehrfähigen Minerva liegt nahe.

Zum Schluß noch ein der späteren Kaiserzeit angehöriges, dem
Verfasser nach unbekanntes Gedicht auf die Genetrix Venus: ‚Per-
vigilium Veneris', wo v. 29—36 über Cupidos Bewaffnung reflektiert
wird. Anth. lat. I, 1. p. 170 Nr. 200 (B—R) 29 ff.:

> Cras amet qui numquam amavit quique amavit cras amet!
> Ipsa Nymphas diva luco iussit ire myrteo:
> ‚Ite, Nymphae, posuit arma, feriatus est Amor'.
> It puer comes puellis; nec tamen credi potest
> Esse Amorem feriatum, si sagittas exuit.
> 'Iussus est inermis ire, nudus ire iussus est,
> Neu quid arcu neu sagitta neu quid igne laederet'.
> Sed tamen, Nymphae, cavete, quod Cupido pulcher est:
> Totus est in armis idem quando nudus est Amor.

Dazu eine Uebertragung Bürgers, der das Gedicht „die Nacht-
feier der Venus" mehrmals übersetzt hat[1]).

> Morgen liebe, wer die Liebe
> Schon gekannt!
> Morgen liebe, wer die Liebe
> Nie empfand!

Schon durchwallt die frohen Haine
Cythereens Nymphenschar.
Amor flattert mit; doch keine
Naht sich ihm und der Gefahr.
'Nymphen, die sein Köcher schreckte,
Wißt ihr nicht, was ihm geschehn,
Daß er heut die Waffen streckte,
Daß er heut muß wehrlos gehn?
Unverbrüchliche Gesetze
Wollen, daß sein Bogen heut
Keiner Nymphe Brust verletze.

---

1) Wolfg. Stammler 'Bürgers Gedicht: Die Nachtfeier der Venus' Bonn
1914 (kl. Texte f. Vorl. u. Uebg. v. Lietzmann 128).

Aber Nymphen scheut, o scheut
Ihn auch nackt! Er überlistet
Er verletzt euch Mädchen doch:
Denn den Waffenlosen rüstet seine ganze Schönheit noch.

Amor und Venus im Kampf mit den Menschen ist ein Bild, das natürlich immer wieder nachgeahmt und in der gesamten neueren Literatur und Kunst verwendet wurde. Daß die speziellen Ovidnachahmer reichen Gebrauch davon machen, wundert uns nicht [1] Mittelalterliche Dichter sprechen öfters von 'diu strâle' (Pfeil) des Liebesgottes. Zwei Beispiele hiefür: Im „Tristan" heißt es:

125. 25: al nâch der minnen quâle
   diu viurînen s t r â l e

der Meisner sagt:

3. 92. a: du schiuz der Minnen strâle mit gewalt
   durchs wîbes ougen in mannes herze.

Aus der neuesten Literatur auch einige typische Fälle: Ueber Aphroditens giftigen Pfeil reflektiert das 'Aphrodite' betitelte Gedicht von Just. K e r n e r. Es schließt mit den Zeilen:

Traue nicht der Meerentstieg'nen,
Oft ein Paradies sie bot,
Während sie mit gift'gem Pfeile
Senkte in ein Herz den Tod.

Amors Waffen: K l e i s t 'Penthesilea' v. 1081 ff.

Die Königin, sagst du? Unmöglich, Freundin!
Von Amors Pfeil getroffen — wann? Und wo?
. . . . .
Die Tochter Mars', der selbst der Busen fehlt,
Das Ziel der giftgefiederten Geschosse.

G o e t h e 'Götz von Berl.' II. 1:

Liebetraut: Mit Pfeilen und Bogen
   Cupido geflogen
   die Fackel in Brand
   wollt mutilich kriegen
   und männilich siegen
   mit stürmender Hand.

---

1) Ich verweise auf das Buch v. K. B a r t s c h Albrecht von Halberstadt und Ovid im Mittelalter besonders S. 51 ff. Quedlinburg und Leipzig 1861.

§ 2.

Das Jagen ist zu Ende,
das Jagen so frank und frei;
mein Herz ist mir zerschossen
mit Pulver und mit Blei.

Ein Mägdlein jung von Jahren
so schlank als wie ein Reh,
hat mich zu Tod getroffen,
mein Herz schreit ach und weh.

Herm. Löns „der verw. Jäger".

Wir haben gesehen: Eros kämpft in eigener Person mit den Menschen. Er sendet sein Geschoß und verfehlt selten das Ziel. Seinem Willen leistet niemand ungestraft Widerstand. In einer nicht-mythologischen Einkleidung bleibt zwar 'die Wunde' der Liebenden als Ausgangspunkt, ein 'Pfeil' als Verursacher, aber es ist nicht Eros, der ihn sendet, sondern die Strahlen der schönen Augen der Geliebten sind verzehrend 'wie Pfeile', sind geradezu Pfeile, die verwunden. Das reizende Mädchen verwundet ganz unbewußt wegen ihrer Schönheit den Liebhaber, beherrscht diesen wie ein Sieger den geschlagenen Feind. Die „Waffen" der Geliebten sind zumeist die Augen. Die Vorstellung, daß die Augen der Urgrund aller Liebeskrankheit sind und die Pforte für die Liebesschmerzen, ist ja von Anfang an in der antiken Literatur weit verbreitet [1]). Auch diesen τόπος sollen einige typische Beispiele veranschaulichen. „Verwundung" durch das Mädchen: A. P. V. 161 (Asklepiades):

'Η λαμπρή μ' ἔ τ ρ ω σ ε Φιλαίνιον [2])

dazu A. P. V. 52; A. P. V. 95.

Mit den Augen „schießt" der schöne Myiskus. Meleager A. P. XII. 101:

Τόν με Πό θ ο ι ς ἄ τ ρ ω τ ο ν [3]) ὑπὸ στέρνοισι Μυΐσκος
ὄμμασι τ ο ξ ε ύ σ α ς , τοῦτ' ἐβόησεν ἔπος·
'Τὸν θρασὺν εἶλον ἐγώ· τὸ δ' ἐπ' ὀφρύσι κεῖνο φρύαγμα
σκηπτροφόρου σοφίας ἡνίδε ποσσὶ πατῶ'. θαμβεῖς;

Selbst Eros kann auf diese Weise besiegt werden: Meleager A. P. XII. 113:

---

1) Vgl. Pindar Nem. 8. 1 ff.; Soph. Ant. 795 f.; Eur. Hipp. 525 f.

2) Nicht selten ist das naheliegende Jagdbild gebraucht. Vgl. A. P. V. 99: θηρευτὴν ὄμμασιν ἰξὸν ἔχων, A. P. V. 192: 'Η τρυφερή μ' ἤγρευσε Κλεώ. Dazu A. P. XII. 113.

3) Beachte den Kontrast!

Καὐτὸς Ἔρως ὁ πτανὸς ἐν αἰθέρι δέσμιος ἦλω,
ἀγρευθεὶς τοῖς σοῖς ὄμμασι, Τιμάριον.

Besonders viel verwertet ist dieses Bild von den Epistolographen: So Aristän. I. 1: *ὁ δὲ χρυσοῦς Ἔρως ἐπαίδευσε τὴν ποθουμένην εὐστόχως ἐπιτοξεύειν ταῖς τῶν ὀμμάτων βολαῖς.* Die Mädchen 'verwundet' sogar der schöne Gesang des Jungen: Aristän. I. 2: *ἐπειδὴ μέλη προσᾴδων καλὰ τὰ δεινὰ τῶν Ἐρώτων ἡμῖν ἐμβέβληκας βέλη.* Philostratos fordert den schönen Knaben auf, endlich einmal aus seinen Augen zu verschwinden. Die Augen sind als Burg gedacht, die der Knabe besetzt hält: Philostr. 11: *ἀπόπτηθι ἤδη ποτὲ καὶ τὴν πολιορκίαν λῦσον καὶ γενοῦ ξένος ἄλλων ὀμμάτων.* Philostr. 12 wird geschildert, wie der Junge des Liebhabers Seele erobert hat: *Πόθεν μου τὴν ψυχὴν κατέλαβες; ἢ δῆλον ὅτι ἀπὸ τῶν ὀμμάτων, ἀφ' ὧν μόνων κάλλος ἐσέρχεται; ὥσπερ γὰρ τὰς ἀκροπόλεις οἱ τύραννοι καὶ τὰ ἐρυμνὰ οἱ βασιλεῖς καὶ τὰ ὑψηλὰ οἱ ἀετοὶ καταλαμβάνουσιν, οὕτω καὶ ὁ ἔρως τὴν τῶν ὀφθαλμῶν ἀκρόπολιν, ἣν οὐ ξύλοις οὐδὲ πλίνθοις, ἀλλὰ μόνοις βλεφάροις τειχίσας ἡσυχῇ καὶ κατὰ μικρὸν ἐς τὴν ψυχὴν ἐσδύεται, ταχέως μὲν ὡς πτηνός, ἐλευθέρως δ' ὡς γυμνός, ἀμάχως δ' ὡς τοξότης.*

Auch die Schönheit an sich wird als „Burg" bezeichnet, die erobert werden muß. Philostr. 38: *καὶ κάλλους ἀκρόπολις πολὺ κρείττων τῶν βασιλέων.* Aehnlich bei den Romanschreibern: Xenophon Ephes. I. 3. 1. Das Mädchen Antheia beim Anblick des Lieblings: *ἁλίσκεται[1] Ἄνθεια ὑπὸ τοῦ Ἀβροκόμου, ἡττᾶται δ' ὑπὸ Ἔρωτος Ἀβροκόμης, κατεῖχε δ' αὐτὸν ἐγκείμενος ὁ θεός.* Habrokomes seinerseits wird vom Mädchen erobert: . . . *ἑάλωκα καὶ νενίκημαι καὶ παρθένῳ δουλεύειν[2] ἀναγκάζομαι,* vgl. Lukian, 'ἐρωτ. διάλ'. 11. 10. Nonn. Dion .XI. 376. Niketas Eugen. II. 243.

Chariton Aphrod.: I. 1. 7: Chaireas, der die schöne Kallirhoe gesehen hat: *Ὁ μὲν οὖν Χαιρέας οἴκαδε μετὰ τοῦ τραύματος μόλις ἀπῄει καὶ ὥσπερ τις ἀριστεὺς ἐν πολέμῳ τρωθεὶς καρδίαν.*

---

[1] Schon Plato gebraucht den Ausdruck Phädr. 253 c: *προθυμία μὲν οὖν τῶν ὡς ἀληθῶς ἐρώντων καὶ τελετή, ἐάνγε διαπράξωνται ὃ προθυμοῦνται ᾗ λέγω, οὕτω καλή τε καὶ εὐδαιμονικὴ ὑπὸ τοῦ δι' ἔρωτος μανέντος φίλου τῷ φιληθέντι γίγνεται, ἐὰν αἱρεθῇ· ἁλίσκεται δὲ δὴ ὁ αἱρεθεὶς τοιῷδε τρόπῳ* . . .
[2] Plato Symp 184 b. c: *ἔστι γὰρ ἡμῖν νόμος, ὥσπερ ἐπὶ τοῖς ἐρασταῖς ἦν δουλεύειν ἐθέλοντα ἡντινοῦν δουλείαν παιδικοῖς.*

Auch hier können wir bemerken, wie diese späten Autoren sich
in größerem Maße als die Alexandriner der Kriegertermini bedie-
nen und wie sie oft anschauliche, aber in allzuweit geführter Pa-
rallelisierung und pedantischer Breite ans Komische grenzende Bilder
entwerfen. Charakteristisch ist für sie ferner, daß sie im Gegensatz
zu ihren Vorbildern meist durchgeführte Bilder und eigentliche
Vergleiche bringen. Letzteres erklärt sich z. T. aus der langen Tra-
dition des τόπος.

Verhältnismäßig selten ist das eben betrachtete Bild in der römi-
schen Erotik. Dem Ausdruck *capere* begegnen wir öfters; er ent-
spricht dem griechischen αἱρεῖν, dem eben die Vorstellung zugrunde
liegt, daß der Liebesdienst ein „Kriegsdienst" bzw. eine „Jagd" ist.
Wenn P l a u t u s von „Pfeilküssen" redet, so steckt das gleiche
Bild dahinter: Trin. 241:

nam qui amat quod amat quom extemplo suaviis sagittatis
perculsus est.

Die schöne Gestalt verwundet:
L u c i l i u s fr. 735 (M):

at metuis porro ne aspectu et forma capiare altera[1]).

Prop. I. 1. 1 f.:

Cynthia prima suis miserum me cepit ocellis

vgl. Prop. II. 3. 44; II. 22. 7; III. 11. 16.

O v i d Am. I. 10. 10:

Nec facies oculos iam capit ista meos

vgl. Ov. Am. I. 2. 27; Ars I. 61; I. 83; I. 159.

Die schöne Geliebte schlägt den Liebhaber in Bande, wie der Herr
den Sklaven oder der Sieger den Kriegsgefangenen: T i b. I. 1. 55:

Me retinent vinctum formosae vincla puellae

T i b. I. 9. 79 f.:

Tum flebis, cum me vinctum puer alter habebit
Et gerit in regno regna superba tuo[2])

---

1) Aus deutscher Literatur zwei Beispiele: Heinrich v. Morungen 141. 16
Fr. V o g t 'des Minnesangs Frühling' 1920):

ir liehten ougen diu hânt âne longen
mich senden verwunt

'Venusgärtlein' S. 118. 9: Der Anschlag war gerathen, er ging gar bald von
staten, denn bald der erste Blick, die Jungfrau thät verwunden, daß sie
ward angebunden, gar hart mit Venusstrick.

2) Das gleiche Motiv: Heinr. v. Morungen 130. 18 ff.:

Der si ansiht
der muoz ir gevangen sîn
und in sorgen leben iemer mê.

vgl. Tib. II. 4. 1 ff. Zum Schluß noch eine Ovidstelle. Das Mädchen verwundet wegen ihrer Keuschheit: O v. ars I. 262 :

Multa dedit populo vulnera, multa dabit

vgl. O v. ars I. 458; I. 462; II. 12 u. a. St.

Ich fasse meine bisherige Untersuchung zusammen: Amor erzeugt den Liebeskrieg. Mit Kriegerwaffen persönlich ausgerüstet führt er bitteren Kampf mit den Menschen. Das Bild des pfeilsendenden Eros trafen wir zum erstenmal bei Euripides ausgebildet vor. Dieses wird besonders von den Alexandrinern gepflegt und weiter ausgewertet, wo es bei Epigrammatikern wie Poseidipp und Meleager die für die folgenden Zeiten maßgebende Gestalt erhalten hat. Die Hauptattribute des Eros sind Flügel, Pfeil, Bogen und Fackel. Mit dieser Ausrüstung tritt er seinen 'Eroberungszug' an. Diese Vorstellungen sind einerseits von den Römern, andererseits von den griechischen Romanschriftstellern und Epistolographen übernommen und inhaltlich nur wenig bereichert worden. Die Allegorie wurde durch alle Jahrhunderte fortgepflanzt und ist heute noch in Kunst und Literatur lebendig.

Bei den Römern stellten wir fest, daß die Bewaffnung Amors mit Vorliebe auch auf Venus selbst übertragen wird. Daß die Römer trotz ihrer motivischen Abhängigkeit dem Bild durchaus ihren individuellen Stempel aufzudrücken wußten, zeigten die Beispiele zur Genüge. Das gleiche Resultat ergab sich aus der Betrachtung des Bildes von der „verwundenden Geliebten", das eine Weiterentwicklung des Primärbildes vom pfeilsendenden Eros darstellt.

Zweites Kapitel.

§ 3.

Bekannt ist die Tatsache, daß die römische Elegie einen gewissen
Vorrat an Gedanken und poetischen Intentionen aufweist, die be-
reits in der griechischen, speziell in der hellenistischen Literatur
Form gewonnen haben. Ich brauche nur an einige wenige zu er-
innern: Der eben behandelte 'Triumphator Amor', der *„exclusus
amator"*, die Kämpfe mit Rivalen, der lästige Aufpasser, die ge-
schlagene Geliebte gehören zum viel verwendeten Motivbestand der
römischen Erotik, der mindestens keimhaft schon in der griechischen
Literatur anzutreffen ist. Ovid sah sich veranlaßt, jedem dieser Ge-
meinplätze eine besondere Elegie in seinen 'Amores' zu widmen und
so kunstvoll abzurunden. Auch der τόπος „Liebesdienst ein Kriegs-
dienst" ist das Thema einer ganzen Elegie; die Formulierung meiner
Abhandlung sind ja die Anfangsworte dieser Elegie. Nicht nur
Ovid, auch seine älteren Genossen Tibull und Properz, sowie andere
Schriftsteller der vor- und nachaugusteischen Zeit befleißigen sich
dieser Metapher. Wir dürfen von vornherein annehmen, daß die
Römer auch hier auf den Schultern der Alexandriner und der Grie-
chen überhaupt stehen. Ist das Bild in der hellenistischen Literatur
nicht aufzuspüren, so können wir daraus noch nicht schließen, daß
es spezifisch römisch ist und aus dem anderen kulturhistorischen
Hintergrund verstanden werden muß; sind doch die nachzuprüfen-
den literarischen Dokumente überaus lückenhaft. Dieser Umstand
erschwert naturgemäß die Uebersicht in der Entwicklung des Motivs.
Zum Glück können wir griechische Autoren zu Hilfe ziehen, von
denen uns Werke größeren Umfangs erhalten sind, und in denen
sich — so dürfen wir nach der bisherigen Forschung annehmen[1]) —

---

1) Erwähnen möchte ich die Arbeiten von Fr. Leo Plaut. Forsch. Berlin
1895, 126 ff.; Th. Gollnisch, *Luaest. elegiacae* Diss. Breslau 1905; M. Heine-
mann, *Epistulae amatoriae quo modo cohaereant cum elegiis Alexandrinis.*
Diss. 1909.

das literarische Leben der Alexandriner widerspiegelt. Das sind die griechischen Romanschriftsteller auf der einen, die Verfasser erotischer Briefe auf der andern Seite, die beiderseits verschiedenen Jahrhunderten der römischen Kaiserzeit angehören. Daß diese von den Römern beeinflußt sind, wäre zeitlich sehr wohl möglich, ist aber aus literarhistorischen Gründen zu verwerfen. Der „Liebeskrieg" ist für sie ein geläufiges Motiv. Wertvoller indes sind natürlich solche Belege, die aus früherer Zeit datieren. Wir werden darnach forschen, wo die Metapher zum erstenmal Platz greift, ob sie Eigentum erst hellenistischer Literatur ist oder ob sie noch früher auftaucht. Wir haben oben gesehen, daß Eros seit dem 4. Jahrh. v. Chr. in Kunst und Literatur zum spielenden Kind degradiert ist und das Problem „Liebe" die buntesten literarischen Erzeugnisse ins Leben ruft. Dieser Umstand könnte die Vermutung nahelegen, daß unsere Metapher ein poetisches Spiel eben jener alexandrinischen Epigrammatiker ist. Das vorhandene Material wird das vielleicht nicht genügend entscheiden lassen. Schließlich müssen wir bedenken, daß das Bild Allgemeingut der Literatur sein kann. Halten wir jetzt in der griechischen Poesie und Prosa Umschau!

Was wir bisher verfolgt haben, war das Bild des Soldaten Eros, der mit den Menschen heftigen Kampf führt, ohne daß diese sich wehren dürfen und können. Der Krieg der Liebenden besteht indes vor allem im aktiven Eingreifen, indem sie auf Eroberungen ausgehen, mit ihrer Geliebten Kämpfe ausfechten, kurz Mühen und Strapazen nach Art der Soldaten zu ertragen haben. Der oberste Kriegsherr in der *militia Veneris* ist Amor. Unter seiner Fahne treten sie den Kriegszug an, er ist für sie der „Feldherr" schlechthin: P o s e i d i p p sagt A. P. V. 212:

> Εἰπὲ δὲ σημεῖον, μεθύων ὅτι καὶ διὰ κλωπῶν
> ἦλϑεν Ἔρωτι ϑρασεῖ χρώμενος ἡ γ ε μ ό ν ι.

Wenn wir den Wurzeln der Metapher nachgehen, so werden wir in erster Linie die Fragmente der alten Lyriker darauf prüfen. In dem berühmten Sapphogedicht „ποικιλόϑρον' ἀϑανάτ' Ἀφρόδιτα" scheint das Bild vorzuliegen. Die Dichterin fordert Aphrodite auf, ihre Liebesschmerzen zu heilen und ihr in der Liebe „σύμμαχος" zu sein. S a p p h o fr. 1. letzte Str.:

> ἔλϑε μοι καὶ νῦν, χαλέπαν δὲ λῦσον
> ἐκ μερίμναν, ὅσσα δέ μοι τέλεσσαι
> ϑῦμος ἰμέρρει, τέλεσον· σὺ δ' αὔτα
> σ ύ μ μ α χ ο ς ἔσσο.

Diese Stelle gestattet jedoch noch nicht ohne weiteres die Annahme, daß unsere Metapher schon dem 7./6. Jahrh. angehört. σύμμαχος ist ein vielgebrauchtes Wort, das ähnlich unserem „Bundesgenosse" in allen Sprachgebieten Verwendung findet. Das Kriegsbild dürfte dabei kaum mehr empfunden werden. Wir denken in obiger Stelle mehr an „Helferin" als an „Mitstreiterin". Weil das Beispiel so vereinzelt ist, ist es nicht ratsam, das —μαχος zu betonen. Denn wie die Lyrik scheint auch die attische Tragödie[1]) die Metapher vom Liebeskrieg nicht gebraucht zu haben. Dagegen finden wir bei Aristophanes im Drama eine schwache Spur davon. Von den Frauen, die den Liebesgenuß gestatten, sagt der Dichter: Ekkl. 621 f.:

$$\vartheta άρρει, \ μὴ \ δείσῃς, \ οὐχὶ \ μ α χ ο ῦ ν τ α ι$$
$$\ldots\ldots τοῦ \ μὴ \ ξυγκαταδαρϑεῖν.$$

Diese Stelle beweist auch noch nicht die technische Bedeutung der Metapher. „Sich wehren" hat zwar militärische Wurzel, aber das Kriegerische wird hier nicht mehr empfunden. Man hört nur „sie sträuben sich nicht" heraus. — Den Ausdruck μάχεσϑαι gebraucht Aristophanes einmal im Sinn des Streites mit einem Rivalen in der Liebe. Der Junge tritt die Hetäre, die er bisher sein eigen nannte, dem Alten willig ab: Plut. 1076:

$$ἐγὼ \ περὶ \ ταύτης \ οὐ \ μ α χ ο ῦ μ α ι \ σοι$$
1079: $νῦν \ δ'ἄπιϑι \ χαίρων \ σ υ λ λ α β ὼ ν \ τὴν \ μείρακα.$

Hier möchte ich gleich eine verwandte Stelle des Epigrammatikers Meleager beifügen. Den Zeus will der Dichter nicht zum Nebenbuhler haben. A. P. XII. 66:

$$κρίνατ' \ "Ερωτες, \ ὁ \ παῖς \ τίνος \ ἄξιος \cdot \ εἰ \ μὲν \ ἀληϑῶς$$
$$ἀϑανάτων, \ ἐχέτω \cdot \ Ζηνὶ \ γὰρ \ οὐ \ μ ά χ ο μ α ι.$$

Das Bild des Liebenden als στρατιώτης liegt also, so weit feststellbar, in der alten Komödie nur keimhaft vor und ist von ihr noch nicht im eigentlichen Sinne als erotische Metapher benutzt. Aristophanes kennt dagegen, wie später gezeigt wird, gymnastische Metaphern fürs Liebesleben und zwar in ausgebildeter Form.

Ein bei Athenäus (XIII. 562 f.) erhaltenes Fragment des Komikers Alexis[1]), der zur mittleren Komödie gehört, beweist zur Genüge,

---

1) Die Tragiker lieben das Bild vom Ackerbau, als Bereich, aus dem sprachliche Wendungen zum Ausdruck sexueller Verhältnisse genommen werden. Vgl. A. Dieterich „Mutter Erde"[3] 1925.

2) Ueber die Zugehörigkeit des Fragmentes siehe Meineke, com. gr. frg. I. 519 f. u. Kock II. 382.

daß unsere Metapher schon griechisch ist. Die Liebenden werden
als „στρατευτικώτατοι" charakterisiert. A l e x i s fr. 234 (K II. 382):

> τίς οὐχὶ φήσει τοὺς ἐρῶντας ζῆν μόνους[1];
> εἰ δεῖ γε πρῶτον μὲν σ τ ρ α τ ε υ τ ι κ ω τ ά τ ο υ ς
> εἶναι, πονεῖν τε δυναμένους τοῖς σώμασιν
> μάλιστα, π ρ ο σ ε δ ρ ε ύ ε ι ν τ' ἀρίστους τῷ πόθῳ,
> ποιητικούς, ἰτάμους, προθύμους, εὐπόρους
> ἐν τοῖς ἀπόροις, βλέποντας ἀθλιωτάτους.

Jedermann, sagt unser Komiker, muß gestehen, daß das Liebes-
leben ein mühevolles Ringen ist. Die Liebhaber müssen die „krie-
gerischsten" Leute sein. Das Folgende ist eigentlich nur nähere
Begründung zum Begriff 'στρατευτικώτατοι'. Der Liebende muß in
besonders hohem Maße körperlichen Anstrengungen gewachsen sein.
'Προσεδρεύειν' ist ein militärischer Terminus und wird gebraucht
für das Belagern von Burgen und Städten. Wie die Soldaten die
Stadt, so müssen die Venuskämpfer tapfer und ausdauernd ihr Ziel
verfolgen und belagern. Das „ποιητικοὺς" v. 5 will Meineke (V. 1. 91)
in νοητικοὺς verbessern. Wir behalten das überlieferte ποιητικοὺς
bei in dem ursprünglichen Sinn — als von ποιεῖν abgeleitet —
gleich erfinderisch, wenn auch das nachfolgende εὐπόρους den
ähnlichen Gedanken enthält. Uebrigens wäre νοητικοὺς inhaltlich

---

1) Kock glaubt das überlieferte μόνους in v. 1 ändern zu müssen, indem
er dazu bemerkt „μόνους poetae non esse potest, cum amantes m i s e r e vivere
dicat." Er will π ό ν ο ι ς einsetzen. Das ist sachlich m. E. keine schlechte
Konjektur, denn programmatisch stände dann der Begriff 'πόνοι amantium'
voran, der in den folgenden Versen näherhin erläutert wird. Vielleicht ist
die Wendung πόνοις ζῆν zu beanstanden. Die Stelle (Pher. 13) στραβήλοις ζῆν,
die Kock zur Stütze beizieht, ist ja kein analoger Fall. Sollte es schon nötig
sein, den Text zu verbessern, würde ich die Lesart ζῆν π ό ν ο υ ς, was der
Ueberlieferung näher käme, vorschlagen. Der Akkusativ der Sache bei ζῆν
kommt einmal in der sog. figura etymologica: ζωὴν (βίον) ζῆν öfters vor
(vgl. Eur. Medea 248 f.); sonst kann ich allerdings nur noch eine Demosthenes-
stelle anführen, wo das Relativpronomen so konstruiert wird: 558: Δῆλον
ὅτι ἐκ τῶν ἄλλων, ὧν (= ἃ) ἔζης, ἄξιος . . . . . Indes glaube ich, daß der
überlieferte Text festgehalten werden kann. Der Dichter sagt: Wer leugnet, daß
eigentlich nur die Liebenden ein wahres, vollhaltiges, wenn auch mühevolles
und kampfreiches Leben zu führen haben. Das in μόνους liegende Hyperbolische
des Gedankens paßt zu der die Strapazen der Liebenden ausmalenden Stelle
wohl besser als das den Text glättende πόνοις (πόνους), zumal das Wort
πονεῖν v. 3 vorkommt. Uebrigens ist nicht so fast das 'm i s e r e vivere' der
amantes betont, wie Kock schreibt, als vielmehr das f o r t i t e r vivere d. h. die
Tapferkeit und Tüchtigkeit, die von denen verlangt ist, welche Amor dienen.

von unserem *ποιητικούς* kaum verschieden. Geschickt, verwegen, voll Mut müssen die Liebhaber sein, in der Not Rat wissen und als recht unglückliche und kampfbeladene Leute in die Welt blicken. Leider bricht das Bruchstück hier ab. Es ist noch zu erwähnen, daß der Titel der Komödie „*Τραυματίας*" (der „Verwundete") zu dem „militat omnis amans" des erhaltenen Fragments gut paßt. Es ist nicht unmöglich, daß das Stück den *τόπος* behandelte, wie der Liebende „verwundet" ist und nur heilbar durch den Verwundenden (*ὁ τρώσας καὶ ἰάσεται*).

Wir fühlen uns an Ovids Elegie (Am. I. 9) erinnert, wo auf ähnliche, nur vielleicht noch ausführlichere Weise die Eigenschaften und Mühen der Liebenden dem Leser vor Augen geführt werden. Daß Ovid und die römischen Elegiker diese Komödie des Alexis gekannt haben. ist unwahrscheinlich. Wir wissen, daß römische Palliatendichter den Alexis benutzt haben (Kaibel, RE II, 1471); Ovid aber müßte das Stück durch Zufall oder etwa seines eminent erotischen Themas wegen in die Hände bekommen haben, was wenig wahrscheinlich ist. Denn ein doctus poeta ist er nicht; er ergreift vielmehr stets das Bereitliegende.

Situationskomik, Wortspiele, Witz, humoristisch-derbe Ausgelassenheit könnten diese Metapher in der Komödie leicht bedingen. Tatsächlich stoßen wir aber in unseren Quellen auf merkwürdig wenig Beispiele. Man würde — zumal wenn man an die Rolle des miles gloriosus seit den Diadochenzeiten denkt — viel mehr erwarten. Ich führe die mir noch bekannt gewordenen Beispiele an. **Menander** „*Περικειρ.*" 232 ff. (Jensen).

Der Sklave Sosias sagt zum Offizier Polemon, bei dem sich das Mädchen Habrotonon aufhält, und zu ihr:

ᾤμην σε ποιήσειν τι · καὶ γάρ, Ἀβρότονον,
ἔχεις τι πρὸς π ο λ ι ο ρ κ ί α ν σὺ χρήσιμον
δύνασαί τ' ἀ ν α β α ί ν ε ι ν, π ε ρ ι κ α θ ῆ σ θ α ι . .

Für diese Sphäre liefert auch der Komiker Machon einiges Material (s. w. u.!). Von seinen „*Χρεῖαι*", einer Sammlung von witzigen, aber stark obszönen Hetärenanekdoten, hat uns Athenäus (XIII, 577 ff.) größere Bruchstücke gerettet[1]). Vielleicht darf folgende Stelle nicht übergangen werden. Athen. 581[b]:

---

1) Abgedruckt bei G. von Wartensleben, Begriff der griechischen Chreia Diss. Heidelberg 1901 p. 128 ff.

Ein alter, vornehmer Satrap wünscht eine Nacht bei der Hetäre Gnathaina zu verbringen. Er fragt sie: 'πόσον ... νυκτός', diese:

> ... εἰς τὴν πορφύραν
> καὶ τὰ δόρατ' ἀποβλέψασα δραχμὰς χιλίας
> ἔταξεν. ὃ δ' ἄφνω καιρίμην πληγείς · 'παπαῖ,
> ζωγρεῖς, γύναι, φήσ', ἕνεκα τοῦ στρατιωτικοῦ ·
> μνᾶς πραξαμένη δὲ πέντε τ ὰ ς σ π ο ν δ ὰ ς π ο ο ῦ
> καὶ στρῶσον ἡμῖν ἔνδον.'

Die Hetäre schließt mit ihrem Opfer einen 'Vertrag': um so witziger, als dieses ein Satrap ist. —

Auch die palatinische Anthologie liefert im ganzen recht wenig Beispiele. Oben habe ich eine Stelle aus Meleager erwähnt. Komödienton tritt uns auch hier entgegen: Meleager A. P. XII. 33:

> 'Ην καλὸς 'Ηράκλειτος, ὅτ' ἦν ποτέ · νῦν δὲ παρ' ἥβην
> κ η ρ ύ σ σ ε ι π ό λ ε μ ο ν δ έ ρ ρ ι ς ὀ π ι σ θ ο β ά τ α ι ς.

(vgl. A. P. XII. 144: Μνίσκος ὁ δ ύ σ μ'α χ ο ς.)

„Δέρρεις" bedeutet sonst Decken, die auf Kriegsschiffen und bei Belagerungen verwendet werden, um die Wirkung der Geschütze zu entkräften, vgl. Thuk. II. 75. 'Ο π ι σ θ ο β ά τ η ς scheint nur an dieser Stelle vorzukommen. Es erinnert an den Terminus ναυβάτης und will das Marinebild verdeutlichen. Ein späterer Epigrammatiker S k y t h i n o s A. P. XII. 22 sagt ähnlich:

> 'Ηλθέν μοι μέγα πῆμα, μ έ γ α ς π ό λ ε μ ο ς, μέγα μοι πῦρ
> 'Ηλισσος πλήρης τῶν ἐς ἔρωτ' ἐτέων.....
> 6: Καὶ τί πάθω; φησὶν γὰρ ὁρᾶν μόνον · ἤ ῥ' ἀ γ ρ υ π ν ή σ ω
> πολλάκι, τῇ κενεῇ κύπριδι χ ε ι ρ ο μ α χ ῶ ν.

Der reizende Helissos steht nämlich in dem fürs Liebesleben reifen Alter, gestattet aber dem Liebhaber nicht, ihn zu berühren; er darf ihn nur anschauen. Die übrigen in Frage kommenden Epigramme gehören alle der späteren Kaiserzeit an. Aus sachlichen Gründen sollen diese erst an späterer Stelle Berücksichtigung finden.

Metaphern, die dem Bereiche der Palästra, dem Leben und Treiben in den Gymnasien entnommen sind, spielen in der griechischen Literatur eine große Rolle. An späterer Stelle soll uns das veranschaulicht werden. Zunächst weiterhin das Kriegsbild bei den Erotikern der Kaiserzeit: Ergiebig für unsere Metapher sind Lukian, vor allem aber die Epistolographen und Romanschreiber. Sachliche

Gesichtspunkte mögen neben der Chronologie [1]) die Anordnung bestimmen.

Lukian ὄνος c. 11 spricht vom „Liebeskrieg": αἰχμάλωτον ἔχεις ἐρωτικῷ πολέμῳ ψυχαγωγοῦσα, eine Stelle, die sonst agonale Bilder aufweist und weiter unten nochmals genannt werden muß. Das Bild ist wenigstens angedeutet Luk. ἑταιρ. διάλ. 10. 4: Eine Hetäre fordert ihre Genossin auf, ihr Hilfe zu leisten im Kampf mit Aristänetus, ihrem Rivalen in der Liebe: Εὖ γε, συστράτευε μόνον, ὦ Χελιδόνιον, κατὰ τοῦ ἀλαζόνος Ἀρισταινέτου. Das Gewand ist eine 'Mauer' bei Bettkämpfen: ἑταιρ. διάλ. 11. 1: καὶ τέλος διετείχιζες τὸ μεταξὺ ἡμῶν τῷ ἱματίῳ δεδιὼς μὴ ψαύσαιμί σου. Ausdrücke wie ἁλίσκεσθαι, ἡττᾶσθαι, νικᾶν u. ä. sind natürlich häufig gebraucht. Weil sie für die *militia Amoris* nicht gerade von weittragender Bedeutung sind wegen der bereits abgeblaßten Metaphern, genügt es, wenn ich nur wenige Fälle anführe: Luk. ἑταιρ. διάλ. 11. 10: καὶ ἑάλωκα ὁ κακοδαίμων καὶ συνείλημμαι πρὸς αὐτῆς ... oder: Heliodor Αἰθίωπ. III. 7. 19 f: ἑάλωκεν ἡ δυσάλωτος καὶ νενίκηται ἡ δυσκαταμάχητος· ἐρᾷ Χαρίκλεια. Chariton Aphrod. I. 4. 2: Γυνὴ δ' εὐάλωτόν ἐστιν, ὅταν ἐρᾶσθαι δοκῇ ... anders II. 8. 2: ἀλλ' ἡ Καλλιρρόη πανταχόθεν ἀήττητος ἦν καὶ ἔμενε Χαιρέᾳ μόνῳ πιστή.

Von den Epistolographen kommen Alkiphron und Aristänetus für das Bild in Frage. Das Spielen mit einem Kriegsausdruck erzeugt die Metapher: Die Hetäre will den Demetrius πολιορκητὴς mit Flötenspiel erobern Alkiphron ἐρωτ. ἐπιστ. 16. 3: νὴ τὴν Ἀφροδίτην, σήμερον αὐτὸν τοῖς αὐλοῖς ἐκπολιορκήσω καὶ ὄψομαι τί με διαθήσει. Aehnlich weiter unten (§ 5): ἐμοὶ γὰρ ἐξ ἐκείνου, μὰ τὴν Ἄρτεμιν, οὐδὲ προσέπεμψαν ἔτι πολλοὶ [οὐδὲ ἐπείρασαν] αἰδούμενοί σου τὰς πολιορκίας. Die Nebenbuhler wagen sich nicht an die Hetäre des Demetrius πολιορκητής. — Ausgeführte Bilder kommen in dieser Spätzeit des öfteren vor. Ein modus des 'Liebeskriegs' besteht vor allem auch darin, daß die Liebenden Gegner haben, mit denen sie mitunter bittere Rivalenkämpfe bestehen müssen. Diese spielen sich meist vor der Türe der Ersehnten ab. Aristänetus II. 19:

---

1) Siehe Christ-Schmid, Lit.Gesch. u. K. Kerényi, Die griech.-orient. Romanliteratur in religionsgeschichtlicher Beleuchtung Tübingen 1927 unter Chronologie.

Πρὸ θυρῶν ἀκήκοα κωμαστῶν ὑπὲρ ἐμοῦ μ α χ ο μ έ ν ω ν ἀωρὶ νυκτῶν, οὐκ ὄναρ, ἀλλ᾽ ὕπαρ [1]).

Eine humorvolle Szene bietet dieser im folgenden: Ein Mann erleidet gleichzeitig zwei Niederlagen. Einmal verliert er beim Würfelspiel all sein Geld, ein größeres Malheur aber bedeutet es für ihn, wenn die Mitspieler das gewonnene Geld nun dazu benützen, dem Verlierer auch noch seine Geliebte zu entreißen. A r i s t ä n. I. 23:

εἶτα πρὸς τὴν ἐρωμένην ἀπιὼν ἐκεῖ δευτέραν ἧ τ τ α ν ὑπομένω καὶ χείρονα τῆς προτέρας. οἱ γὰρ εὐτυχεῖς ἀντερασταί, ἅτε δή με τὰ τοσαῦτα νενικηκότες, φιλοτιμότερον δωροῦνται τῇ ποθουμένῃ, καὶ προκρίνονταί μου τοῖς δώροις, κᾆτα ἀπὸ τῶν ἐμῶν με π ο λ ε - μ ο ῦ ν τ ε ς μεταπεττεύουσί μου τῆς φιλίας κύβον.

Beinahe jeder Romanschriftsteller macht von unserer Metapher, die nunmehr zum *τόπος* geworden ist, Gebrauch. Bemerkenswert ist die Tatsache, daß diesen Autoren die Kriegsbilder geläufiger sind als den Schriftstellern des Hellenismus. Der Grund dafür dürfte z. T. darin zu suchen sein, daß Roms Militärmacht auch für Griechen den Sprachschatz mit militärischen Ausdrücken bereicherte — wie ja die römische Dichtung (Elegie) freigebiger damit geschaltet hat.

Von der militia Amoris ganz im allgemeinen hören wir in diesen Stellen: H e l i o d o r *Αἰθιοπ.* VII 10. 30 ff.: Der Anblick des eingetroffenen hübschen Fremdlings hat die Königin in rasende Leidenschaft versetzt. Dieser hat noch einen heftigeren „Krieg" heraufbeschworen, als es der kurz zuvor wirklich ausgefochtene Kampf war... *ὁ γάρ τοι πόλεμος ὁ πρὸ τῶν τειχῶν τήμερον ὀλίγου μὲν συγκροτηθεὶς ἀθρόον δὲ καταστᾱλεὶς τοῖς μὲν ἄλλοις ἀναίμακτος ἀπεφάνθη καὶ εἰς εἰρήνην κατέστρεψεν, ἐμοὶ·δὲ ἀρχή τις ἀ λ η - θ ε σ τ έ ρ ο υ π ο λ έ μ ο υ καὶ τ ρ α ῦ μ α οὐ μέρους μόνον ἢ μέλους ἀλλὰ καὶ ψυχῆς αὐτῆς γέγονε.* Ein feiger Soldat im Liebeskrieg A c h. T a t. II. 5. 1: *Μέχρι τίνος, ἄνανδρε, σιγᾷς; τί δὲ δειλὸς εἰ σ τ ρ α τ ι ώ τ η ς ἀνδρείου θεοῦ;* E u s t a t h i u s sagt einmal VII. 5. 1: *Ταῦθ᾽ ἡμεῖς ἐ ρ ω τ ι κ ῶ ς ἐ μ α χ ό μ ε θ α καὶ παίζοντες* [2]) *ἐσπουδάζομεν.* Das erinnert an L o n g u s past. II.

---

1) Zum Philostratusbrief 29 bemerkt der Scholiast (Hercher p. 488): . . . . *ἧς ἔργα θυραυλίαι καὶ χαμαικοιτίαι καὶ ἡ πρὸς θάλπος καὶ χειμῶνα ἀντίταξις καὶ ἡ ʻμʼ ἀνάρειοʼ ἢ ʻἐγώσεʼ πρὸς τὸν ἀντεραστὴν μάχη.*

2) *παίζειν* (*ludere* bei den Römern) begegnet öfters im Sinne von Liebesstreit vgl. E u s t a t h. V. 1. 4: *καὶ θέλων παίζειν ἐρωτικῶς τὸ λουτρὸν ἐξεπύρωσε.*

39. 1, der den neutralen Ausdruck 'ἔρις' gebraucht: πρὸς ἀλλήλους ἤριζον ἔριν ἐρωτικήν . . .

Breit ausgeführt ist folgender Rivalenstreit, bei dem das Kriegs-und Agonbild nebeneinander verwendet wird. C h a r i t o n A p h r o d. I. 2. 1 ff: Die Nebenbuhler, die bisher einander befehdet hatten, einigen sich nunmehr zum Kampf gegen den Triumphator:

Οἱ γὰρ μνηστῆρες ἀποτυχόντες τοῦ γάμου λύπην ἐλάμβανον μετ᾽ ὀργῆς. Τέως οὖν μ α χ ό μ ε ν ο ι πρὸς ἀλλήλους ὡμονόησαν τότε, διὰ δὲ τὴν ὁμόνοιαν, ὑβρίσθαι δοκοῦντες, συνῆλθον εἰς βου-λευτήριον κοινόν· ἐ σ τ ρ α τ ο λ ό γ ε ι δ᾽ αὐτοὺς ἐπὶ τὸν κατὰ Χαι-ρέου π ό λ ε μ ο ν ὁ φθόνος. Einer von den Freiern hält folgende Rede:. . . εἰ μέν τις ἐξ ἡμῶν ἔγημεν, οὐκ ἂν ὠργίσθην, ὥσπερ ἐν τοῖς γ υ μ ν ι κ ο ῖ ς ἀ γ ῶ σ ι ν ἕνα δεῖ ν ι κ ῆ σ α ι τ ῶ ν ἀ γ ω ν ι-σ α μ έ ν ω ν· ἐπεὶ δὲ παρευδοκίμησεν ἡμᾶς ὁ μηδὲν ὑπὲρ [τοῦ] γάμου πονήσας, οὐ φέρω τὴν ὕβριν. Ἡμεῖς δὲ παρετάθημεν αὐλείοις θύραις π ρ ο σ α γ ρ υ π ν ο ῦ ν τ ε ς, καὶ κολακεύοντες τίτ-θας καὶ θεραπαινίδας καὶ δῶρα πέμποντες τροφοῖς πόσον χρόνον δεδουλεύκαμεν καί, τὸ πάντων χαλεπώτατον, ὡς ἀντεραστὰς ἀλλή-λους ἐμισήσαμεν· ὁ δὲ πόρνος καὶ πένης καὶ μηδενὸς κρείττων βασιλέων ἀ γ ω ν ι σ α μ έ ν ω ν αὐτὸς ἀκονιτὶ τὸν στέφανον ᾖρατο. Ἀλλὰ ἀνόνητον αὐτῷ γενέσθω τὸ ἆ θ λ ο ν καὶ τὸν γάμον θάνατον τῷ νυμφίῳ ποιήσωμεν.

Kampf mit dem Mädchen: A c h. T a t. II. 10. 3. Der schüchterne Liebhaber hatte endlich den Mut gefaßt, bei Eintritt der Dunkel-heit auf seine Ersehnte zu lauern:

Ἐπιτηρήσας οὖν ὅτε τὸ πολὺ τῆς αὐγῆς ἐμαραίνετο, π ρ ό σ ε ι μ ι θρασύτερος γενόμενος ⟨πρὸς αὐτὴν⟩ ἐκ τῆς πρώτης π ρ ο σ β ο-λ ῆ ς, ὥσπερ σ τ ρ α τ ι ώ τ η ς ἤδη ν ε ν ι κ η κ ὼ ς καὶ τοῦ π ο-λ έ μ ο υ καταπεφρονηκώς· πολλὰ γὰρ ἦν τὰ τότε ὁ π λ ί ζ ο ν τ ά με θ α ρ ρ ε ῖ ν, οἶνος, ἔρως, ἐλπίς, ἐρημία. Mit erstaunlicher Naivi-tät und Anschaulichkeit weiß der zu den spätesten griechischen Romanschreibern gehörende Byzantiner Eustathius eine Liebesszene vor unseren Augen zu entrollen. III. 7. 3 ff.:

Γίνομαι καὶ περὶ τὸ στέρνον τῆς κόρης· ἡ δ᾽ ἀ ν τ έ χ ε τ α ι μάλα γενναίως καὶ ὅλη ξυστέλλεται καὶ ὅλῳ σώματι π ε ρ ι τ ε ι χ ί ζ ε ι τὸν μαστὸν ὡς π ό λ ι ν ἀ κ ρ ό π ο λ ι ς. καὶ χερσὶ καὶ τραχήλῳ καὶ πώγωνι τοὺς μαστοὺς κ α τ α φ ρ ά τ τ ε ι καὶ π ε ρ ι φ ρ ά τ τ ε ι· καὶ κάτωθεν μὲν ἀνέχει τὰ γόνατα, ὡς ἐξ ἀ κ ρ ο π ό λ ε ω ς δὲ τῆς κεφαλῆς ἀ κ ρ ο β ο λ ί ζ ε ι τὸ δάκρυον, μονονοὺ λέγουσα 'ἢ φιλῶν μαλαχθῇ μοι τοῖς δάκρυσι ἢ μὴ φιλῶν ὀκνήσεις τὸν π ό λ ε-

μον'. Ἐγὼ δὲ μᾶλλον τὴν ἧτταν αἰδούμενος ἀντέχομαι βιαιό
τερον καὶ μόλις νικῶ, καὶ νικῶν ἡττῶμαι καὶ ὅλος ἀμβλύνομαι.

Das Liebesleben ist auch insofern eine Art Kriegsleben, als die
Wohnung belagert und bestürmt, evtl. die Geliebte entführt werden
muß: Heliodor IV. 17. 6 ff.: καὶ εἰς τὴν ἑξῆς τοιάδε ἐγίγνετο·
ἐπειδὴ μέσαι νύκτες ὕπνῳ τὴν πόλιν ἐβάστιζον, ἔνοπλος κῶμος
τὴν οἴκησιν τῆς Χαρικλείας κατελάμβανεν. ἐστρατήγει
δὲ Θεαγένης τὸν ἐρωτικὸν τοῦτον πόλεμον κτλ.

Nicht gar so ernsthaft, aber interessanter verlief das Abenteuer,
das Agathias Scholasticus, ein Rechtsanwalt und Epigrammatiker
des sechsten nachchristlichen Jahrhunderts, in sehr originellem
Tone schildert. Dabei sind sowohl militärische wie agonale Bilder
verwertet. Passend gelobt der Dichter am Schluß, der Kypris Tropaiophoros für den Fall seines Erfolgs Siegeskränze, A. P. V. 293:

Ἡ γραῦς ἡ φθονερὴ παρεκέκλιτο γείτονι κούρῃ,
 δόχμιον ἐν λέκτρῳ νῶτον ἐρεισαμένη
προβλὴς ὥς τις ἔπαλξις ἀνέμβατος· οἷα δὲ πύργος
 ἔσκεπε τὴν κούρην ἁπλοῖς ἐκταδίη.
καὶ σοβαρὴ θεράπαινα πύλας σφίγξασα μελάθρου
 κεῖτο χαλικρήτῳ νάματι βριθομένη.
ἔμπης οὔ με φόβησαν, ἐπεὶ στρεπτῆρα θυρέτρου
 χερσὶν ἀδουπήτοις βαιὸν ἀειράμενος
φρυκτοὺς αἰθαλόεντας ἐμῆς ῥιπίσμασι λώπης
 ἔσβεσα, καὶ διαδὺς λέχριος ἐν θαλάμῳ
τὴν φύλακα κνώσσουσαν ὑπέκφυγον· ἦκα δὲ λέκτρου
 νέρθεν ὑπὸ σχοίνοις γαστέρι συρόμενος,
ὠρθούμην κατὰ βαιόν, ὅπῃ βατὸν ἔπλετο τεῖχος·
 ἄγχι δὲ τῆς κούρης στέρνον ἐρεισάμενος
μαζοὺς μὲν κρατέεσκον, ὑπεθλίφθην δὲ προσώπῳ
 μάστακα πιαίνων χείλεος εὐαφίῃ.
ἦν δ' ἄρα μοι τὰ λάφυρα καλὸν στόμα, καὶ τὸ φίλημα
 σύμβολον ἐννυχίης εἶχον ἀεθλοσύνης.
οὔπω δ' ἐξαλάπαξα φίλης πύργωμα κορείης·
 ἀλλ' ἔτ' ἀδηρίτῳ σφίγγεται ἀμβολίῃ.
ἔμπης ἢν ἑτέροιο μόθου στήσωμεν ἀγῶνα,
 ναὶ τάχα πορθήσω τείχεα παρθενίης,
οὐδ' ἔτι με σχήσουσιν ἐπάλξιες. ἢν δὲ τυχήσω,
 στέμματα σοὶ πλέξω, Κύπρι τροπαιοφόρε[1]).

---

[1] Ich verweise auf die geschmackvolle Uebersetzung Kiefers bei Licht,
Sittengesch. der Griechen I. p. 290 f.

Zwei Epigramme, sog. Centonen, wären an diesem Orte noch zu berücksichtigen. Unter einem Cento versteht man ein aus verschiedenen Versen anderer Dichtungen zusammengesetztes Gedicht. Der Reiz solcher Centonen liegt darin, daß die aus andern Dichtern entlehnten Verse im Cento oft einen ganz andern (z. B. obszönen) Sinn ergeben als im Original [1]). Einen solchen haben wir von dem Epigrammatiker Leon Philosophus, der einen Nachtkampf erzählt. Diese translationes von ἔγχος, ξίφος u. ä. auf den Phallus kamen wohl schon in der griech. Komödie vor und gehören wahrscheinlich der Vulgärsprache an. Textkritisch behandelt ist das Stück von Leo Sternbach „Anthologiae Planudeae appendix Barberino-Vaticana" Leipzig 1890 p. 84 ff.:

Μῆτερ ἐμὴ δύσμητερ, ἀπηνέα θυμὸν ἔχουσα
λίην ἄχθομαι ἕλκος, ὅ με βροτὸς οὔτασεν ἀνὴρ
νύκτα δι' ὀρφναίην, ὅτε θ' εὕδουσι βροτοὶ ἄλλοι,
γυμνὸς ἄτερ κόρυθός τε καὶ ἀσπίδος, οὐδ' ἔχεν ἔγχος.
Πᾶν δ' ὑπεθερμάνθη ξίφος αἵματι· αὐτὰρ ἔπειτα
οὐρόν τε προέηκεν ἀπήμονά τε λιαρόν τε.

Der genannte Cento benützt in der Hauptsache homerische Worte und Wendungen [2]); folgender ist aus sieben Versen des Quintus Smyrnäus und Homer zusammengestoppelt. Adespoton (Sternb. p. 7 ff.).

Αἶψα δ' ὅγ' ἀντιθέην κούρην βάλε · τῆς δὲ διαπρὸ
ἦλθε δόρυ στιβαρὸν κατὰ νηδύος, ἐκ δέ οἱ ὦκα
κήκιεν αἷμα μέλαν, φύροντο δὲ δέμνια καλά·
ἔγχεϊ δ' ὀξυόεντι μεσηγὺ κόρην βάλε μηρῶν,
εὐσφυρον, ἀδμήτην, διὰ δὲ φλεβας αἱματοέσσας
κέρσε · μέλαν δέ οἱ αἷμα δι' ἕλκεος οὐταμένοιο
ἔβλυσεν ἐσσυμένως, δάμνα δὲ ἑ νεύρινον ἔγχος.

Ausdrücke wie Krieg, Kampf, Getümmel u. ä. sind nicht bloß für das harmlose Liebesgetändel, sondern auch für das tumultuarische Eheleben verwendet, wo der Vergleich oft recht nahe liegt. Die Dichter klagen öfters über die Kriegsszenen zu Hause. A. P. XI. 6 (Adespoton):

---

1) Ueber die Centonen der griech. u. röm. Lit. handelt Crusius Realenzykl. III. 1929 ff. Auf den *Cento nuptialis* des Ausonius komme ich unten zu sprechen.

2) Ein Beispiel: Im letzten Vers soll dadurch eine Pointe erzielt werden, daß der Dichter des Cento das Wort für Wind = οὖρος (vgl. Homer Od. V. 268) im Sinne des gleichklingenden οὐρὸς = menschlicher Samen gebraucht.

Πτωχοῦ ἐστι γάμος κυνέα μάχα, εὐθὺ κ υ δ ο ι μ ό ς, λοιδορίαι, πλαγαί, ζημία, ἔργα, δίκαι.

Die Heirat eines Armen hat also a priori eine unglückliche Ehe zur Folge. Ein sehr witziges Epigramm des Palladas: A. P. IX. 168: Der Grammatiker hat täglich seine Doppelschlacht zu schlagen. Einmal muß er den Jungen das Epos vom Trojanerkrieg, *μῆνιν ἄειδε* einhämmern, auf der anderen Seite hat er mit seiner Frau den Krieg :

Μῆνιν οὐλομένην γαμετὴν ὁ τάλας γεγάμηκα
καὶ παρὰ τῆς τέχνης μήνιδος ἀρξάμενος.
ὤμοι ἐγὼ πολύμηνις, ἔχων διχόλωτον ἀνάγκην,
τέχνης γραμματικῆς καὶ γαμετῆς μαχίμης[1]).

Ein humorvolles Wortspiel bietet ein anderes Epigramm des Palladas. A. P. V. 70 :

Πρωτομάχου πατρὸς καὶ Νικομάχης γεγαμηκὼς
θυγατέρα, Ζήνων, ἔνδον ἔχεις π ό λ ε μ ο ν.
Ζήτει Λ υ σ ί μ α χ ο ν μοιχὸν φίλον, ὅς σ'ἐλεήσας
ἐκ τῆς Π ρ ω τ ο μ ά χ ο υ λύσεται 'Α ν δ ρ ο μ ά χ η ς.

Der Patriarch Johannes Chrysostomus, der mit Vorliebe die Bilder dem militärischen Leben entnimmt[2]), nennt auch gelegentlich die Ehe einen „Krieg". De Virg. 108. 36 ff. : Er fordert die Eheleute auf, *φέρειν γενναίως τὸν ἀ κ ή ρ υ κ τ ο ν π ό λ ε μ ο ν.* Die Dienstboten nützen die Streitigkeiten der Eheleute aus: De Virg. 122. 47 :

Οὐ μικρὰν ἀφορμὴν τῆς οἰκείας βδελυρίας τὸν ἐκείνων λαμ-βάνουσιν π ό λ ε μ ο ν[3]).

---

1) Auf Ausonius' Namen gefälscht ist folgende Naçhahmung (Epigr. app. III):
Arma virumque docens atque arma virumque peritus
   non duxi uxorem, sed magis arma domum.
   namque dies totos totasque ex ordine noctes
   litibus oppugnat meque meumque larem ;
   atque, ut perpetuis dotata a Marte duellis,
   arma in me tollit, nec datur ulla quies.
   iamque repugnanti dedam me, ut denique vitet
   iurgia ob hoc solum, iurgia quod fugiam.
Die schlagende Kürze der Vorlage ist dabei verloren gegangen.
2) Vgl. H. D e g e n , Die Tropen u. Vergl. bei J. Chrys. Diss. Freiburg i. Schw. 1921.
3) Schon im Gilgameschepos fand ich eine Stelle, wo vom Lieben und Heiraten wegen der Folter Weib abgeraten wird:

Die Untersuchung zeigt, daß die Griechen die Urheber der Metapher sind. Komiker und Epigrammatiker bedienten sich beiderseits des Bildes. Auf Grund des vorliegenden Materials möchte ich folgende Entwicklungslinie ziehen: Die Metapher *'militat omnis amans'* hat ihre ersten Wurzeln in der griechischen Komödie, die ihrerseits vielleicht den erotischen Jargon des Volkes übernimmt. Der Umstand, daß namentlich in der neueren Komödie die Figur des Soldaten als Liebhaber eine wichtige Stelle einnimmt, hat zur Ausbreitung und stärkeren Verwurzelung der Metapher beigetragen. Die Beispiele allerdings sind nicht zahlreich. Die Epigrammatik und vielleicht auch andere Zweige der alexandrinischen Literatur haben das Bild übernommen. Hier gewinnt es dem Charakter eines Epigramms entsprechend nur um seiner selbst willen Gestalt und wird schließlich zu einem beliebten, in allen Variationen auftretenden τόπος. Diese Entwicklung ist wohl in der hellenistischen Zeit vollzogen. Dafür spricht die Motivverwandtschaft zwischen der späteren griechischen Epigrammatik, Roman- und Briefliteratur auf der einen, und der römischen Elegie auf der anderen Seite. Historisch-genetisch gesehen wäre ich bei der Verfolgung meines Motivs zum gleichen Resultat gekommen wie schon die Arbeit Hölzers[1]). Wenn gleich das Material gering ist, das den Beweis stützen soll, pflichte ich der Ansicht bei, daß die attische Komödie die Urheberin einer Reihe von Gedanken und Bildern ist, die in der Erotik seit den Alexandrinern immer wieder auftauchen. Ich glaube, durch meine Arbeit diese These bekräftigt zu haben.

Bevor die römische Literatur in den Kreis meiner Betrachtung gezogen wird, sollen hier kurz die Bilder aus dem Gymnasion, die in der erotischen Sprache Eingang fanden, gestreift werden. Das Leben in der Palästra spielte ja bei den Griechen eine Hauptrolle. Die Metapher hat dementsprechend in der Gymnastik ein beson-

---

Liebe nicht, mein Herr, liebe nicht!
Das Weib ist ein Brunnen,
Das Weib ist ein eiserner Dolch, ein scharfer,
der dem Mann den Hals abschneidet.
Gressmann „altor. Texte" unter Sprüche p. 286.

1) Hölzer „*De poesi amatoria a comicis exculta, ab elegiacis imitatione expressa*" *pars prior* Diss. Marburg 1890.

Die motivische Uebereinstimmung der röm. Kom. des Plautus u. Terenz mit der august. Elegie führt er wie Leo u. a. eben darauf zurück, daß die Alexandriner, die näheren Vorbilder der römischen Elegie, ihre Motive vielfach der Komödie entnommen haben.

ders ergiebiges Feld gefunden. Unter den verschiedenen Uebungen sind **vor** allem das Ringen und Laufen die Bilder, die in den einzelnen Sprachzonen am meisten ausgebeutet werden [1]). Im ganzen betrachtet nützen die griechischen Erotiker, wenigstens der vorchristlichen Jahrhunderte (vgl. o. p. 35), die Agonbilder stärker aus als die Kriegs- oder Jagdmetaphern. Die Römer dagegen greifen, wie wir sehen werden, ungleich öfter zu ihrem vertrautesten Gebiet, dem Kriegs- und Soldatenleben. Da die zum Bereiche der Palästra gehörenden Bilder nicht zu meinem eigentlichen Thema gehören, will ich nur wenig Beispiele zusammenstellen, die das Gesagte veranschaulichen sollen.

Zum erstenmal scheint das Bild des Ringkampfes für eine Liebesszene bei Aristophanes zu begegnen. Während das Kriegsbild bei ihm eine ganz untergeordnete Rolle spielt (vgl. p. 30), ist das Palästrabild voll entwickelt. Daß er das Vorbild für spätere Autoren abgegeben hat, dürfte wohl fraglos erscheinen: A r i s t. pax 894 ff.:

> ἔπειτ' ἀγῶνά γ' εὐθὺς ἐξέσται ποιεῖν
> ταύτην ἔχουσιν αὔριον καλὸν πάνυ,
> ἐπὶ γῆς παλαιειν, τετραποδηδὸν ἐστάναι
> καὶ παγκράτιόν γ' ὑπαλειψαμένοις νεανικῶς
> παιειν, ὀρύττειν, πὺξ ὁμοῦ καὶ τῷ πέει [2]).
> Τρίτῃ δὲ μετὰ ταῦθ' ἱπποδρομίαν ἄξετε,
> ἵνα δὴ κέλης κέλητα παρακελητιεῖ.

Lucta, pugilatus und *certamina equestria* sind hier in die Sprache der Erotik übertragen. Zum Bild der Rennbahn vergleiche A r i s t. vesp. 501; Lysistr. 60; D i o s k o r i d e s A. P. V. 54. 53; A s - k l e p i a d e s (?) A. P. V. 201; bei den Römern: M a r t. XI 104. 14; H o r. Od. I. 25. 13 f., vgl. auch schon Ibykos frg. 7 und Pindar frg. 123, 127.

Van Leeuwen glaubt mit Recht, daß das bei den Tragikern begegnende ‘πῶλος ἄζυξ’ von Aristophanes ins Komische gewendet sei. Er verweist ferner auf das Anakreonlied (fr. 70), wo ein Mädchen mit „πῶλε Θρηϊκίη“ angeredet wird [3]).

Die folgenden Beispiele bewegen sich auf derselben Linie und

1) H. B l ü m n e r „Stud. zur Geschichte der Metapher im Griechischen" 1. Heft Leipzig 1891 p. 95 ff.
2) In diese Region gehört nach A. A b t (Philol. 1910 p. 147 ff.) auch das Papyrusfrg. von Oxyrynchos (VI. 201).
3) Vgl. Alkman fr. 1, 45 f. — 59. Theognis v. 1249 ff., 1267 ff.

sind fast durchweg obszön zu verstehen. Die Obszönität soll eben
durch die metaphorische Wendung in etwas verschleiert werden:
Der Komiker T i m o k l e s sagt (fr. 22) (K. II 461):

> .... δεῖν δέ τι
> ἀ γ ω ν ι ᾶ σ α ι καὶ ῥαπισθῆναί τε καὶ
> πληγὰς λαβεῖν ἀπαλαῖς χερσίν¹).

Bei dem schon oben erwähnten Komiker Machon begegnet uns
auch das Athletenbild ähnlich pointiert wie das Kriegsbild (s. p. 63 f.):
Athenäus XIII. 578 f. :

> .... μηθέν, φησί, σοί,
> ψυχή, μελέτω. μαθεῖν γὰρ αἰσθέσθαι θ'ἅμα
> Ὀλυμπιονικῶν νυκτὸς ἀθλητῶν δυεῖν
> πληγὴν ⟨παρὰ πληγὴν⟩ τί δύναταί ποτ' ἤθελον.

Hier liegt in den Personen der Grund für das gewählte Bild:
Die Hetäre Mania tröstet mit diesen Worten ihren bevorzugten
Liebhaber, den Pankratiasten Leontiskos, den sie mit dem Olym-
pioniken Antenor einmal betrogen hatte.

Rivale in der Liebe: M e l e a g e r A. P. XII. 68:

> Οὐκ ἐθέλω Χαρίδαμον·... τί δέ μοι τὸν ἐπουρανίων βασιλῆα
> ἄ ν τ α θ λ ο ν νίκης τῆς ἐν ἔρωτι λαβεῖν.

Ein Gegenstück zu dem oben zitierten Epigramm des Meleager
A. P. XII. 66 (p. 57), vgl. Chariton V. 10. 7.

Noch einige Beispiele aus späterer Zeit. Die Verfasser erotischer
Briefe und der Romane kennen mehr die Kriegs- als die Agonbilder.

In der bekannten Stelle bei Plutarch, wo dieser vom παρακλαυ-
σίθυρον spricht, heißt es (Ἐρωτ... Ἐρωτ. 753ᴮ):

> ἐρᾶται γὰρ αὐτοῦ νὴ Δία καὶ κάεται· τίς οὖν ὁ κωλύων ἐστὶ
> κωμάζειν ἐπὶ θύρας, ᾄδειν τὸ παρακλαυσίθυρον, ἀναδεῖν τὰ εἰ-
> κόνια, π α γ κ ρ α τ ι ά ζ ε ι ν πρὸς τοὺς ἀντερραστάς;

Auch die oft zitierte Lukianstelle möchte ich hier anführen
(ὄνος 576). Das Mädchen Palaistra sagt zum Gast:

> Τοῦτο μὲν δὴ πάντως δεῖ σε μνημονεύειν, ὦ νεανίσκε, ὅτι εἰς
> Π α λ α ί σ τ ρ α ν ἐμπέπτωκας, καὶ χρή σε νῦν ἐπιδεῖξαι, εἰ γέγονας
> ἐν τοῖς ἐφήβοις γοργὸς καὶ π α λ α ί σ μ α τ α πολλὰ ἔμαθές ποτε.

---

1) Vgl. A. P. V. 274 (Paul. Silent.), wo der neutrale Ausdruck μάρνασθαι
verwendet ist:

> ἡ παῖς ἐξ ὕπνοιο διέγρετο, χερσὶ δὲ λευκαῖς
> κράτος ἡμετέρου πᾶσαν ἔτιλλε κόμην·
> μαρναμένης δὲ τὸ λοιπὸν ἀνύσσαμεν ἔργον ἔρωτος.

'Αλλ᾽ ..... ἤδη π α λ α ί ω μ ε ν .. Es folgt nun eine detaillierte
Angabe von σχήματα Ἀφροδίτης *(modi Veneris)*, alles in *termini
technici* der Palaestra; sie kommandiert wie ein Sportlehrer. 579 :
ἐν τοιαύταις ἡδοναῖς καὶ παιδιαῖς π α λ α ι σ μ ά τ ω ν ἀ γ ω ν ι -
ζ ό μ ε ν ο ι νυκτερινοὺς ἀ γ ῶ ν α ς ἐστεφανούμεθα. Ueber die ent-
sprechende Stelle bei Apuleius s. unten p. 76.
Longus past. III. 19. 2: Χλόη δὲ σ υ μ π α λ α ί ο υ σ ά σοι
ταύτην τὴν π ά λ η ν. Vgl. Ach. Tat. V. 3. 5. A.P. V. 90 (Adespoton).
„Athlet" in der Liebe : A c h. T a t. II. 4. 4: δέδοικα δὲ μὴ
ἄτολμος καὶ δειλὸς ἔρωτος ἀ θ λ η τ ή ς γένωμαι.
Sieg im Kampf mit dem Nebenbuhler : C h a r i t o n I. 2. 4:
ἀλλ᾽ αὐτῷ γενέσθω τὸ ἆ θ λ ο ν ..
Nachtkämpfe : P a u l. S i l e n t. A. P. V. 258 : εἰ μὲν παννυ-
χίησιν ἡμιλήσασα π α λ α ί σ τ ρ α ι ς ὅς σε π ε ρ ι π λ έ γ δ η ν ἔχε
πήχεσιν .... vgl. A g a t h. S c h o l a s t. V. 293 (oben ausge-
schrieben) ; N i k e t a s III. 246 : Εἰ μὲν π α λ α ί σ τ ρ α ι ς ὡμί-
λησας παννύχοις.

Olympische, isthmische und nemeische Kämpfe erlebt hier der
Dichter mit seiner streitsüchtigen Frau. Ein Gegenstück zur Ehe
als Kriegsschauplatz (s. p. 39): L u k i l l i o s A. P. XI. 79 :

Π ύ κ τ η ς ὢν κατέλυσε Κλεόμβροτος · εἶτα γαμήσας
ἔνδον ἔχει πληγῶν ᾿Ι σ θ μ ι α καὶ Ν έ μ ε α
γραῦν μ α χ ί μ η ν, τ ύ π τ ο υ σ α ν ᾿Ο λ ύ μ π ι α, καὶ τὰ παρ᾽ αὐτῷ
μᾶλλον ἰδεῖν φρίσσων ἢ ποτὲ τὸ σ τ ά δ ι ο ν.
᾿Αν γὰρ ἀναπνεύσῃ, δέρεται τὰς παντὸς ἀ γ ῶ ν ο ς
πληγὰς, ὡς ἀποδῷ · κἂν ἀποδῷ, δέρεται.

Unsere Metapher klingt auch in mehreren Hetärennamen an. Ge-
rade auch sie verraten, wie die Metaphern aus der Gymnastik dem
Griechen besonders geläufig waren. Ganz unproblematisch dürfte
die Erklärung der Namen Παλαιστὼ und Παλαίστρα sein. Π α λ α ι -
σ τ ὼ begegnet uns auf einem Psykter des Euphronios und gehört
zu den vier nackten Zecherinnen [1]), die alle ihrem Handwerk ihren
Namen verdanken. Vgl. Lukian deor. dial. 20. 14 : Λευκὴ μέν,
οἷαν εἰκὸς ἐκ κύκνου γεγενημένην, ἀπαλὴ δέ, ὡς ἐν ᾠῷ τραφεῖσα,
γ υ μ ν ὰ ς τὰ πολλὰ καὶ π α λ α ι σ τ ι κ ή ... Daß das obszöne
παλαίειν dahintersteckt, sah zuerst Kretschmer [2]). Der Name „P a -

---

1) K l e i n Meistersign. ² 138.
2) K r e t s c h m e r, gr. Vaseninschriften p. 209 vgl. K. S c h m i d t
Hermes 37 (1902) p. 175 ff.

l ä s t r a" kommt öfters vor, schon bei dem Komiker Alkaios [1]), dann in Plautus' Rud., Lukians ὄνος, CIL II 2281 u. s.). Ihr Gebaren ist das der gemeineren Sorte von Hetären und zwingt uns dieselbe Deutung auf wie Παλαιστώ. Zweifellos gehören auch die Hetären Γυμνάσιον, Ἀγωνίς, Ἰσθμιάς, Νεμεάς, Ὀλυμπιάς und Πυθιάς [2]) unter diese Rubrik. Sprachlich wie sachlich kommen ja mehrere Möglichkeiten, sie zu deuten, in Frage. So kann beispielsweise Ἰσθμιάς ein Geburtstagsname sein und kann ebensogut die Tochter (Sklavin) eines Isthmiensiegers bezeichnen [3]). Daß der Name aber auch erotisch-obszön verstanden werden kann, hat Bechtel schon gesehen (p. 126 f.) und gewinnt durch meine Untersuchung an größerer Wahrscheinlichkeit (vgl. p. 43). „Aniketos" (Alkiphron II. 6 J. G. III. 1223 u. s.) bedeutet die in der Liebe Unbesiegbare [4]). Mehr Schwierigkeiten bereitet die Interpretation des bei Plautus im Epidikus begegnenden Hetärennamen A k r o p o l i s t i s. Die Handschriften überliefern so.

Schmidt weist in dem oben genannten Aufsatz darauf hin, daß diese Form (Akropoli s t i s) aus sprachlichen wie inhaltlichen Kriterien unhaltbar sei. Er dachte an die Lesart „Akrobolistis", also = Plänklerin. Nun aber kommt das Wort ἀκροβολίζομαι, wie Schmidt auch sieht, nirgends in der erotischen Sprache vor. Er sieht sich deshalb veranlaßt, die Ueberlieferung Akropolistis in Akropoli s c i s abzuändern. Der Name wäre nach Schmidt Kosenamen einer Hetäre, die den lokalen Namen Akropolis trägt, der einigemal belegt ist. Es fragt sich, ob wir hier nicht auch eine erotische Pointe suchen müssen. Der Ausdruck ἀκρόπολις kommt ja öfters in der Erotik vor (vgl. p. 48 f. u. 25, wo das Mädchen, spez. ihre Augen, eine vom Liebhaber zu erobernde „Burg" genannt wird) [5]). Da πολιστής der „Erbauer einer Stadt" ist, wäre ἀκροπολιστίς die „Erbauerin einer Burg", doch wohl nicht ungeeignet für eine Hetäre, die sich ihre Einnahme etwas kosten läßt.

---

1) F r. B e c h t e l „Die hist. Personennamen d. Griech." Halle 1917 p. 610.
2) Ich verweise auf den Aufsatz „Hetären" in RE von K. S c h n e i d e r und die dort angegebene Literatur.
3) Vgl. Fr. B e c h t e l „Die attischen Frauennamen" Göttingen 1902 p. 53; K. M r a s „Die Personennamen in Lukians Hetärengesprächen" WSt 38 (1916) p. 337.
4) Vgl. C. Th. S o n d a g „de nominibus apud Alciphronem propriis" Diss. Bonn 1905 p. 24.
5) Eine Entsprechung bei Plautus 'Truc'. 170 f. s. u.

Die Metapher aus dem Leben der Gymnastik treffen wir gelegentlich auch bei den Römern an. Worte wie *luctari, colluctari* gehören ja ursprünglich auch in diese Sprachsphäre. P r o p. II. 1. 13:

seu nuda erepto mecum l u c t a t u r amictu.

Andere Beispiele aus der Elegie werden besser später eingereiht. S e n. contr. I. 2. 6: Die *virgo sacerdos* wird gefragt: *Numquid hoc negas c o n l u c t a t a m te tamen cum viro, quem in illa volutatione necesse est prius super te fuisse* [1]). Vgl. M a r t. V. 46; . IV. 22. A p u l. 2. 17; 9. 5; L a c t. I. 17, 11, ff.

Gräzismen: M a r t. X. 55. 4:

Jdem (penis) post opus et suas p a l a e s t r a s.

Den Ausdruck *κλινοπάλης* gebraucht nach Sueton der Kaiser Domitian als erotischen *terminus technicus.* S u e t. Dom. 22: *Libidinis nimiae assiduitatem concubitus velut exercitationis genus „κλινοπάλην"* vocabat, vgl. A u r e l. V i c t. 11, 5 (Caes.); *ἐπικλινοπάλη* M a r t. XIV. 201, 2. Das Fechterleben war den Römern vertrauter. Im folgenden werde ich gelegentlich auch die Bilder aus der Fechtkunst berücksichtigen.

§ 4.

Daß unsere Metapher in der römischen Elegie eine besonders wichtige Rolle spielt, ist bereits erwähnt. Es fragt sich, ob sie auch von römischen Schriftstellern der voraugusteischen Zeit gekannt und verwendet ist. Die Elegiker, insbesondere Properz und Ovid, rühmen sich, Schüler der Alexandriner zu sein. Daß sie die einheimische Dichtung auch kannten, ist wohl selbstverständlich, und daß sie von dieser bisweilen formell und inhaltlich beeinflußt sind, ist unbestreitbar. Uns interessiert vor allem, ob die Sprache der Palliatendichter, des Plautus und Terenz voran, das Bild aufweist. Sie bewegen sich ja in den Bahnen der *νέα*, und sind z. T. nur Uebersetzer attischer Geistesschöpfungen und Bühnenerzeugnisse, in

---

1) Dem *παλαίειν, luctari* entspricht unser „ringen" im erotischen Sinn: Bechtel (att. Frauenn. 67) zitiert eine Wolframstelle: 193/4:

. . 'welt ir iuch êren
sölhe mâze gein mir kêren
daz ir mit mir r i n g e t niht,
nûn ligen aldâ bî in geschiht'

sagt Conduiramur zu Parzifal. Ein Beispiel aus neuerer Literatur. L e n a u „Faust" Der Tanz S. 113:

Die badende Jungfrau, die lange g e r u n g e n,
wird endlich vom Mann zur Umarmung gezwungen.

deren Mittelpunkt Liebes- und Hetärenszenen stehen. Oben lernten wir einige Stellen aus der griechischen Komödie kennen, in denen unser Kriegsbild mehr oder weniger ausgebildet vorliegt. Da dieses zweifellos öfters auch den Zweck hat, nackte Obszönitäten durch die bildhafte Wendung zu verdecken, dürfen wir wohl annehmen, daß es in der urbaneren Diktion der griechischen Komödie zahlreicher vorkam als in der naiv-derben Redeweise der altrömischen Komiker, zumal eines Plautus. Sehen wir uns nach Plautus, Terenz und den anderen Dichtern ihrer Zeit um!

Mit der Allegorie des „kriegerischen" Amor ist die Komödie, wie der erste Abschnitt zeigte, fast gar nicht vertraut. Pichon in seiner zu Beginn zitierten Dissertation gibt die richtige Erklärung dafür p. 14: *comici qui minus fabulosas Graecorum religiones curant quam elegiarum auctores, rarius sagittas Amoris aut faces describunt aut regnum aut dominationem.* Nicht einwandfrei aber ist, was er weiter unten behauptet: *Translationes quoque quasdam non frequenter usurpant, nec militiae certaminibus et victoriis fortunam amantium adsimulare solent.* Gewiß, durchgeführte Vergleiche dürfen wir wenig erwarten; ebenso fehlt die Fülle und Variation in der Gestaltung des Motivs, wie sie den Elegikern eigen ist. Die plautinischen Beispiele überwiegen weit. Das dürfte damit zusammenhängen, daß von Plautus viel mehr Stücke vorliegen als von Terenz.

Vom „Liebeskampf" redet der von Liebesschmerzen gepeinigte Sklave: Plaut.[1]) Persa 26: *saucius factus sum in Veneris proelio.* Das gewonnene Mädchen ist eine Kriegsbeute: Men. 435: *habe praedam* vgl. Men. 441; Cas. 113 und 114. Praeda bedeutet zunächst die im Krieg erworbene Beute, ist dann aber in abgeblaßter Form für Beute oder Gewinn ganz allgemein benützt. Das Kriegsbild braucht hier also nicht unbedingt dem Dichter und Leser vorzuschweben.

'Feind' ist dem Mann die Frau, falls er sie nur gezwungen besitzt: Stich. 140:
  hostis est uxor invita quae ad virum nuptum datur.
Dazu Men. 132; Terenz Hek. 789: *Nam nupta meretrici hostis est* (Feindin der Nebenbuhlerin).

Die Frau soll 'Siegerin' im Ehekampf sein: Cas. 819 f.:
tuaque ut potior pollentia sit vincasque virum victrixque sies tua vox superet tuomque imperium vir te vestiat, virum
despolies.

---

1) Ich zitiere nach der Ausgabe von Lindsay.

Ein Wortspiel: Das Mädchen sträubt sich nicht, wenn man es fein behandelt: Cas. 851:

> *at mihi, qui belle hanc tracto, non b e l l u m facit.*

In den genannten Stellen ist das Bild nur angedeutet wie auch in folgenden zwei stark obszönen Fällen: Persa 232:

> . . . *at confidentia*
> *illa m i l i t i a m i l i t a t u r multo magi' quam pondere.*

Die Frechheit wiegt mehr in solchem „Dienst" als das Gewicht, sagt der keusche Knabe zur Magd, die sein Glied prüft.

Das Mädchen Casina ist v. 660 ff., 751 f. mit einem Schwert bewaffnet, um den ihr aufgezwungenen Gemahl zu ermorden. Als letzterer nun v. 909 mit der vermeintlichen Casina — denn es ist ihm statt der Casina der Sklave Chalinus als Braut zugeführt worden — die Hochzeitsnacht feiern will und aus Befürchtung, sie könnte, wie sie gedroht, das Schwert irgendwie versteckt haben, diese untersucht, stößt er an etwas langes und ruft überrascht aus: Cas. 909 f.:

> *Dum gladium quaero ne habeat, arripio c a p u l u m,*
> *sed quom cogito, non habuit g l a d i u m, nam esset frigidus* [1]).

Für *gladius* = Phallus gebraucht Catull 67. 21 *s i c u l a* (kleiner Dolch). Spätere wechseln zwischen *arma, telum, mucro, hasta* u. a. Kriegsausdrücken. (s. u.!)

Mehr oder weniger ausgeführt wird unser Bild im Folgenden: Der Kampf mit dem Nebenbuhler um eine Hetäre bedeutet eine „denkwürdige Schlacht". Pseud. 524 ff:

> Ps. *priu'quam istam p u g n a m p u g n a b o* [2]), *ego etiam prius*
> *dabo aliam p u g n a m c l a r a m et c o m m e m o r a b i l e m.*
>
> Si. *Quam p u g n a m?* Ps. *Em ab hoc lenone vicino tuo*
> *per sycophantiam atque per doctos dolos*
> *tibicinam illam tuo' quam gnatus deperit,*
> *ea circumducam levide lenonem.*

Vgl. Men. 128 f.: *qui p u g n a v i f o r t i t e r.* Der Mann, welcher seine Frau vertrieben und seine Blicke nach einem jungen Mädchen

---

1) Die folgenden Metaphern zeigen, daß das erigierte Glied des Chalinus gemeint ist. Zu *gladius* vgl. ξίφος S. 38.

2) Der erste Kampf (*ista pugna*) besteht in Herbeischaffung von Geld. Uebrigens verwertet Plautus die Worte *pugna* und *pugnare* in verschiedenstem Sinn. Capt. 585: „*aliquid pugnae edidit*" bedeutet nichts anderes als „er hat dir mitgespielt" vgl. Bacch. 270. Pseud. 525.

gerichtet hat, fordert seine Freunde auf, ihm zu diesem Sieg zu gratulieren. Zur Wendung „*dabo pugnam*" (Pseud. 525) soll hier gleich eine Parallelstelle bei T e r e n z eingereiht werden. Diese ist jedoch anders pointiert: Eunuch. 899:

Dabit hic p u g n a m aliquam denuo. Daß *pugna* hier mit *res venerea* identifiziert werden muß, ergibt sich aus dem Zusammenhang; auch bemerkt der Donatkommentar zu der Stelle '*pugnam*' *pro stupro.* Vgl. Lucilius fr. 1323 (M.).

Plautus überträgt das Kriegsbild auch aufs Essen und Trinken, z. B. Persa 112 oder Men. 181 ff.[1]). Letztere Stelle führe ich an, weil in ihr auch unsere Metapher vorkommt. Das Mädchen Erotium kommt zu seinem Schatz: „*Animi mi, Menaechme, salve*". Der Parasit, der den Menächmus begleitet, fühlt sich zurückgesetzt, weil er keinen Gruß bekommt: *Quid ego?* Die Hetäre erwidert: *extra n u m e r u m es mihi.* Der Parasit: *idem istuc aliis a d s c r i p t i v i s fieri ad l e g i o n e m solet.* Der Parasit also wird als zweiter *amans* behandelt wie der Rekrut, wenn er bei der Musterung fürs Heer durchfällt. Hernach wird das Schlachtbild ausführlich auf das Trinkgelage übertragen:

M e n.: *ego istic mihi hodie apparari iussi apud te proelium.*
E r.: *hodie id fiet.* M e n.: *in eo uterque proelio potabimus,*
uter ibi melior bellator erit inventus cantharo,
tua est legio: adiudicato cum utro hanc noctem sies.
Der Sieg im Trinkduell entscheidet demnach über den Besitz des Mädchens.

Krieg im Eheleben: P l a u t. Amphit. 476 ff.:

> *nam Amphitruo actutum uxori t u r b a s c o n c i e t*
> *atque insimulabit eam probri; tum meu' pater*
> *eam s e d i t i o n e m illi in tranquillum conferet.*

Ganz ähnlich bei T e r e n z: Andria 829 f.:

> . . . *ut homini adulescentulo*
> *in alio occupato amore, abhorrenti a re uxoria,*
> *filiam ut darem in s e d i t i o n e m atque in incertas nuptias.*

Dazu ein Fragment des Komikers S t a t i u s C a e c i l i u s (f. 19):

> *Ea est s e d i t i o s a, ea cum viro b e l l u m g e r i t.*

Zum Schluß noch ein Gleichnis bei Plautus, das wir schon bei den Griechen kennengelernt haben (ἀκρόπολις-Motiv p. 25). Der

---

1) Auch das ist griechisches Erbe: Poseid. 27 (K III. 344); Antiphanes 80. 11 (K II 44) sagt vom Parasiten, er sei ein στρατιώτης ἀγαθός.

Liebhaber wird mit einer feindlichen Befestigung verglichen; je rascher er gekapert wird, um so vorteilhafter ist das für die Hetäre. Truc. 170 f.:

amator similest o p p i d i h o s t i l i s . . . . .
Quam primum e x p u g n a r i potis[est], tam id optumum est amicae.

Außer den bereits erwähnten Stellen kommen bei Terenz nur mehr wenige in Frage: Ein andermal führt zwar der Dichter den Vergleich nicht aus, nennt aber die Vergleichspunkte. Eun. 59 ff.:

> *In amore haec omnia insunt vitia: iniuriae,*
> *suspiciones, inimicitiae, i n d u t i a e ,*
> *b e l l u m , p a x rursum* . . . . .

Horaz übernimmt das später fast wörtlich: Sat. II. 3, 267:

> *In amore haec sunt mala, bellum, pax rursum.*

Zu 'pax' vgl. Eun. 53: *I n f e c t a p a c e ultro ad eam venies* . . . .
Eun. 55: *Eludet*[1]*), ubi te v i c t u m senserit.* Triumph der Hetäre über den *amans*, weil er sie beschenkt hat. Eun. 392 ff.:

> . . . *Non tam ipso quidem*
> *dono quam abs te datum esse: id vero serio t r i u m p h a t* . . . .

Unsere Metapher ist bei Terenz wohl Uebersetzung der Vorlage. Das werden wir besonders in Eun. 59 ff. annehmen, wo das Bild geradezu in Sentenzenform gebracht ist. Merkwürdigerweise kommen fast nur im Eunuchus Beispiele vor. Das mag sich daraus erklären, daß hier ja eine Hauptszene die Belagerung des Hauses bildet (v. 755 u. 771 ff.). Das wäre eine Erscheinung, auf die wir noch besonders bei den Elegikern stoßen, wo öfters wirkliche Kriegsbilder mit übertragenen kontrastieren. Zusammenfassend ist über Plautus zu sagen, daß er die Metapher sehr originell und geschickt verwendet. Denn während sie bei den Elegikern zum Vorrat der immer wiederkehrenden und teilweise — ich denke an Ovid — doch in allzu gekünstelter Weise gehandhabten τόποι gehört, führen bei Plautus witzige Wortspiele (Cas. 851), spannende Kontraste (Pseud. 524), derbe Situationskomik (Cas. 909; Persa 232) zur Anwendung dieses Bildes. Aehnliches hatten wir schon bei den attischen Komikern festzustellen, deren lückenhafte Ueberlieferung diese Tatsache nicht so greifbar macht, wie die erhaltenen Palliaten des Plautus oder Terenz. Bei letzterem müssen wir vielleicht auch an plautinische Reminiszenzen denken.

---

1) Ein Ausdruck des Fechterjargons.

Bei den übrigen Palliatendichtern und Komikern überhaupt hat der „Liebeskrieg" sicherlich auch Ausdruck gefunden. An früherer Stelle (p. 48) bekamen wir ein solches Fragment des Cäc. Statius zu Gesichte, das die Metapher kennt. Ein zweites gehört wohl auch hierher. Cäc. Stat. fr. 2 Hymnis (R. 53).

.... *sine blanditie nihil agit in amore inermus.*

Ist mit dem Fragment an sich schon wenig anzufangen, so ist es dazu noch korrupt überliefert [1]). Was ist der Sinn? Etwa: wer nicht schmeichelt, erreicht im Liebesleben nichts, denn er ist waffenlos, so daß die *blandities* quasi die Waffe in der Hand des Liebhabers ist. Oder bedeutet *arma* Geld [2])? Wer zahlen kann, braucht nicht zu schmeicheln? Wir wissen es nicht.

In der sonstigen voraugusteischen Literatur tritt die Metapher nur sporadisch auf. Der Togatendichter Titinius sagt p. 176 fr. 3: *Qui ex tanta factione atque opibus puellam sum ausus adgredi* Lucilius fr. 1323 (M):

vicimus, o socii, et magnam pugnavimus pugnam.

Daß es sich hier um die *pugna amatoria* handelt, lehrt der Donat-kommentar zur oben behandelten Terenzstelle Eun. 899: „*Dabit hic pugnam aliquam*" : *pugnam pro stupro .... ut Lucilius „vicimus .... pugnam*". Donat bemerkt außerdem zu Adelphoe 859: *„vitam duram quam vixi'* : ἀρχαισμός, *ut Lucilius „magnam .... pugnam*". F. Marx glaubt, daß hier ein Enniusvers von Lucilius parodiert sei. Er bemerkt (II. 425): *Ennii versu quodam per irrisionem usum esse poetam suspiceris ideo quod Lucanus VI. 164 priore usus est hemistichio in re seria 'vicimus, o socii; veniet, qui vindicet arces, dum morimur'.*

Lukrez gebraucht für den Akt der Umarmung den Ausdruck *potiri* IV. 1076:

etenim potiundi tempore in ipso.

Ovid ahmt das nach: Met. IX. 997; IX. 265; IX. 753.

Cicero spricht einmal voll Ironie vom „weiblichen Kriegsdienst" Verr. 5. 104:

contubernium muliebris militiae.

---

1) Lindsay schreibt in seiner Ausgabe des Nonius Marc.:
   sine † blanditiae nihil agit
   In amore inermus.
2) Vgl. unten S. 59 Anm. 1.

Zum Schluß noch die bekannten *versus populares* (Frg. poet. Lat. B. 330. 1):

> *Gallias Caesar subegit, Nicomedes Caesarem:*
> *ecce Caesar nunc triumphat, qui subegit Gallias.*
> *Nicomedes non t r i u m p h a t, qui s u b e g i t Caesarem.*

Solche an die Komödie erinnernden, witzigen Wortspiele werden wohl in größerer Zahl dem Volksmund geläufig gewesen sein.

Unser Bild ist bis auf die Zeit Catulls, sofern wir von Plautus und Terenz absehen, sehr selten. Das erklärt sich freilich auch daraus, daß Werke wie die Satiren des Lucilius oder des Varro, die wohl am meisten in Frage gekommen wären, nur in geringfügigen Resten vorliegen.

Mit Catull und dem Neoterikerkreis erwacht bekanntlich das regste Interesse an den Erzeugnissen alexandrinischer Dichter. Lyrik, Epyllion und vor allem die Kleinkunst des Epigramms werden am Musenhof von Alexandria und an anderen geistigen und kulturellen Zentren der damaligen Welt in reichstem Maße angebaut und gepflegt. Bei der Prüfung der uns geretteten Dokumente konnten wir ja für unsere Metapher wenig gewinnen. Ganz anders bei den römischen Elegikern. Daß diese als Söhne des geborenen Kriegsvolkes sich in höherem Maße der aus dem Soldaten- und Lagerleben geflossenen Bilder und Vergleiche befleißigen als die Griechen, liegt nahe. Denn die Kriegsausdrücke waren dem Dichter wie dem Publikum stets gegenwärtig. Wir werden sehen, daß das Bild der *militia Veneris* bei Tibull und Properz nicht nur von Zeit zu Zeit angedeutet wird, sondern eigentlichen τόπος-Charakter annimmt und kompositionstechnische Funktion erhält. Ovid vollends gibt ihm die variationsreichste und kunstvollste Gestaltung; in dessen Dichtung fließt alles bisherige, hinsichtlich des „Liebeskriegs" Geformte zusammen, und Ovid selbst weiß den τόπος in einer Weise zu bereichern, daß alle spätere Dichtung damit gespeist werden konnte.

§ 5.

Mit Catull stoßen wir auf den ersten Römer, bei dem die Metapher relativ reichlicher vorkommt. Daß er sie aus der griechischen Dichtung kennt, ist sehr wahrscheinlich, wenn sich auch kaum direkte Parallelen finden lassen. Das Bild ist bei Catull zumeist nur angedeutet, und das Liebesleben ist nie direkt in nähere Beziehung gebracht zu den Mühen und Aufgaben der Krieger. Die

Worte: *bellum, proelium, pugnare* usw. stehen gewöhnlich im Sinn des Duells mit dem Mädchen und entbehren weiterer Ausführung. Analoge oder verwandte Beispiele bei späteren Autoren werde ich jeweils gleich anschließend zitieren, im übrigen aber die einzelnen Dichter in chronologischer Reihenfolge getrennt behandeln. So dürften wohl individuelle Verschiedenheiten am deutlichsten hervortreten. Wenden wir uns zu Catull!

Das Mädchen, für das der Dichter schwere Kämpfe bestanden hat, ist untreu geworden. Cat. 37. 11 ff.:

> *Puella nam mi, quae meo sinu fugit,*
> *Amata tantum quantum amabitur nulla,*
> *Pro qua mihi sunt m a g n a b e l l a p u g n a t a*[1]*),*
> *Consedit istic . . . . .*

Gedacht ist hier an die üblichen Pflichten des Liebhabers wie Rivalenkampf, Postenstehen vor der Tür der Geliebten a. ä. In dem Ausdruck *magnum bellum* haben wir das Pendant zu „μέγας πόλεμος" des Epigrammatikers Skythios (p. 33).

Spezialisiert sind die „Kämpfe" in folgenden Stellen. Cat. 62. 59 f.: Die Braut sträubt sich gegen die Forderungen des Gemahls:

> *At tu ne p u g n a cum tali coniuge virgo.*
> *Non aequomst p u g n a r e, pater cui tradidit ipse . . .*

Ganz ähnlich heißt es bei Fronto, dem Epigrammatiker des 2. Jahrh. n. Chr. A. P. XII. 174: Μέχρι τίνος π ο λ ε μ ε ῖ ς με, wo der Ausdruck zu den „kriegerischen Namen" dieses Epigramms paßt: K y r o s, K a m b y s e s, M e d o s, S a k k a s, A s t y a g e s, die zum Teil, wie πολεμεῖς einen erotischen Tropus, so ihrerseits einen obszönen darstellen. Das ähnlich pointierte „*pugnare*" findet sich ferner: T i b. I. 4. 54; I. 8. 37; P r o p. I. 10. 21; O v. Am. I. 5. 14 f; ars I. 561, 661; Met. II. 436; IV. 358. M a r t. Epig. V. 46; IV. 22.

Nächtliche Abenteuer. Cat. 66. 11 ff.:

> *Qua rex tempestate novo auctus hymenaeo*
> *Vastatum finis iverat Assyrios,*
> *Dulcia n o c t u r n a e portans vestigia r i x a e*
> *Quam de virgineis gesserat e x u v i i s.*

Rixa ist kein eigentlicher Kriegsausdruck, wird aber von den Erotikern des öfteren wie *pugna* verwendet. Vgl. C a t. 40. 3 f.; H o r.

---

1) Hier sind die gewöhnlichen *figurae etymologicae* „*pugnam pugnare*" und „*bellum bellare*" gemischt. Vgl. K ü h n e r gr. lat. III. p. 209.

Od. I. 13. 9 ff. Der Grieche sagt oben „ἐννυχίη ἀεϑλοσύνη"
(p. 37). Hier möchte ich Vergils einzige Stelle anführen, die unser
Bild kennt. Statt „nocturnae rixae" gebraucht dieser den Tropus
„nocturna bella". Aeneis XI. 735 f. :

> Quo ferrum ? quidque haec geritis tela irrita dextris
> At non in Venerem segnes nocturnaque bella.

Vgl. Ov. Am. I. 9. 45.

Die Metapher ist hier wie so oft aus dem Kontrast erwachsen.
Tarcho fordert die vor der Heldin Kamilla fliehenden Scharen zum
Kampfe auf. Um Kampf handelt es sich und zwar mit einem Weibe.
Wie nahe lag das Bild des anderen, gewöhnlichen „Kampfes"
mit einer Frau!

Zur obigen Catullstelle vergleiche noch: Prop. II. 15. 4 f.; III. 8. 1.

Für pugna gebrauchen die Erotiker auch gelegentlich den Ter-
minus 'proelium' Cat. 66. 19 f. :

> Id mea me multis docuit regina querellis
> Invisente novo proelia torva viro

vgl. Tib. I. 3. 63 f.; Prop. II. 1. 44 f.

Beachten wir, daß Catulls Gedicht auf die „Locke der Berenike"
(c. 66), eine freie Uebersetzung der Kallimacheischen gleichnamigen
Dichtung, in zwei Stellen das Kriegsbild aufweist. Da bisher nur
der Schluß des Originals auf Papyrus gefunden ist, läßt sich nicht
feststellen, ob es hier genau entsprechende Bilder enthielt.

Oefters und mannigfaltiger begegnet unsere Metapher bei Tibull
und seinen Dichtergenossen. Catull und, was schon hier betont sein
soll, auch Properz begnügen sich mit gelegentlicher, für die Struktur
eines Gedichtes weniger bedeutenden Verwendung des Motivs. Bei
Tibull aber gewinnt letzteres eine Bedeutung für die Architektur
und Gesamtkomposition eines Gedichtes. Freilich, diese innerstruk-
turelle Bedeutung ist nicht überall vorhanden. Die berühmteste und
konstruktiv wichtigste Stelle steht in Tibulls Programmgedicht :
I. 1. 73 ff. :

> Nunc levis est tractanda Venus, dum frangere postes
> non pudet et rixas inseruisse iuvat.
> Hic ego dux milesque bonus: vos signa tubaeque
> Ite procul, cupidis vulnera ferte viris.

Um die Bedeutung der Metapher hier genügend zu verstehen,
muß der Gedankengang und Aufbau des ganzen Gedichtes ins Auge

gefaßt werden[1]). Im Proömium (1—6) werden wir mit dem Thema
bekannt: Reichtum mag sich erwerben, wer der *vita mili-
taris* lebt, ich, sagt der Dichter, begnüge mich mit beschei-
denem Auskommen und genieße dafür das ruhig-behag-
liche Glück der *vita rustica.* Dieser Gegensatz des Kriegs- und
Landlebens durchzieht das ganze Gedicht. In einem ersten Teil
schildert er uns den βίος auf dem Land: Pflanzen, Ernten und den
gnädigen Göttern für ihren Segen danken ist sein Wunsch (7—24).
Emphatisch hebt er dieses sein Ideal hervor (25—28). Gerne will
er den Karst zur Hand nehmen, Freude macht es ihm, die Lämmer
und Kühe zu weiden und gegen die wilden Tiere zu schützen; auch
spendet er gern einen Teil der eingeheimsten Güter den Göttern
(v. 29—40). Nochmals weist er energisch den Reichtum zurück,
denn *parva seges satis est, satis est requiescere lecto* (v. 43). Zum
Inhalt des Landlebens tritt nun auch die Liebe und das Leben mit
der Geliebten hinzu. In diesem zweiten Teile (v. 41—74), der im
Gegensatz zum ersten, mehr 'bukolisch' gefärbten T., des öfteren
'erotisch' genannt wurde, kommt der Dichter auf sich und seine
Liebe zu Delia zu sprechen. Wiederum verzichtet er ausdrücklich
auf Kriegsdienst und Reichtum (v. 51—54). Einem Mann wie Mes-
salla mag das anstehen, mir ist ein anderes Los beschieden v. 55 f.:

> *me retinent vinctum formosae vincla puellae*
> *et sedeo duras ianitor ante fores.*

Der Dichter will sich den Aufgaben des Liebhabers widmen, er
will lieben bis zum Tode (51—68). Weil aber das graue Alter und
der Tod allzu früh dem Menschen drohen, will er die Zeit nützen,
die für den Cupidodienst geeignet ist (69—74) 73 f.:

> *nunc levis est tractanda Venus, dum frangere postes*
> *non pudet et rixas inseruisse invat.*

Die Ausführung gipfelt in des Dichters Bekenntnis: *hic ego dux
milesque bonus,* was scherzhaft klingt, aber durchaus ernst genom-
men sein will. Der fein angekündigte und durch stufenweise Be-
tonung dem Bewußtsein des Lesers immer näher gebrachte Ge-
danke und Wunsch, Amor dienen zu wollen in der Sphäre des

---

1) Mit dem Aufbau der ersten Tibullelegie befaßten sich besonders die
Aufsätze von F. Jacoby Rh. Mus. 65 (1910) 22 ff. u. 64 (1909) 601 ff.;
R. Reitzenstein Hermes 47 (1912) 60 ff.; A. Reinert: *De Tibulli
elegia prima cum aliorum poetarum laudationibus vitae comparanda.* Diss. Jena
1914; O. Weinreich Hermes 56 (1921) 337 ff.

ruhigen und zufriedenen Landes, errreicht in der Metapher seinen
Höhepunkt. Noch mehr! Das Kriegsbild ermöglicht in dem kurzen
Epilog (75—78) den Gegensatz des Einganges wieder aufzunehmen
und so das Gedicht geschickt abzurunden [1]). Der Schluß ist nicht
banal, wie Jacoby meint, sondern durchaus gelungen. *Hic ego dux
milesque bonus* steht im engsten Zusammenhang mit dem voraus-
gehenden, das den Inhalt des Liebeskriegs kurz nennt, andererseits
bildet der Halbvers mit dem folgenden das programmatische Be-
kenntnis und den eindrucksvollen Abschluß. Im ganzen betrachtet
ist also die Bedeutung der Metapher an dieser Stelle eine ganz
hervorragende.

Tibulls Lebensideal besteht wesentlich im Kampf um und für das
Mädchen. Darin ist er nicht nur *miles*, sondern geradezu *dux*.
Die Formulierung: *hic ego dux milesque bonus* erinnert an P r o p.
II. 22. 34:

> *Hic ego Pelides, hic ferus Hector ego.*

War Tibull das Vorbild? Properz hat dann den Vers auf seine
Weise umgeformt: mit dem bei ihm beliebten Mythengleichnis
hat er konkretere Fassung angestrebt. Das ergab sich aus der
Situation, 29 ff.:

> *quid? cum e complexu Briseidos iret Achilles
> num fugere minus Thessala tela Phryges?
> quid? ferus Andromachae lecto cum surgeret Hector,
> bella Mycenaeae non timuere rates?
> ille vel hic classes poterant vel perdere muros:
> hic ego Pelides, hic ferus Hector ego.*

Die metaphorische Wendung erwächst auch hier aus dem Gegen-
satz. Aufs nächste mit der Tibullstelle verwandt ist diese: P r o p.
I. 6. 29 f.:

> *non ego sum laudi, non natus idoneus armis:
> hanc me militiam fata subire volunt.*

O v i d ahmt das nach: Her. 16. 254 ff.

> *Bella gerant fortes, tu, Pari, semper ama!
> Hectora, quem laudas, pro te pugnare iubeto!
> Militiast operis altera digna tuis.*

---

1) Der Kontrast des ersten Teils (Kriegstaten in aller Welt — an die
Scholle gebundenes Landleben) erhält also auch im erotischen Teil seinen
Kontrast: ländliches Idyll mit der Geliebten — Liebesabenteuer d: r *levis
Venus* im städtischen Milieu. Weil I. 1 „Programmgedicht" ist, werden all
diese Motive kunstvoll verschlungen.

Den Inhalt der Venuskämpfe bilden die in der Erotik überaus beliebten Gemeinplätze. Tibull erwähnt oben das „*postes frangere*". Diesen Motiven nachzugehen gehört nicht zu meiner Aufgabe. Weil sie mit dem Bild des Liebeskriegs aufs engste zusammenhängen, möchte ich aber einige Beispiele vor Augen führen. Sie sind schon in der griechischen Komödie zu Hause. Nachtschwärmen, Türerbrechen der Jungen: A r i s t. Ekkl. 976 ff.:

> οὗτος, τί κόπτεις; μῶν ἐμὲ ζητεῖς; .....
> καὶ τὴν θύραν γ' ἤραττες .....
> τοῦ δαὶ δεόμενος δᾷδ' ἔχων ἐλήλυθας;

T h e o k r. II. 127:

> εἰ δ' ἀλλᾷ μ' ὠθεῖτε καὶ ἁ θύρα εἴχετο μοχλῷ,
> πάντως κα πελέκεις καὶ λαμπάδες ἦνθον ἐφ' ὑμέας.

Vgl. Her. II. 65.

Oft klagen die Liebhaber über das schlechte Wetter, bei dem sie durchnäßt oder frierend im Freien warten müssen, bis sie ihre „Eroberung" machen können. A s k l e p i a d e s A. P. V. 189 oder A s k l e p. A. P. V. 166:

> Ὑετὸς ἦν καὶ νὺξ καὶ ἐπιρρέπον ἄχθος ἔρωτι,
> οἶνος, καὶ Βορέης ψυχρός, ἐγὼ δὲ μόνος.
> ..... αἱ σὺ γὰρ οὕτως
> ἦλυες, οὐδὲ θύρην πρὸς μίαν ἡσυχάσας.

T e r., Adelph. 102: ...... *neque fores ecfringere,*

T i b. I. 2. 31 ff.:

> *Non mihi pigra nocent hibernae frigora noctis*
> *Non mihi, cum multa decidit imber aqua.*
> *Non labor hic laedit, reseret modo Delia postes.*

P r o p. III. 3. 47 ff.:

> *Quippe coronatos alienum ad limen amantes*
> *Nocturnaeque canes ebria s i g n a f u g a e,*
> *Ut per te clausas sciat excantare puellas,*
> *Qui volet austeros arte ferire viros.*

O v. Am. I. 9. 15 f.:

> *Quis nisi vel miles vel amans et frigora noctis*
> *Et denso mixtas perferet imbre nives?*

Tibull spricht oben ganz allgemein von „*rixas inseruisse*". Diese „*rixae*" können die Streitigkeiten der Rivalen sein, die sich oft vor

der Tür der Ersehnten abspielen: Bei Properz spricht die Tür I,
16. 5: *num ego, nocturnis potorum saucia rixis*, vgl. P r o p. II. 19. 5;
O v. ars III. 71:

Nec tua frangetur nocturna ianua rixa O v. Rem. 31. Die „*rixae*"
bestehen ferner in dem Kampf mit dem Mädchen, der bald ernsterer,
bald harmloserer Natur ist. Dieser muß da sein, wenn wahre Liebe
herrschen soll. O v. Am. I. 8. 55: *Non bene, si tollas p r o e l i a,
durat amor*. Große Freude macht es bisweilen dem „Eroberer",
wenn er in heißem Mühn den Sieg erringen muß, vgl. P r o p. II.
15. 4 ff. Gewöhnlich ist ja das Sträuben des Mädchens nur schein-
bar, vgl. O v. Am. I. 5. 13 ff.[1]). Ernster geht es hier zu: O v.
Her. 5. 140 ff.:

> *Ille meae s p o l i u m virginitatis habet,*
> *Id quoque l u c t a n d o; rupi tamen ungue capillos,*
> *Oraque sunt digitis aspera facta meis.*

Ein andermal kommt Tibull in ähnlichem Zusammenhang auf
die Liebeskämpfe zu sprechen. Dabei werden diese eingehender ge-
schildert als im Programmgedicht. Dem Kriegsleben sind die Vor-
teile des Friedens gegenübergestellt. Frieden sehnt der Dichter
mehr als einmal herbei. Hält aber Mars Ruhe, dann mögen der
Venus' Kriege nur immer entbrennen: T i b. I. 10. 53 ff.:

> *Sed V e n e r i s tunc b e l l a calent, scissosque capillos*
> *femina perfractas conqueriturque fores.*
> *flet teneras subtusa genas, sed v i c t o r et ipse*
> *flet sibi dementes tam valuisse manus.*
> *at lascivus Amor r i x a e mala verba ministrat*
> *inter et iratum lentus utrumque sedet.*
> *a, lapis est ferrumque, suam quicumque puellam*
> *verberat: e caelo deripit ille deos.*
> *Sit satis e membris tenuem rescindere vestem,*
> *sit satis ornatus dissoluisse comae,*
> *sit lacrimas movisse satis: quater ille beatus,*
> *quo tenera irato flere puella potest.*

Wie der Krieger Tränen verursacht, so triumphiert der „krie-
gerische" Liebhaber erst dann, wenn dem Mädchen die Tränen
fließen. Doch der Dichter bereut, sein Mädchen auf so schimpfliche

---

1) Vgl. 'Venusgärtlein' p. 118. 13: 'Hierbey kan man nun spüren, wenn
sich die Jungfrawen wehren, daß es nur sey ein Schertz, ob sie schon hoch
erheben, das Kloster und Nonnenleben, ist ihnen doch nicht umbs Hertz.

Weise besiegt, ihr die Haare zerrauft und die Wangen zerkratzt zu haben. Er selbst weint. Zwischen den Weinenden sitzt Amor; dessen Sinnen geht nicht dahin, Frieden zu stiften, sondern er schürt Krieg und Streitigkeiten. Eine anschauliche Szene, lebendig empfunden und bildhaft zugleich.

Statt „*bella Veneris*" sagt O v i d Am. II. 10. 29 : *Felix, quem Veneris certamina mutua perdunt.*

Mit Tibull I. 10. 53 ff. gehört eng zusammen Properz II. 5. 19 ff. Es fragt sich, ob Properz nicht durch die Tibullstelle beeinflußt ist. P r o p. II. 5. 19 ff.:

> *Non solum taurus ferit uncis cornibus hostem,*
> *Verum etiam instanti laesa repugnat ovis.*
> *Nec tibi periuro scindam de corpore vestes,*
> *Nec mea praeclusas fregerit ira fores,*
> *Noc tibi conexos iratus carpere crines*
> *Nec duris ausim laedere pollicibus.*
> *Rusticus haec aliquis tam turpia p r o e l i a quaerat.*

Properz ist m. E. von Tibull abhängig. Psychologisch dürfte diese Mäßigung der Affekte eher zu Tibull passen, als zu dem temperamentvollen, extremen Properz, für den es auch stilistisch *nil medium* gibt.

Zum Gedanken vergleiche O v. ars II. 160 ff.; ars III. 568 ff.; Am. I. 7. Anders P r o p. III. 5. 2:

> *Sat mihi cum domina proelia dura mea.* O v. ars II. 346:
> *Asperitas odium s a e v a q u e b e l l a movet.*

Der Sieg bei derartigen Gefechten ist bisweilen dem Mädchen beschieden. So triumphiert Cynthia nach gewonnener „Schlacht" P r o p. IV. 8. 63 ff.:

> *Cynthia gaudct in e x u v i i s v i c t r i x q u e recurrit*
> *Et mea p e r v e r s a s a u c i a t o r a m a n u*
> *imponitque notam c o l l o m o r s u q u e c r u e n t a t*
> *praecipueque oculos, qui meruere, ferit.*

67 : *Atque ubi iam nostris lassavit bracchia p l a g i s* . . . . .

Wie eine Tigerin wütet sie, wie eine Amazone verfolgt sie ihr Opfer (den Amazonenvergleich führt Ovid ein ars III. 1).

82 : *riserat imperio facta superba dato.*

Die Versöhnung aber weiß der Mann herbeizuführen v. 88 :

> . . . . *et toto s o l v i m u s a r m a toro.*

Das Bett schlichtet auch bei Ovid den Streit. ars II. 461 ff.:

Cum bene saevierit, cum certa videbitur hostis,
Tum pete concubitus foedera: mitis erit,
Illic depositis habitat Concordia telis,
Illo, crede mihi, Gratia nata locost.

Der Erfolg im Liebeskrieg richtet sich oft nach der Finanzlage des Liebhabers. Große Geschenke sprengen die Türen: T i b. III. 4. 33:

Sed pretium si grande feras, custodia victa est,
Nec prohibent claves, et canis ipse tacet.

Properz nennt den Reichtum direkt „Waffen" [1]) Prop. III. 13. 9 f.:

haec autem clausas expugnant arma pudicas,
quaeque terunt fastus . . . . .

Die Kleider sind „*spolia*", die das Mädchen von ihrem Galan geschenkt bekam. P r o p. III. 13. 12:

et spolia opprobrii nostra per ora trahit.

Das Kriegsbild auf Reichtum und Kleider übertragen ist individuell-properzisches Gut.

Die bisher erwähnten properzischen Stellen finden mindestens gedanklich bei Tibull ein Analogon. Das psychologische Element wird zwar das Problem der Abhängigkeit mehr oder weniger klären helfen aber im ganzen ist es recht schwer zu sagen, welcher Dichter und wie weit dieser vom andern beeinflußt ist. Denn ihre Vorbilder, die für uns leider zu wenig greifbar sind, konnten ja gemeinsame sein. Der einzelne Elegiker wird im wesentlichen das ihm selbst Kongeniale übernommen und ausgemünzt haben. Freilich dürfen wir keineswegs an sklavische Abhängigkeit denken. Dafür sind doch Tibull, noch mehr Properz viel zu kraftvolle Dichterpersönlichkeiten. Beachten wir außerdem, daß der kulturelle Hintergrund ihrer Poesie ein anderer ist als für die alexandrinische Literatur; die römischen Elegiker denken und fühlen als Angehörige der augusteischen Zeit. — Mit großer Meisterschaft ist die Metapher von den Römern gehandhabt; mit seltenem Geschick besonders von Tibull in die Gesamtkomposition eines Gedichtes verwoben. Von Properz sind noch einige Beispiele aufzuführen: P r o p. IV. 1. 137 ff.:

1) Der Philosoph Krantor läßt den Reichtum sagen: ἐν δὲ πολέμοις νεῦρα τῶν πράξεων γένομαι (b. Sext. Emp. adv. eth. (Mutschmann p. 387)) Bion nennt ihn νεῦρα πραγμάτων (b. Diog. Laert. IV. 7. 3. 48), Cicero analog *nervos belli* (Phil. V. 2. 5) siehe G. Büchmann „geflügelte Worte" Berlin 1918 S. 359 f. Vgl. auch oben S. 50.

Militiam Veneris blandis patiere sub armis
Et Veneris pueris utilis hostis eris.
Nam tibi victrices, quascumque labore parasti,
Eludet[1]) *palmas una puella tuas.*

Der Aufforderung seiner Gönner, sein Dichtertalent in den Dienst der Epik zu stellen, ist Properz wieder nicht nachgekommen. Von der Liebe und Liebespoesie vermag er nicht Abschied zu nehmen. Denn er ist zu nichts anderem als zur „*militia Veneris*" geboren. Eine Stelle, die wiederum für die Struktur des Gedichtes sehr wichtig ist, haben wir vor uns. Der Inhalt der Elegie gipfelt nämlich — vergleiche Tibull I. 1. — in dem metaphorisch geformten Gedanken, der sein Lebensprogramm verkünden soll. Angedeutet ist dieser Höhepunkt mit Vers 135:

Et tu fige elegos, fallax opus (*haec tua castra*).

Mit „*castra*" wird das Bild eingeleitet und vorbereitet. Also nicht bloß als Liebhaber ist der Dichter Soldat der Venus, sondern auch als Liebes- und Elegiendichter. Ovid, der alle seine Vorgänger auszubeuten weiß, hat auch diesen, dem Properz zuzuschreibenden Gedanken, übernommen und geschickt verwertet. Ovid als Sänger der „*Amores*" und der „*ars amatoria*" ist ein Soldat im Lager Amors. Wenn er nun später „*remedia amoris*" dichtet, kommt er in Konflikt mit dem Liebesgott, seinem obersten Feldherr. Ov. Rem. 2 ff.:

'*bella mihi, video, bella parantur*', *ait,*
parce tuum vatem sceleris damnare, Cupido,
tradita qui totiens te duce signa tuli.

Dagegen gibt der Poet als ἐρωτοδιδάσκαλος, als Lehrer der Liebeskunst, den Liebenden Waffen in die Hand, mit denen sie ihre Beute machen können. Der Dichter verabschiedet sich vom Leser, indem er ihm viel Erfolg und Glück im Liebeskrieg wünscht. Kämpfer sollen sie sein vom Schlage Achills: Ov. ars II. 741 ff.:

Arma dedi vobis; dederat Vulcanus Achilli:
Vincite muneribus, vicit ut ille, datis!
Sed quicumque meo superarit Amazona ferro,
Inscribat spoliis 'Naso magister erat'.

vgl. ars III. 812.

---

1) *Eludere* gehört der Fechtersprache an und bedeutet „einen Schlag parieren". Außerdem ist *ferire* ein Fechterterminus:
vgl. Prop. III. 3. 50: *arte ferire viros*
Prop. IV. 5. 44: *ferit astutos moecho Getas.*

In diesem Bild fährt der Dichter zu Beginn des dritten Buches
weiter. ars III. 1 f.:

Arma dedi Danais in Amazonas: arma supersunt,
Quae tibi dem et turmae, Penthesilea, tuae.

Die Danaer d. h. die Jünglinge hat er bewaffnet. Nun sollen auch
die Mädchen, die Amazonen, kriegsfähig werden. Eine raffinierte
Weiterführung der seit ars II. 735 ff. begonnenen Vergleiche! Der
Dichter fährt fort ars III. 3 ff.:

Ite in bella pares: vincant, quibus alma Dione
faverit et, toto qui volat orbe, puer!
Non erat armatis aequum concurrere nudas:
Sic etiam vobis vincere turpe, viri.

'Nudae' d. h. waffenlos sind noch die Mädchen, solange sie vom
Poeten nicht über die „Kunst zu lieben" informiert sind. *Armatus*
hat auch obszönen Sinn (ars III. 46). Wenn einem Diener ein Brief
anvertraut ist, so kann dieser ihm auch eine „Waffe" sein. Ov.
ars III. 492:

armaque in armatos sumere iura sinunt.

Hier muß auch Horaz genannt werden. Denn für ihn ist die ero-
tische Dichtung ebenfalls ein Kampf unter Cupidos Fahne. Hor.
Od. III. 26. 1 ff.:

Vixi puellis nuper idoneus
et militavi non sine gloria
nunc arma, defunctumque bello
barbiton hic paries habebit . . .

Scherzhaft und witzig klingt es, wenn der Lyriker bei der Wieder-
aufnahme seiner Liebesdichtung sagt. Hor. Od. IV. 1. 1:

Intermissa, Venus, diu rursus bella moves.

Zweifellos kannte Ovid die Stellen. Woher aber hat Horaz das
Bild? Dieser wird außer der alten griechischen Lyrik auch die
hellenistischen Dichter gelesen haben. Ferner wissen wir, daß Horaz
mit Tibull befreundet war, von dem er angeregt sein könnte. Schließ-
lich ist es nicht nötig, literarische Abhängigkeit zu konstruieren:
damals war das Bild doch schon Gemeinplatz geworden.

Als Properz mit der Liebespoesie Schluß machen will, bittet er
Bacchus als Λύσιος, ihn von den Leiden der Liebeskriege zu befreien
und ihm den Frieden zu verschaffen: Prop. III. 17. 2:

da mihi pacato vela secunda pater.

Sonstige Beispiele bei Properz, die meist das Bild nur andeuten Prop. II. 1. 13: Ein hübsches Doppelbild

> *seu nuda erepto mecum luctatur amictu,*
> *tum vero longas condimus Iliadas*

P r o p. III. 8. 31 f.:

> *Dum vincunt Danai, dum restat barbarus Hector,*
> *ille Helenae in gremio m a x i m a b e l l a g e r i t.*

Eine lange Zeit mißverstandene, durch Rothstein zweifellos richtig gedeutete Stelle ist P r o p. I. 3. 16:

> *osculaque ad mota sumere et a r m a manu*

arma hier im Sinn von Liebesspiel vgl. P r o p. III. 20. 20:

> *dulcia quam nobis concitet a r m a Venus!*

Prop. II. 34. 6:

> *Et bene concordes tristia ad a r m a vocat.*

Seine Geliebte aufgeben und einem anderen Mädchen nachjagen heißt 'castra movere' P r o p. IV. 8. 27 f.:

> *cum fieret nostro totiens iniuria lecto,*
> *mutato volui c a s t r a m o v e r e toro.*

„Feind" im Liebesleben, P r o p. II. 8. 3 f.:

> *Nullae sunt inimicitiae nisi amoris acerbae:*
> *Ipsum me iugula, lenior h o s t i s ero.*

vgl. P r o p. III. 16. 7 f.; O v. ars II. 461 ff.; ars III. 667; Her. VI. 82; VII. 62.

P r o p. IV. 8. 17 f.:

> *Appia, dic quaeso, quantum te teste t r i u m p h u m*
> *egerit effusis per tua saxa rotis,*
> *turpis in arcana sonuit cum r i x a taberna:*

Eindrucksvolle Antithesen sprachlich sowohl wie inhaltlich: P r o p. II. 1. 44 f.:

> *Et numerat miles vulnera, pastor oves,*
> *nos contra, angusto v e r s a n t e s p r o e l i a lecto.*

Rivalenkämpfe P r o p. II. 9. 51 f.:

> *Quam, mihi si media liceat p u g n a r e puella,*
> *mortem ego non fugiam morte subire tua.*

Die Geliebte ist der Kampfpreis für die beiden Nebenbuhler.

Auch in der Horazstelle handelt es sich um solche Kämpfe.
Hor. Od. III. 13. 5:

> ... *et Venerem et proelia destinat*

Prop. III. 8. 20 f.:

> *hostibus eveniat lenta puella meis!*
> *in morso aequales videant mea vulnera collo,*

vgl. Ov. Am. II. 10. 16; Am. III. 11. 16; Her. 15. 217.

Der Besitz des Mädchen ist dem Dichter wertvoller als die Siegesbeute im Kampf gegen die Parther, Prop. II. 14. 22 ff.:

> *Mecum habuit positum lenta puella caput.*
> *Haec mihi devictis potior victoria Parthis,*
> *haec spolia, haec reges, haec mihi currus erunt.*
> *Magna ego dona tua figam, Cytherea, columna,*

Für seinen Sieg widmet der Dichter wie der sieggekrönte Heerführer der Gottheit Opfergaben:

> 27 f.: '*has pono ante tuas tibi, diva, Propertius aedes*
> *exuvias, tota nocte receptus amans.*'

Dabei spielt der Dichter mit dem Stil des Votivepigrammes. Bei Trophäen pflegte man ja die Beute an Häusern, besonders an Tempeln aufzuhängen. In der palat. Anthologie finden sich eine Reihe von Epigrammen, in denen vor allem auch Hetären der Kypris Weihegeschenke darbringen, vgl. A. P. XVI. 17, 18, 19, 20, 59, 208, 209, 210 und mehr.

A. P. VI. 71 will ich vorführen: Ein Liebhaber namens Anaxagoras weiht der stolzen Lais Kränze u. dgl. *spolia*:

> Σοὶ τὰ λιποστεφάνων διατίλματα μυρία φύλλων,
> σοὶ τὰ νοοπλήκτου κλαστὰ κύπελλα μέθης,
> βόστρυχα σοὶ τὰ μύροισι δεδευμένα τῇδε κονίῃ
> σκῦλα ποθοβλήτου κεῖται Ἀναξαγόρα,
> σοὶ τάδε, Λαΐς, ἅπαντα. παρὰ προθύροις γὰρ ὁ δειλὸς
> τοῖσδε, σὺν ἀκρήβαις πολλάκι παννυχίσας, ...

. . . .

Während Properz oben den Inhalt der Beute aufzählt, schildert Ovid in ähnlicher Ausführung die Funktion, die er auf seinem Feldzug hatte. Ov. Am. II. 12. 13 f.

> *Me duce ad hanc voti finem, me milite veni;*
> *Ipse eques, ipse pedes, signifer ipse fui.*

Der erstere Vers erinnert seinerseits an das Tibullische *hic ego dux milesque bonus* (I. 1. 75).

Ovid hat dem τόπος des Liebeskriegs eine ganze Elegie gewidmet. In dieser gibt er eine ausführliche Begründung und Erklärung des bei anderen Dichtern nur metaphorisch angedeuteten oder bloß einen Vergleichspunkt herausstellenden Bildes. Er zieht hier die Summe der Vergleichspunkte. Die Grundlage dafür bieten die in der Liebespoesie viel behandelten Gemeinplätze. Das Motiv des *exclusus amator*, des *postes frangere* u. a. sind schon von Ovids Vorgängern mit dem Kriegsleben in Beziehung gesetzt worden. Ovid aber faßt hier alle zusammen, modifiziert sie und fügt, dank seines Spürsinns und seiner Phantasie, noch neue Gedanken bei. O v. Am. I. 9:

> *Militat omnis amans, et habet sua castra Cupido:*
> *Attice, crede mihi, militat omnis amans.*
> *Quae bellost habilis, Veneri quoque convenit aetas:*
> *Turpe senex miles, turpe senilis amor* [1]);
> 5   *Quos petiere duces animos in milite forti,*
> *Hos petit in socio bella puella viro;*
> *Pervigilant ambo; terra requiescit uterque:*
> *Ille fores dominae servat, at ille ducis;*
> *Militis officium longast via: mitte puellam,*
> 10   *Strenuus exempto fine sequetur amans;*
> *Ibit in adversos montes duplicataque nimbo*
> *Flumina, congestas exteret ille nives,*
> *Nec freta pressurus tumidos causabitur Euros*
> *Aptaque verrendis sidera quaeret aquis.*
> 15   *Quis nisi vel miles vel amans et frigora noctis*
> *Et denso mixtas perferet imbre nives?*
> *Mittitur infestos alter speculator in hostes,*
> *In rivale oculos alter, ut hoste, tenet.*
> *Ille graves urbes, hic durae limen amicae*
> 20   *Obsidet; hic portas frangit, at ille fores* [2]).

___

1) Nachgeahmt im „Venusgärtlein" p. 184: „Eine junge Wittbe zu einem lüstren Greisen":

„Im Alter soll den Krieg und auch die Liebe lassen, weil Mars u. Venus ihn als einen toten hassen, es liegt nicht nur an Muth, er muß auch Krafft erweisen, sonst ist er nicht für gut, in seinem Thun zu preisen."

2) Vgl. 'Venusgärtlein' p. 11. 6: 'Jetzt steh' ich vor ihr Thür, voll Getrühr, macht dar ein groß Turnier, kann ich dann kein Trost erwerben, so muß ich, so muß ich, von Trawren sterben' oder p. 22 Tochter:

Saepe soporatos invadere profuit hostes
  Caedere et armata vulgus inerme manu:
Sic fera Threicii ceciderunt agmina Rhesi,
  Et dominum capti deseruistis equi;
Saepe maritorum somnis utuntur amantes,   25
  Et sua sopitis hostibus arma movent.
Custodum transire manus vigilumque catervas
  Militis et miseri semper amantis opus.
Mars dubius nec certa Venus: victique resurgunt,
  Quosque neges umquam posse iacere, cadunt.   30
Ergo desidiam quicumque vocabat amorcm,
  Desinat: ingeniist experientis amor.
Ardet in abducta Briseide magnus Achilles:
  Dum licet, Argivas frangite, Troes, opes!
Hector ab Andromaches complexibus ibat ad arma   35
  Et, galeam capiti quae daret, uxor erat.
Summa ducum, Atrides, visa Priameide fertur
  Maenadis effusis obstipuisse comis;
Mars quoque deprensus fabrilia vincula sensit:
  Notior in caelo fabula nulla fuit.   40
Ipse ego segnis eram discinctaque in otia natus:
  Mollierant animos lectus et umbra meos;
Impul ignavum formosae cura puellae
  Iussit et in castris aera merere suis:
Inde vides agilem nocturnaque bella gerentem.   45
  Qui nolet fieri desidiosus, amet!

Meine Arbeit erfordert eine eingehendere Interpretation dieser Elegie.
Den Kommentar zum Motivgeschichtlichen liefert ja schon großen-
teils die bisherige Untersuchung. Aber auch das stilistische Moment
und die Frage des Aufbaus mögen besondere Beachtung finden [1]).
Die in Ovids Dichtung wiederkehrenden Parallelen müssen z. T.
beigezogen werden. Mit diesem Gedicht taucht das Motiv zum ersten-
mal bei Ovid auf. Seine spätere Poesie ist sehr reich damit ge-
schmückt; dabei ist die Metapher teils im obigen Stil, teils im
neuen Sinne gestaltet:

'Ho, Ho mit diesem Narrengedicht, bringt ihr mich nicht an den Tantz,
Nonnenfleisch ist mir gewachsen nicht, kein Alter mir auch wenig Frewde
anriht, ein Junger gewinnt die Schantz'.
1) Im übrigen verweise ich auf den Kommentar von Brandt.

Vers 1: Einleitung und Themastellung. Wie ernst es Ovid dabei ist, dem Leser den Gedanken recht tief einzuprägen, zeigt die Wiederaufnahme der Einleitungsworte in chiastischer Form und das emphatische „*crede mihi*" (v. 2). Das Lieben, will er sagen, ist keineswegs eine leicht zu nehmende Spielerei; es ist geradezu ein mühevoller Soldatendienst. Diesen Gedanken klarzulegen, ist seine Absicht. Er bildet den Höhepunkt der Elegie (v. 31 f.) und mit ihm nimmt der Dichter Abschied vom Publikum.

Der *amans* ist dem Kommando Cupidos unterstellt. In dessen Lager dient er vgl. O v. ars III, 559: *Hic rudis et c a s t r i s nunc primum notus A m o r i s;* Her. VII. 32: *c a s t r i s militet ille tuis;* Am. II. 9. 4: *et in c a s t r i s vulneror ipse meis;* ars II. 236: *Mollibus his c a s t r i s et labor omnis inest.*

V. 3 ff. führt der Dichter die einzelnen Beziehungen auf, die zwischen Liebes- und Kriegsleben bestehen. Zunächst ist die Person des Liebhabers charakterisiert (v. 3—6): Dieser muß in einem gebührend jugendlichen Alter stehen, von Mut und Tapferkeit beseelt sein. — Der Hinweis auf die ähnliche Altersstufe findet kein Analogon, wohl aber ist in dem oben behandelten Eupolisfragment von Mut und Entschlossenheit die Rede (p. 31); letzteres wird vom Soldaten und Liebhaber in gleicher Weise verlangt.

V. 7 ff. werden die Mühen und Aufgaben der Krieger bzw. Liebenden aufgezählt. Beide müssen Nachtwachen halten, weite Märsche zurücklegen — die „*longae viae*" der Soldaten werden sogar übertrumpft von dem sein „Ziel" verfolgenden Liebhaber: *exempto fine sequetur amans* (v. 10 ff.). Ferner müssen beide in der Kälte der Nacht und bei strömenden Regen draußen stehen und warten. Mit dem Fragesatz (v. 15 f.) schließt die Gedankenreihe ab, die im wachsenden Maße der Liebenden Strapazen vor uns entwickelt. Die *officia amantium* werden fortgeführt: Die Folgenden machen nun nicht so fast Anspruch an die körperlichen Leistungen als an das ingenium, die List, Vorsicht und Klugheit derselben (v. 17 ff.): Späherdienst, jener belagert Städte, dieser die Tür seines „Verlangens"[1]); Tore erbricht der Soldat, Türen der Kavalier[2]); Ueberfälle auf ihr Opfer, wobei beide den Schlaf der Gegner ausnützen[3]);

---

1) Vgl. O v. ars II. 526: *quid nostras o b s i d e t iste fores?* H o r. Od. III. 15: *filia rectius e x p u g n a t iuvenum domos.*

2) Die Elegie Am. I. 6 ist diesem Thema gewidmet.

3) v. 26 ist eine von Ovid auch sonst beliebte Doppeldeutigkeit (vgl. Am. III. 7. 71. (*arma = mentula*)) nach der Ansicht von Brandt (s. p. 70).

Wachtposten zu hintergehen, ist beider Bemühen. Diese Einzelmotive sind in der Erotik so viel besungen, daß weitere Bemerkungen dazu unnötig sind. Bei all diesen Unternehmungen, fährt der Poet weiter, ist der Ausgang auf beiden Seiten recht ungewiß. V. 31 f. resumiert Ovid. Damit wäre eigentlich die *propositio* entwickelt und bewiesen. Der Dichter aber führt noch einige Kriegsrecken aus dem Mythenbereich vor, gleichsam um seine Behauptungen durch berühmte Beispiele zu bekräftigen. Hier also (v. 33—40) geht er zu konkreten Fällen über; man könnte jetzt den Stil wenden und sagen: *miles omnis amat*, nach Ovid wenigstens für die vorbildlichen Helden zutreffend [1]). Der Begriff „*miles*" wird gesteigert zum Soldaten κατ' ἐξοχὴν mit Achill u. a. mythologischen Heroen, ja selbst zum Kriegsgott Mars, der *miles*-Vorbild ist im Kampf und *miles*-Vorbild in der Liebe. So baut sich das alles ganz konsequent und mustergiltig auf. Von hier aus gewinnt auch das „*crede mihi*" in v. 2 noch Bedeutung: Der Satz ist wahr und erweislich aus irdischer Vergangenheit, heroischer Vorzeit, selbst aus göttlicher Welt. Also macht er — Ovid — keine Ausnahme (v. 41 ff.). So verbindet sich mit dem Objektiv-Deskribierenden und mit dem Mythologisch-Exemplifizierenden das Subjektiv-Bekenntnishafte und das ἐρωτοδιδάσκαλος-Element (Schlußvers).

Im ganzen gesehen zeigt sich Ovid in der Art, wie er das Bild durchführt und erläutert, als Meister rhetorischer Interpretationskunst. Zwar sind viele Gedanken übernommen und ein der Erotik gemeinsames Gut, aber sie sind so passend verwendet, in so guten Zusammenhang gebracht, daß man an dem eleganten παίγνιον, das so gar nicht pedantisch wird, seine Freude haben kann.

Eine nähere Parallele zu der eben besprochenen Elegie haben wir in Ov. ars II. 233 ff. Dabei wird der τόπος in ähnlicher, nur viel kürzerer Weise dem Leser veranschaulicht:

Militiae species amor est: discedite segnes!
Non sunt haec timidis signa tuenda viris;

---

1) Diese Tatsache, daß der Soldat in erster Linie auch ein Mädchenjäger ist, bildet großenteils ein Thema der Komödien der Alten. Ein deutsches Sprichwort sagt:
'Der Soldat, hat in jeder Stadt eine andere Mad'
(E. M. Kronfeld ‚Krieg u. Soldat in der Spruchweisheit' p. 25.
Abraham a Santa Clara schimpft (daselbst p. 33):
'so seynd die Offiziere, sie nehmen lieber ihr Quartier zu Frauheim, als zu Mannheim'.

Nox et hiemps longaeque viae saevique dolores
Mollibus his c a s t r i s et labor omnis inest;
Saepe feres imbrem caelesti nube solutum,
frigidus et nuda saepe iacebis humo [1]).

Auch hier also mit Emphase betont: *discedite segnes!* Trotz aller
ernsthaften Gebärde schimmert doch eine gewisse Ironie durch in
„*m o l l i b u s castris*".

Dem unerfahrenen „Rekruten" steht der erprobte „Veteran" gegen-
über: Ov. ars III. 559 ff.:

Hic r u d i s et c a s t r i s nunc primum notus Amoris,
Qui tetigit thalamos p r a e d a novella tuos

. . . . .

Effuge rivalem! v i n c e s, dum sola tenebis.
Non bene cum s o c i i s r e g n a Venusque manent.
Ille v e t u s m i l e s sensim et sapienter amabit
Multaque t i r o n i non patienda feret.
Nec franget postes nec saevis ignibus uret

. . . . .

Vom „Kriegsdienst" der Liebenden hören wir noch in folgenden
ovidischen Stellen: ars II. 673 f.:

Aut latus et vires operamque adferte puellis:
Hoc quoque m i l i t i a s t, hoc quoque quaerit opes.

Am. II. 12. 27 f.:

Me quoque, qui multos, sed me sine caede, Cupido
Iussit m i l i t i a e s i g n a m o v e r e suae.

vgl. Hor. c. IV. 1. 15 f.:

et centum puer artium
late s i g n a feret m i l i t i a e tuae.

„Soldat" unter Amor: Ov. ars I. 36:

Qui nova nunc primum m i l e s in a r m a venis!

Am. II. 9. 3:

Quid me, qui m i l e s numquam tua s i g n a reliqui,

Der Dichter, der von der Tragischen Muse (Medea) zur Liebes-
poesie zurückkehrt, glaubt auch hiemit „Kriegsmelodien" anzu-
stimmen. Am. II. 18. 11 f.:

Vincor, et ingenium sumptis revocatur ab armis,
Resque domi gestas et mea b e l l a cano.

_____

1) H o r a z sagt c. IV. 1. 4. . . *flectere m o l l i b u s iam durum i m p e r i i s.*

Aehnlich **H o r a z**: Varius wird deine Siege, Agrippa, verherrlichen, ich bin dazu erkoren, von unblutigen Kämpfen Verliebter zu singen. Od. I. 6. 17:

> *nos convivia, nos p r o e l i a virginum*
> *sectis in iuvenes unguibu*s *acrium*
> *cantamus.*

Wer Amor untreu wird, ist ein „Deserteur" Ov. Her. 18. 157:

> *In tua c a s t r a redi, socii d e s e r t o r a m o r i s!*

An den Schluß seien noch einige Beispiele gerückt, die individuell-ovidisch sind. Gerade sie zeigen, wie unser Bild dem Denken und der Phantasie des Dichters immer gegenwärtig ist, und daß er geradezu darnach hascht, dieses, wenn irgend möglich, anzubringen. Des Eindrucks der Verkünstelung können wir uns nicht erwehren, wenn das Gebären einer Frau „Kriegsdienst" genannt wird. Her. XI. 48:

> *Et r u d i s ad partus et n o v a m i l e s eram*

oder, wenn er gar für das Abtreiben der Leibesfrucht das Kriegsbild gebraucht. Am. II. 14. 5 f.:

> *Quae prima instituit teneros convellere fetus*
> *M i l i t i a fuerat digna perire sua!*

Wie der besonnene Feldherr jeden Centurio an seinen gebührenden Posten stellt, so sollt ihr Mädchen eure Liebhaber an die ihnen zukommenden Plätze bringen. Der Vergleich ist m. E. an den Haaren herbeigezogen. Ars III. 527 ff.:

> *Dux bonus huic centum commisit vite regendos,*
> *Huic equites, illi signa tuenda dedit:*
> *Vos quoque, de nobis quem quisque erit aptus ad usum,*
> *Inspicite et certo ponite quemque loco!*
> *Munera det dives . . .*

Bei den nachaugusteischen Autoren kommt die Metapher wohl noch ab und zu vor, aber zumeist nur im obszönen Sinn. Namentlich sprechen sie gern von der *mentula* bildhaft. Ob sie hierin von Ovid abhängig sind, ist fraglich. Wir haben früher diesen Tropus der Vulgärsprache zugeschrieben (Vgl. Goldbacher, Glotta 18, 45). Auch die *carmina Priapea* scheinen dafür zu sprechen.

Die *mentula* ist die „Waffe" des Mannes im Liebeskrieg. Ist sie nicht leistungsfähig, so ist der Mann „entwaffnet". Ov. Am. III. 7. 71:

> *Tu dominum fallis, per te deprensus i n e r m i s*
> *Tristia . . .   tuli.*

Brandt glaubt, es liege in Ov. Am. I. 9. 26:

Et sua sopitis hostibus a r m a movent

bewußte Doppeldeutigkeit vor, „*arma*" habe auch obszönen Sinn. Das ist nicht unmöglich. Indes kann „*arma*" ebensogut als „Liebesspiel" gefaßt werden (vgl. Prop. I. 3. 16, wo der *amans* sein „Liebesspiel" mit der Schlafenden treibt).

Telum, hasta, arma etc. für Phallus ist besonders den Priapeendichtern geläufig. Griechische Priapdichtungen mögen auch da Vorbild gewesen sein: Ein Beispiel kann ich zur Stütze dieser Annahme anführen. Es stammt von dem Epigrammatiker Erykios von Kyzikos, der etwa bis zu Beginn der augusteischen Zeit dichtete [1]). Die Manier ist dieselbe, wie sie uns in der lateinischen Priapeensammlung so oft entgegentritt. Der Dichter fordert den Gartengott auf, keinen Anstoß zu erregen. A. P. XVI. 242:

Ὡς βαρὺ τοῦτο, Πρίηπε, καὶ εὖ τετυλωμένον ὅ π λ ο ν [2])
πᾶν ἀπὸ βουβώνων ἀϑρόον ἐκκέχυκας
εἰς γάμον οὐκ ἀνέτοιμον · ἔχει δέ σε δίψα γυναικῶν,
ὦ 'γαϑέ, καὶ σπαργᾷς ϑυμὸν ἅπαντα πόϑοις.

. . . . .

Carm. Priap. 9 (B—H):

Cur obscena mihi pars sit sine veste requiris?
quaere, tegat nullus cur sua t e l a deus.

. . . . .

Nec mihi sit crimen, quod mentula semper aperta est:
hoc mihi si t e l u m desit, i n e r m i s ero.

vgl. 55. 4.

43: *Velle quid hanc dicas, quamvis sim ligneus, h a s t a m*

. . .

'*utetur veris viribus h a s t a rudis*'.

„*Arma*" begegnet auch in einem Priapeum, das ziemlich wahrscheinlich dem Virgil gehört [3]) 86. 15f.

1) Vgl. Christ-Schmid: Lit.Gesch. II, 1 ⁶ 329 u. R. Reitzenstein: Realenzykl. VI. 565.

2) Schon bei Nikander aus Kolophon hat ὅπλον einmal diese Bedeutung b. Athen. XV. 683. e.

3) Das Versmaß läßt vermuten, daß der junge Vergil der Verfasser des nebst zwei andern in der *appendix Vergiliana* überlieferten Priapeums ist. Unser Gedicht ist im *metrum Priapeum* gedichtet, das in der römischen Literatur zuerst bei Catull Eingang gefunden hat, als dessen Nachahmer sich Vergil in seiner Jugendzeit erweist vgl. P. Sommer: *De P. Verg. M. Catalepton carm. quaest.* cap. III. Diss. Halle 1910.

Sanguine haec etiam mihi-sed tacebitis- a r m a
barbatus linit hircutus . . .

vgl. **P r i a p.** 31,3; **M a r t.** VI. 73. 6; **M a x i m i a n** 5. 77?

Von Ovid müssen noch wenige Beispiele vorgeführt werden. In diesen spielt er mit Kriegsausdrücken ars I. 131 f.:

> *Romule, militibus scisti dare commoda solus!*
> *Haec mihi si dederis commoda, m i l e s ero.*

Es ist auf die Szene angespielt, wo bei Gelegenheit einer Theateraufführung die Sabinerinnen von Romulus geraubt werden (*commoda*). ars II. 709 f.:

> *fecit in Andromache prius hoc fortissimus Hector*
> *nec solum b e l l i s utilis ille fuit;*

Eine etwas versteckte Andeutung: ars I. 143:

> *Hic tibi quaeratur s o c i i sermonis origo,*
> *et moveant primos publica verba sonos.*

Die Gespräche mit der Geliebten sind ein „Bundesgenosse" im Kampf um sie, gleichsam die erste Etappe im „Feldzug". Rem. 281 ff.

(Circe sagt zu Odysseus, den sie zu längerem Verweilen auf ihrer Insel bewegen will):

> *. . . non hic nova Troia resurgit;*
> *non aliquis socios rursus ad arma vocat;*
> *hic amor et p a x est, in qua male v u l n e r o r una,*
> *totaque sub r e g n o terra futura tuo est.*

Desselben γένος wegen möchte ich gleich Maximian, den Elegiker des 6. nachchristlichen Jahrhunderts, anschließen. Wie er sich sonst als immerhin beachtenswerter Epigone der augusteischen Elegie erweist, so auch mit unserem Bild, das er nicht ungeschickt zu benützen weiß. Eleg. V. 1 ff.:

> *Missus ad Eoas legati munere partes,*
> *Tranquillum cunctis nectere pacis opus,*
> *Dum studeo gemini componere foedera regni*
> *Inveni cordis b e l l a n e f a n d a mei.*

Auf der Reise nach Osten, wo er fürs Reich Frieden holen wollte, fand er eine Liebe, holte für sich also den „Krieg". Liebeskampf el. V. 61 f.:

> *'Quae te crudelis rapuit mihi femina?' dixit,*
> *'Cuius ab amplexu fessus ad a r m a redis?'*

Lykoris nennt den alten Liebhaber *i m b e l l i s* el. II. 6.

el. V. 77 f.:

> *En longo confecta situ tibi t r a d i m u s a r m a*
> *a r m a ministeriis quippe dicata tuis.*

Gewisse Worte, die ursprünglich nur dem Kriegsleben angehören, sind wie im übrigen Sprachleben auch in der Liebesdichtung zu Hause. Sie sind Allgemeingut der Volks- und Literatursprachen. Als Metaphern werden sie kaum mehr empfunden. Deshalb genügt es, wenn ich auf die Dissertation von R. Pichon über den *sermo amatorius* verweise, der unter *capere, captare, vincere, victoria, victor, pax, foedus, repugnare, resistere* das Material der römischen Elegie tabellenmäßig zusammengestellt und unter Rubriken gebracht hat. Ich fasse das Ergebnis aus der römischen Elegie kurz zusammen. Der Neoteriker Catull steht unter dem Einfluß der Alexandriner, ist freilich zum kleinsten Teil nur Uebersetzer. Er kennt unsere Metapher, verwendet sie aber noch seltener, wenig ausgebaut und variiert. Erst Tibull und Properz gebrauchen das Bild in einer Mannigfaltigkeit, daß sie nur mehr von Ovid übertroffen werden. Das Bild bei den Griechen weist selbst in den Romanen bei weitem nicht diesen Reichtum in der Ausgestaltung des Motives auf; ebensowenig bei Catull und in der römischen Komödie des Plautus und Terenz. Denn während es hier überall fast nur einseitig-obszönen Charakter trägt, ist es in der römischen Elegie und in der Lyrik des Horaz vor allem auch durch Vergleich mit den Mühen und Leiden des Kriegers bunter und dem Leser gleichzeitig erfreulicher gestaltet.

Mit Recht, glaube ich, nehmen wir an, daß erst die Elegiker der augusteischen Zeit die Metapher so meisterhaft zu behandeln verstanden. Die Erklärung hiefür liegt in den teilweise schon erörterten Momenten. Als nicht unwesentlich tritt die Tatsache hinzu, daß die Erotiker sich öfters gegen ihre Gönner zu verteidigen haben, welche sie bald zur Teilnahme an Feldzügen, bald zur erhabeneren, episch-heroischen Dichtung anfeuern wollen [1]). Denn dadurch sahen sich die Elegiker veranlaßt, ihre Dichtung und ihr Lebensideal der *militia Amoris* zu rechtfertigen und dies als schwere Aufgabe, als einen Kriegsdienst seiner Art zu proklamieren und zu charakteri-

---

1) Vgl. die kürzlich gefundene K a l l i m a c h u s e l e g i e: O x y r h. P a p. XVII. 2079 (Maas, DLZ 1928 Heft 2; Pfeiffer, Hermes 63, 302 ff.). Hier wehrt sich der Dichter gegen die Nörgler, die ihm vorwerfen, kein zusammenhängendes Epos auf Könige oder Heroen in vielen Chiliaden von Versen verfaßt zu haben.

sieren. Bei Tibull, Properz und Ovid ist der „Liebeskrieg" zu einem innerhalb ihrer Poesie immer wiederkehrenden, thematisch und kompositionell überaus bedeutsamen τόπος geworden. *Militare sub Amore* ist auf das Banner dieser Erotiker geschrieben. Dieses Lebensziel verteidigen sie mit dem oftmaligen Hinweis auf die Freuden, die das Liebesleben mit sich bringt. Allerdings müssen diese Freuden errungen und durch harten Kampf erkauft werden. Kriegsleben und Liebeständelei stehen zwar einander feindlich gegenüber, aber dennoch sind Berührungspunkte da. Daher ist eine doppelte Struktur möglich: entweder werden Waffendienst und Liebesdienst als Motive parallel oder sie werden antithetisch beim Aufbau der Elegie verwendet. An besonders wichtige Stellen ist der τόπος deshalb öfters gerückt, weil das Gedicht wiederholt in dem Gedanken des Dichters kulminiert, ein Priester Amors sein zu wollen, ein Bekenntnis, das in pikant-scherzhafter verwendet ist. Bei Tibull bewundern wir die elegante und gefällige Weise, wie er das Motiv ins Gesamtgedicht verwebt. In der Formulierung aber verrät Properz mehr Kraft und Lebendigkeit als Tibull, der in Wortwahl und Rythmus die μεσότης anstrebt. Durch O v i d s Elegie ist das Bild in virtuoser Weise ausgeführt und am vollkommensten zur Darstellung gekommen. Ovid versteht es zugleich wie keiner, bei all seinen Vorgängern zu Gaste zu gehen und sie für sein eigenes Dichten auszubeuten. Inhaltlich wie formell dankt er am meisten seinen wenig älteren Kollegen Properz und Tibull. Dazu weiß seine reiche Phantasie, sein Humor und Witz dem Motiv noch neue Seiten abzugewinnen. Schließlich kommt ihm eine staunenswerte Sprachbeherrschung, ein außergewöhnliches Formtalent zugute, so daß wir in Ovid den Meister in der Verwendung unserer Metapher erblicken müssen.

Nach Ovid ist, wenn wir von Apuleius und Petron absehen, selbst stilistisch nichts Neues für unsere Metapher geschaffen worden. Das Bild beginnt, in der Hauptsache sich auf Anspielungen zu beschränken, andererseits fast nur für Ausmalung von Obszönitäten zu dienen. Im nächsten und letzten Abschnitt soll ein Ueberblick über das Nachleben des Motives gewonnen werden.

§ 6.

Die Satiriker Juvenal und Persius machen von unserer Metapher keinen Gebrauch. Ihre Themata würden an sich wohl Gelegenheit dazu gegeben haben. Allerdings sind sie nicht Erzähler eigener

Liebeserlebnisse, üben vielmehr an den morschen Sitten und nicht
zuletzt am degenerierten Liebes- und Eheleben ihrer Zeitgenossen
strengste Kritik. Was sie aber in dieser Beziehung anzuklagen und
darzustellen haben, wird nicht in Metaphern gekleidet und mit
Bildern geschmückt; ihre Sittenschilderungen sind durch krassen
Naturalismus, durch fürchterliche Nacktheit der Darstellung gekenn-
zeichnet. Juvenal sagt Sat. VI. 268:

> *semper habet lites alternaque iurgia lectus*
> *in quo nupta iacet . . .*

Er gebraucht also die gewöhnlichen, eigentlichen Worte für die
Sache. Vgl. Sat. VI. 35.

Ganz anders Petrons Werk. Sein genialer und humorgesättigter,
sprachlich und kulturgeschichtlich überaus interessanter Abenteurer-
roman hat eine sehr bilder- und metaphernreiche Sprache. Er bietet
mehrere Beispiele für meine Arbeit. Wäre der Roman uns ganz
erhalten, hätte er fraglos eine reiche Ausbeute für die *„militia
Amoris"* gewährt. Petron ist stark von Ovid und der römischen
Elegie beeinflußt; er kann aber auch bei seinen spezielleren Vor-
bildern, bei Varro und im griechischen Roman den τόπος vorge-
funden haben. Beachtenswert ist, daß er im Gegensatz zur römi-
schen Elegie mit Vorliebe aus der Fechtersprache seine Tropen
für die Erzählung erotischer Abenteuer nimmt [1]). Schon darin zeigt
sich eine gewisse Selbständigkeit Petrons. Denn diese Bilder hatten
die Römer bisher, wenigstens in erotischer Sphäre, nicht gekannt,
und noch viel weniger die Griechen, bei denen bekanntlich das
Fechten recht spät seinen Einzug hielt.

Die Metapher hat, um es nochmals hervorzuheben, in der Kaiser-
zeit zumeist einseitig-obszönes Gesicht. Die Obszönitäten, die bei
früheren römischen Autoren meist nur in Kriegsausdrücken ange-
deutet waren, werden bei Petron und noch mehr bei Apuleius unter
Beibehaltung des Bildes ausgemalt. Das Material soll das beleuchten.
Einzelne Kriegsausdrücke: Petr. c. 80. 1 ff.:

Askylt und Enkolp bemühen sich beiderseits um den *puer* Giton.

---

1) Zur Beliebtheit der Bilder aus dem Fechterleben vgl. M. Wiegandt
„De metaphorarum usu quodam Ciceroniano" p. 30 ff.; D. Wollner *„Die
von der Beredsamkeit aus der Krieger- u. Fechtersprache entlehnten bild-
lichen Wendungen in den rhetorischen Schriften des Cicero, Quintilian und
Tacitus"* Progr. Landau 1886; Straub, *De tropis et figuris, quae inveniuntur
in orationibus Demosthenis et Ciceronis"* Progr. Würzburg 1883.

Askylt: *non frueris, inquit, hac praeda.* Der besiegte Enkolp c. 80. 8: *attulissem mihi damnatus manus si non inimici victoriae invidissem: egreditur superbus cum praemio Ascyltus* . . . . vgl. c. 85. 3; c. 97. 4; c. 98. 8; c. 87. 3; c. 109. 2; c. 20. 8; c. 83. 5 c. 85. 6; c. 88. 8; c. 113. 6.

Mentula militans: c. 24. 7: *mox manum etiam demisit in sinum et pertrectato vasculo tam rudi „haec, inquit, belle cras in promulside libidinis nostrae militabit, hodie enim post asellum diaria non sumo."*

Enkolp schreibt der Circe, sich wegen seiner Impotenz entschuldigend, c. 130. 4:

paratus miles arma non habui c. 91: cum duos armatos viderem (armatus hier wohl doppeldeutig!). Die 'Waffe' ist näherhin gekennzeichnet. c. 129. 1: *funerata est illa pars corporis, qua quondam Achilles eram.* Das *tertium comparationis* ist die *longa hasta.* Berühmt war ja der Achillesspeer [1]). Im griechischen ist uns das analoge ξίφος begegnet. Ἔγχος scheint ähnliche Verwendung gefunden zu haben: Sueton berichtet über den Kaiser Vespasian c. 22: *Expugnatus antem a quadam, quasi amore suo deperiret, cum perductae pro concubitu sestertia quadringenta donasset, admonente dispensatore, quemadmodum summam rationibus vellet inferri, Vespasiano, inquit, adamato. Utebatur et versibus Graecis tempestive satis, et de quodam procerae staturae improbiusque nato:*
Μακρὰ βιβάς, κραδάων δολιχόσκιον ἔγχος [2]).

Askylt schilt seinen Genossen Enkolp. (Petr. c. 9. 8 f.): *Non taces, inquit, gladiator obscene, quem de ruina harena dimisit? non taces, nocturne percussor, qui ne tum quidem, cum fortiter faceres, cum pura muliere pugnasti.* Das Fechterbild bei Petron außerdem: c. 21. 2: *Quartilla alte cincta iussit infelicibus dari missionem.* Die Liebhaber werden abgeschoben, wie den besiegten Gladiatoren ‚*missio*' erteilt wurde, vgl. Apul. Met. 2. 17.

Petr. c. 19: *Et praecincti certe altius eramas: immo ego sic iam paria composueram, ut, si depugnaudum foret, ipse cum Quartilla consisterem, Ascyltus cum ancilla, Giton cum virgine,* vgl. c. 22; c. 107.

Apuleius hat viele Bilder und Motive der römischen Elegie ent-

---

1) Zur eigentlichen Bedeutung vgl. etwa Ovid Her. III. 126: *Transeat Hectoreum Pelias hasta latus.*

2) Auch die Spanier sagen obszön: *armar (armado).*

lehnt [1]). Er kennt auch unsere Metapher. Die *pugna Venerea* schildert er so ausführlich wie kein Römer zuvor; in den griechischen Romanen indes stießen wir auf ähnliche Szenen. Apul. Met. 2. 18: *tamen comiter a m a t o r i a e m i l i t i a e brevem commeatum indulsit.* Die „Kämpfe" sind durchweg eindeutig: Met. 5. 21: *Nox erat et maritus aderat primisque v e n e r i s p r o e l i i s v e l i t a t u s, in altum soporem descendit.* Met. 2. 10: *Ac te c o m p a r a, tota enim nocte tecum f o r t i t e r et ex animo p r o e l i a b o r.* Met. 2. 17: *p r o e l i a r c, inquit, et f o r t i t e r p r o e l i a r e, nec enim tibi c e d a m nec t e r g a v o r t a m c o m m i n u s in aspectum, si vir es, derige et g r a s s a r e n a v i t e r* [2]) *et o c c i d e m o r i t u r u s, hodierna p u g n a non habet m i s s i o n e m* [3]). Met. 2. 16: *miserere, inquam, et s u b v e n i maturius. nam ut vides p r o e l i o, quod nobis sine fetiali officio i n d i x e r a s . . ., arcum meum . . . tetendi.* Met. 9. 20: *. . . commodum novis amplexibus Amori rudi litabant, commodum p r i m a s t i p e n d i a Veneri m i l i t a b a n t* [4]) *n u d i m i l i t e s.*

Apuleius verwendet das Bild sehr originell. Auch die Formulierung ist individuell; denn Wendungen wie *terga vertere, proelium indicere, prima stipendia militare* u. a. waren in der erotischen Sphäre bis dahin nicht begegnet. Die Redeweise der Elegiker war noch gemäßigter. Apuleius steigert diese Tradition.

Nur Petron und Apuleius also vermögen die „*militia Veneris*" noch einigermaßen selbständig zu behandeln. Sie begnügen sich keineswegs mit dem abgegriffenen Sprachschatz und Bilderschmuck, wie die übrigen ihnen weit unterlegenen Schriftstellertalente dieser Zeit.

Martial und Ausonius soll uns noch kurz beschäftigen: M a r t i a l bezeichnet folgendes Distichon als ein Erzeugnis des Kaisers Augustus: Epig. XI. 20: (Fulvia zu Octavian):

A u t futue, aut p u g n e m u s, ait. Quid, quod mihi vita carior est ipsa mentula? S i g n a c a n a n t.

---

1) Vgl. M. B e r n h a r d: Stil des Apul. Stuttg. 1927. 354 in den „Tübinger Beitr. z. Altertumswiss." II.

2) Wirkliche Kampfschilderung: *cuspide turmas grassatus* (angreifen) S t a t. Theb. VIII. 570.

3) *missio* = Befreiung der Gladiatoren vom ferneren Fechten vgl. M a r t. XII. 28. 7: *Nuper cum Myrino peteretur m i s s i o laeso.* Vgl. oben S. 75.

4) In eigentlicher Bedeutung: *sub initia s t i p e n d i o r u m meorum* Vell. II. 101 *qui honestis iam s t i p e n d i i s contra Latinos m i l i t a r a t* Eutr. I. 18. Die übrigen hier vorkommenden Kriegerworte sind so üblich, daß es sich erübrigt Belege beizubringen.

Unmöglich ist das nicht: Die Kaiser und Hofleute pflegten, wie wir wissen, z. T. mit Vorliebe solche literarischen *nugae* [1]). Gehen wir nun über zu Martials eigenen Ausdrücken. Wie Ovid spricht Martial vom „Rekruten" im Lieben. Epig. XI. 78: *Ergo Suburanae tironem trade magistrae* . . . Der Schule der Dirnen in der Subura soll der Junge übergeben werden.

Nachtabenteuer: Epig. X. 38:

> *O quae p r o e l i a, quas utrimque p u g n a s*
> *Felix lectulus et lucerna vidit.*

Aus der Situation und Kontrastierung erklärt sich folgende Stelle (Epig. IX. 56): Der schöne Spendophorus soll mit seinem Herrn in den Krieg ziehen. Der Dichter fordert daher den bewaffneten Cupido auf, seine Waffen jenem zu leihen. Ohne Panzer, Helm und Schild soll Spendophorus, schön wie Parthenopäus, seine „Venuskämpfe" ausfechten:

> *Tutus ut invadat p r o e l i a, nudus eat.*
> *Non iaculo, non ense fuit laesusve sagitta,*
> *Casside dum liber Parthenopaeus erat.*
> *Quisquis ab hoc fuerit f i x u s, morietur amore.*
> *O felix, si quem tam bona fata manent.*

Waffe *mentula*: Epig. XI, 78:

> *Dum metuit t e l i v u l n e r a prima novi.*

Von Ausonius besitzen wir einen *cento nuptialis*, in dem vergilische Verse obszöne Bedeutung annehmen. Der eigentliche Witz soll eben darin liegen, daß der k e u s c h e Vergil dazu die Verse liefern soll. A u s. cento nupt. 116 ff.:

> *et super incumbens nodis et cortice crudo.*
> *intorquet summis adnixus viribus h a s t a m*
> . . . . . .
> *illa manu moriens t e l u m trahit, ossa sed inter*
> *altius ad vivum persedit v u l n e r e m u c r o.*

vgl. oben die Homercentones (p. 38).

Die *libido* ist die Urheberin der Liebesgefechte: Aus. epig. 107

> . . . *ubi cassa libido*
> *femineos coetus et non s u a b e l l a l a c e s s i t,*

vgl. Cento nupt. 83 f.; Cento nupt. 101 ff.:

---

1) Anders T e u f f e l RLG 220. 5, der es Martial selbst zuschreibt.

Postquam congressi sola sub nocte per umbram
et mentem Venus ipsa dedit, nova p r o e l i a temptant
tollit se arrectum: conantem plurima frustra
o c c u p a t os faciemque, pedem pede fervidus urget.

Damit verwandt: C l a u d. C l a u d i a n u s fesc. 14. 28 f.:

Tum victor madido prosilias toro
nocturni referens v u l n e r a p r o e l i i

epith. 10. 111: *quae p r o e l i a sudas improbe?*

Das Bild ist in dieser Spätzeit, wie gesagt, schon recht abge-
griffen. Ovid, der bis ins späte Mittelalter sehr viel Gelesene, Martial,
Apuleius u. a. sind die Vorbilder, die nachgeahmt werden. Forberg
bringt in seinem Buch ‚Hermaphrodit des Antonio Beccadelli'
Kob. 1824 eine Rede des Kaisers Elagabal an seine Hetären, die
sicher fingiert ist (Einl. p. V. Anm. c). Diese ist stark von unserer
Metapher beeinflußt. Wenn es darin heißt „*militat profecto omnis
amans*", so beweist das, wie Ovids Worte nunmehr zu einem geflü-
gelten Wort, zum Allgemeingut mindestens der literarisch gebil-
deten und interessierten Welt von damals geworden ist. Obige Rede
dankt wohl ihre Entstehung einer Nachricht des Historikers Lam-
pridius über das Treiben des Kaisers Elagabal: c. 26 *omnes de circo,
de theatro, de stadio et omnibus locis et balneis meretrices collegit
in aedes publicas, et apud eas c o n t i o n e m h a b u i t q u a s i
m i l i t a r e m, dicens eas c o m m i l i t o n e s disputavitque de gene-
ribus schematum et voluptatum.*

Bis ins späteste Mittelalter hinein war unsere Metapher gepflegt.
Besonders wandelten die lateinschreibenden Poeten der Renaissance
in den Bahnen der gezierten Obszönitäten eines Ovid oder Apuleius [1]).
Die Erscheinung des Minnedienstes gab auch den Minnesängern
des Mittelalters reichliche Gelegenheit von dem Bilde Gebrauch zu
machen [2]). Aus späterer und neuester deutschen wie ausländischen
Literatur ließen sich wohl viele Beispiele für den „Liebeskrieg"
auffinden. Wir brauchen dabei nicht immer nach Vorbildern

1) Ich verweise auf das Lexikon *eroticum* von P i e r r u g u e s, wo unter
hasta etc. typische Beispiele vorliegen oder auf die *lascivae paginae* einer
gewissen *Aloisia Sigaea* aus der Humanistenzeit (s. Forberg p. 313—16 u.
sonst).

2) Eine sprechende Illustration zum Bild zeigt eine aus dem 14. Jhdt
stammende, im Museum von Florenz sich befindende Spiegelgarnitur, die auf
dem Deckel darstellt: *le siège du château d'amour.* Abgebildet in „*histoire
de la littérature française*" par B é d i e r - H a z a r d I. 19.

zu suchen oder an Abhängigkeit zu denken: Das Bild ist letzten Endes wie viele andere Bilder Gemeingut der Völker und Literaturen [1]), wenn es auch bei den Griechen und besonders bei den Römern eine ausnahmsweise wichtige Rolle spielte.

---

1) In einem türkischen Schwank wird eine humorvolle „Liebesschlacht" ziemlich ausführlich erzählt. W e s s e l s k i : Der Hodscha Nasreddin I. Nr. 236. Dazu R. K ö h l e r: kleinere Schriften II. 594 ff.

Lebenslauf.

Geboren bin ich, Alfons Spies, am 24. Juli 1905 in Ertingen, OA. Riedlingen, als Sohn des Anton Spies und seiner verstorbenen Ehefrau Monika, geb. Hepp. Herbst 1914 trat ich ins Progymnasium Riedlingen ein, machte 1919 das Landexamen. Darauf besuchte ich das Gymnasium Ehingen a. D., wo ich Frühjahr 1924 das Reifezeugnis erhielt. Um mich dem Studium der klass. Philologie und der Germanistik zu widmen, bezog ich die Universität Tübingen. Während der beiden ersten Semester studierte ich auch Musik und Philosophie. Das vierte und fünfte Semester verbrachte ich in München. Mai 1928 legte ich in Tübingen das Doktorexamen und im darauffolgenden Frühjahr die erste humanistische Dienstprüfung ab. Philosophische Vorlesungen hörte ich bei folgenden Herren Professoren:

a) in Tübingen: Bohnenberger, Focke, v. Garbe, Mewaldt, Schmid, Schneider, Vogt, Watzinger, Weinreich.

b) in München: Kutscher, Rehm, Schwartz, Strich, Stroux, Weymann.

Ihnen allen, besonders aber den Herren Professoren Focke, Mewaldt, Schmid und Weinreich, spreche ich für die mannigfachen Förderungen und Anregungen meinen herzlichen Dank aus.